Learning MS Dynamics AX 2012 Programming

Develop and customize your very own Microsoft Dynamics AX solution quickly and efficiently

Mohammed Rasheed

Erlend Dalen

BIRMINGHAM - MUMBAI

Learning MS Dynamics AX 2012 Programming

Copyright © 2014 Packt Publishing

All rights reserved. No part of this book may be reproduced, stored in a retrieval system, or transmitted in any form or by any means, without the prior written permission of the publisher, except in the case of brief quotations embedded in critical articles or reviews.

Every effort has been made in the preparation of this book to ensure the accuracy of the information presented. However, the information contained in this book is sold without warranty, either express or implied. Neither the authors nor Packt Publishing, and its dealers and distributors will be held liable for any damages caused or alleged to be caused directly or indirectly by this book.

Packt Publishing has endeavored to provide trademark information about all of the companies and products mentioned in this book by the appropriate use of capitals. However, Packt Publishing cannot guarantee the accuracy of this information.

First published: December 2009

Second edition: December 2014

Production reference: 1221214

Published by Packt Publishing Ltd.
Livery Place
35 Livery Street
Birmingham B3 2PB, UK.

ISBN 978-1-78217-126-3

www.packtpub.com

Credits

Authors
Mohammed Rasheed
Erlend Dalen

Reviewers
Deepak Agarwal
Harish Mohanbabu
Umesh Pandit
Nasheet Ahmed Siddiqui

Commissioning Editor
Martin Bell

Acquisition Editor
Greg Wild

Content Development Editor
Rikshith Shetty

Technical Editors
Pramod Kumavat
Rohith Rajan

Copy Editors
Roshni Banerjee
Shambhavi Pai

Project Coordinator
Kinjal Bari

Proofreaders
Ting Baker
Paul Hindle

Indexer
Priya Sane

Graphics
Sheetal Aute
Valentina D'silva

Production Coordinator
Shantanu N. Zagade

Cover Work
Shantanu N. Zagade

About the Authors

Mohammed Rasheed is a Dynamics AX solutions architect and a self-proclaimed Dynamics AX evangelist. He has had a remarkable career as a Dynamics AX expert and has made key contributions to the success of a number of leading Microsoft partners such as IBM (UK), HSO (UK), and Crowe Horwath LLP (USA).

Listed as one of the *most influential people* by `http://www.dynamicsworld.co.uk/`, Mohammed considers himself fortunate to have met and worked with the most amazing team of people. He attributes his success to his parents, his family, and his team—a team of leaders with the zeal to redefine an industry, managers with the resolve to achieve their aspirations, and young consultants with limitless energy.

Mohammed calls Chicago his home, where he lives with his wife, Sakeena, and their beautiful baby daughter, Zara.

Erlend Dalen started working as a developer with the first version of Axapta in 1998. He was then working with some of the first Axapta implementations in Norway and was also part of a team that created an advanced product configurator for Axapta. From 2000 to 2002, he worked on developing e-commerce, mobile, and integration solutions in Java for a Norwegian IT consultancy company. He joined Columbus IT in 2002, working first as a senior developer in Norway and in the USA and then as the technology manager of the Norwegian branch, where his responsibilities included implementing new technology areas, creating an e-commerce solution for Dynamics AX, and being the technology solution architect in internal and external projects.

For the past four years, Erlend has been working as a web developer for Norsk Test AS, where he spends his days programming in Python using the Django web framework.

> I would like to thank my wife, Benedikte, for backing me up on this project. Whenever I felt that things moved slowly, she motivated me to push forward to finish the project. I would also like to thank Columbus IT, Norway, for letting me take some time off to write the book and my coworkers at Columbus IT, Norway, for helping me out whenever I had a question. Last but not least, I would like to thank my daughter, Ellinor, for forcing me to take breaks every now and then. You put a smile on my face when I was struggling with the book.

About the Reviewers

Deepak Agarwal is a Microsoft Certified Professional and is currently working professionally on Dynamics AX. He has worked with different versions of Axapta, such as AX 2009, AX 2012, R2, and R3. He has held a wide range of development, consulting, and leading roles while always maintaining a significant role as a business application developer. Though his strengths are rooted in X++ development, he is a highly regarded developer and has solid knowledge of the technical aspects of Dynamics AX development and customization.

He was awarded the Most Valuable Professional (MVP) on Dynamics AX by Microsoft in 2013 and 2014. He has also worked on the following books by Packt Publishing:

- *Microsoft Dynamics AX 2012 Reporting Cookbook*
- *Microsoft Dynamics AX 2012 R3 Reporting Cookbook*

Deepak shares his experience on Dynamics AX on his blog `http://theaxapta.blogspot.in/`.

> A big thanks to my dear brother, Naveen Agarwal, for his motivational support and best wishes.

Harish Mohanbabu is an independent Dynamics AX consultant with focus on everything related to technical aspects in Dynamics AX.

He has 15 years of experience in software engineering, consulting, and management, out of which the last 12 years have been spent working on Microsoft Dynamics AX. He has held various software development management positions at Capgemini, Charteris plc, and Lebara. He has also been the technical reviewer of three books on Dynamics AX, including *Microsoft Dynamics AX 2009 Programming: Getting Started*, *Packt Publishing*.

He is currently working on a number of complex international AX projects. Harish lives in Hertfordshire, England, with his wife, Chelvy, and their two children, Swetha and Rahul.

Umesh Pandit is a Microsoft Dynamics AX Deployment Specialist currently working with one of the top Microsoft Dynamics players. He has completed his Master of Computer Applications degree with first division specializing in ERP from Ideal Institute of Technology, Ghaziabad.

He is also a Microsoft Certified Professional for:

- Microsoft Dynamics AX 2009 Installation and Configuration
- Microsoft Dynamics AX 2012 Installation and Configuration
- Server Virtualization with Windows Server Hyper-V and System Center
- Microsoft Dynamics AX 2012 Development Introduction I
- Microsoft Dynamics POS 2009
- Administering Microsoft SQL Server 2012 Databases

In the past, he has successfully reviewed *Microsoft Dynamics AX 2012 Reporting Cookbook* by Kamalakannan Elamgovan and *Developing SSRS Reports for Dynamics AX* by Mukesh Hirwani.

He has worked with top IT giants, such as KPIT Technologies, Capgemini India, and Google India, and a cable manufacturing company called Cords Cable Industries.

Umesh also has a deep understanding of ERP systems, such as SAP and Microsoft Dynamics AX. He has worked with different versions of Axapta, such as AX 3.0, AX 4.0, AX 2009, AX 2012, AX 2012 R2, and AX 2012 R3. Also, he has good knowledge of Microsoft technologies, such as SQL, CRM, TFS, Office 2013, Windows Server 2003, Window Server 2008, Windows Server 2012, Office 365, Microsoft Dynamics NAV, SSRS, Cubes, Management Reporter, SSAS, VSS, and Visual Studio.

> I would like to give special thanks to my friends Pramila, Sunil Wadhwa, and Rohan Sodani who encouraged me to pursue my passion.

Nasheet Ahmed Siddiqui studied Computer Science at the University of Karachi, Pakistan. He has over 8 years of consulting experience, playing a variety of roles such as software engineer, senior software engineer, team lead, and technical consultant in Dynamics AX and other Microsoft technologies.

Nasheet started working in 2006 for e-Creatorz, where he developed and managed web applications. He started his Dynamics AX career with MazikGlobal (subsidiary of Tyler Technology Ltd., USA, and Microsoft Corporation). He was the core developer in the development of the Dynamics AX 2012 and AX 2012 R2 features for Microsoft. He was directly involved with the Microsoft team while building the features for AX 2012 and AX 2012 R2. Since 2012, Nasheet has been working for Othaim Markets, where he is responsible for the customizations, development, and implementation of new verticals (Property Management System, Vendor Contract Management, and Maintenance Management System) and integration with other applications.

Nasheet was also the reviewer of *Dynamics AX 2012 Reporting Cookbook*, *Packt Publishing*. Nasheet has solid knowledge and skills of the technical aspects of Dynamics AX 2009 and 2012. He also works as a freelance Dynamics AX technical consultant. He has also provided development training services to many organizations in Pakistan, Saudi Arabia, and Canada. Nasheet is also a Microsoft Certified Professional (MCP) for Dynamics AX Development and Morphx Solution.

Nasheet lives in Riyadh, Saudi Arabia, with his wife and son, Abdullah. He is always happy to share useful AX development tricks on his blog `nasheet.wordpress.com`. He can be contacted via LinkedIn at `http://sa.linkedin.com/in/nasheet`.

> I want to thank my father, mother, and my wife as they are always motivating me and praying for me.

www.PacktPub.com

Support files, eBooks, discount offers, and more

For support files and downloads related to your book, please visit www.PacktPub.com.

Did you know that Packt offers eBook versions of every book published, with PDF and ePub files available? You can upgrade to the eBook version at www.PacktPub.com and as a print book customer, you are entitled to a discount on the eBook copy. Get in touch with us at service@packtpub.com for more details.

At www.PacktPub.com, you can also read a collection of free technical articles, sign up for a range of free newsletters and receive exclusive discounts and offers on Packt books and eBooks.

https://www2.packtpub.com/books/subscription/packtlib

Do you need instant solutions to your IT questions? PacktLib is Packt's online digital book library. Here, you can search, access, and read Packt's entire library of books.

Why subscribe?

- Fully searchable across every book published by Packt
- Copy and paste, print, and bookmark content
- On demand and accessible via a web browser

Free access for Packt account holders

If you have an account with Packt at www.PacktPub.com, you can use this to access PacktLib today and view 9 entirely free books. Simply use your login credentials for immediate access.

Instant updates on new Packt books

Get notified! Find out when new books are published by following @PacktEnterprise on Twitter or the *Packt Enterprise* Facebook page.

Table of Contents

Preface   1

Chapter 1: Understanding Dynamics AX 2012   7
  Understanding the development environment   7
    Programming language   8
    MorphX   8
    Application Object Tree   8
      Data Dictionary   9
      Macros   10
      Classes   10
      Forms   10
      Datasets   10
      SSRS Reports   10
      Reports   10
      Report Libraries   11
      Queries   11
      Jobs   11
      Menus   11
      Menu Items   11
      Web   11
      Services   11
      Workflow   12
      Resources   12
      System Documentation   12
    Application Developer Documentation   12
    Properties   13
    X++ code editor   14
    Compiler   16
    Labels   19
  Creating your first AX program   19
  Utilizing the different development tools   20
    Cross-references   21

MorphX version control	23
Setting up the MorphX version control	24
Using the MorphX version control	26
The debugger	28
Dissecting the AX architecture	**29**
Application object layers	29
Network tiers	30
Case study – Carz Inc.	**31**
Summary	**32**
Chapter 2: The X++ Language	**33**
Introduction	**33**
Datatypes	**34**
Primitive datatypes	35
String	35
Integer	37
Real	38
Boolean	40
Date	40
Enum	40
The timeofday datatype	42
The utcdatetime datatype	43
The anytype datatype	43
Composite datatypes	44
Container	44
Class	46
Table	47
Array	49
Statements and loops	**50**
The for loop	50
The continue statement	50
The break statement	51
The while loop	51
The do-while loop	51
The if-else if-else loop	52
The switch statement	53
Exception handling	53
Operators	**54**
Assignment operators	55
Relational operators	55
Arithmetic operators	56
Classes and methods	**57**
Method access	58
The RunOn property	58

Static methods	59
The default parameter	60
The Args class	60
Inheritance	62
The construct method	64
The main method	64
The RunBase framework	65
The SysOperation framework	66
The collection classes	70
Array	70
List	71
Map	71
Set	72
Struct	73
Macros	**74**
Events	**75**
Summary	**76**
Chapter 3: Storing Data	**77**
Extended datatypes	**77**
Creating an extended datatype	78
Tables	**82**
Creating a table	82
Adding fields to a table	87
Adding fields to a field group	89
Creating an index	90
Creating a relation	92
Creating a delete action	93
Table browser	94
Table inheritance	96
Querying data on inherited tables	99
Valid time state tables	100
Summary	**103**
Chapter 4: Data User Interaction	**105**
Forms	**105**
Main components of a form	106
Methods	106
Data sources	107
Designs	109
Creating a form with one data source	110
Form templates	110
Creating the form	111
Adding the data source	112

Table of Contents

Creating a form design	112
Creating a form with two data sources	**114**
Separating the design using a form splitter	**115**
Display and edit methods	**120**
Edit methods	122
Considerations	123
Caching display methods	123
Creating a lookup form	**124**
Creating a lookup form by adding a new form in AOT	124
Creating a lookup in the lookup method	125
Parts	126
Reports	**127**
Reporting Services	128
Creating an AX report using Visual Studio	128
Menu items	**133**
Creating a menu item	133
Using a menu item as a button in a form	134
Navigation pages	**135**
List pages	136
Creating a list page	137
Menus	**139**
Summary	**141**
Chapter 5: Searching for Data	**143**
Queries	**143**
Creating a static query using AOT	143
Adding a sort order to the query	145
Adding a range to the query	145
Joining data sources in the query	146
Creating a dynamic query using X++	148
Using a query	150
Views	**152**
Creating a view	152
The select statement	**154**
CarTable	156
RentalTable	156
CustTable	156
How to write a simple select statement	157
How to use sorting in the select statements	162
How to use joins in a select statement	163
The inner join	164
The outer join	165
The exists join	166
The notexists join	167

[iv]

How to write aggregate select statements	168
sum	168
avg	169
count	169
minof and maxof	170
Group by	171
Optimizing data retrieval	**173**
Using the correct data retrieval method	173
Field selects	173
Indexing	174
Using views to optimize data retrieval	174
Other ways to improve data retrieval	174
Summary	**175**
Chapter 6: Manipulating Data	**177**
The validation methods	**178**
Record-based manipulation	**179**
Insert	179
Update	180
Delete	183
Set-based data manipulation	**184**
The insert_recordset operator	184
The update_recordset operator	186
The delete_from operator	189
Unit of work	**190**
Direct handling	**193**
Summary	**195**
Chapter 7: Integrating Data	**197**
Text files	**198**
Writing data to a text file	199
Reading from a file	202
Binary files	**203**
XML files	**204**
Creating an XML file and writing to it	204
Reading an XML from a file	207
Open Database Connectivity	**209**
Reading data from the database:	209
Reading from a database using ODBC	209
Writing to a database using ODBC	211
The import/export activity	**212**
The ImpExpFileDialog class	213
The classDeclaration method	214

The dialog method	214
The getFromDialog method	215
The pack method	215
The run method	216
The unpack method	216
The main method	217
The ImpExpFile class	**217**
The classDeclaration method	217
The new method	218
The openFile method	218
The readFile method	219
The run method	219
The writeFile method	220
The construct method	220
The ImpExp_Cars class	**220**
The classDeclaration method	221
The readFile method	221
The writeFile method	222
The ImpExp_Rentals class	**222**
The classDeclaration method	222
The readFile method	223
The writeFile method	224
Summary	**224**
Chapter 8: Integrating with Standard AX	**225**
The inventory module	**225**
The InventTable entity schema	226
The InventTrans entity schema	228
Understanding main class hierarchies	**229**
The InventMovement classes	229
The InventUpdate classes	231
The InventAdj classes	231
The InventSum classes	232
Working with inventory dimensions	**232**
Finding an inventory dimension	232
Finding the current on-hand information	233
Finding on-hand information by a specific date	234
Entering and posting an inventory journal from code	235
The Ledger module	**236**
Posting ledger transactions	238
Entering and posting a LedgerJournal class	238
Entering and posting a LedgerVoucher class	240

Understanding the Accounts Receivable / Accounts Payable modules	**241**
Entity schema – base data and orders	242
Entity schema – transactions	244
The trade agreements	**245**
Finding the price of an item for a specific customer	**245**
Posting and printing sales/purchase updates	**246**
The voucher settlement	**248**
Summary	**251**

Chapter 9: Creating a New Module — 253

Setting up a number sequence reference	**254**
The parameter table	**257**
Setting up the number sequence	260
Using the number sequence	262
The security framework	**263**
License codes	263
Configuration keys	264
The security hierarchy	266
Code permission	267
Privileges	267
Duties	267
Policies	267
Roles	268
Process cycles	268
Summary	**270**

Chapter 10: Working with .NET and AX — 271

Common Language Runtime	**271**
Adding a reference to a .NET class in AX	273
Assembly existing in the Global Assembly Cache	273
Assembly not in Global Assembly Cache	274
Using a .NET class in X++	274
.NET Business Connector	**278**
Using .NET Business Connector in .NET classes	278
Creating a static method in AX in the global class	278
Creating a new project in Visual Studio and adding it to AOT	279
Application Explorer	280
Inserting data in an AX table	282
Reading data from an AX table	284
Exception classes	286
Summary	**289**

Chapter 11: Web Services — 291
- **Exposing AX logic using web services** — 292
  - Creating a web service that exposes the AX logic — 292
  - Publishing a web service to IIS — 298
- **Accessing logic in an external web service** — 304
  - Creating a service reference — 304
  - Creating a class that consumes the web service — 306
- **Summary** — 308

Chapter 12: Enterprise Portal — 309
- **Creating a dataset** — 310
- **Creating a new Visual Studio project** — 311
- **Creating a grid** — 312
- **Creating a new Web Part page** — 318
- **Creating a tunnel/wizard** — 321
- **Summary** — 327

Appendix A: Links — 329
- **Websites** — 329
  - Official Microsoft websites — 329
  - Blogs — 330
  - Other relevant websites — 330

Appendix B: Debugger — 331

Index — 335

Preface

Microsoft Dynamics AX 2012 R3 is unique in the fact that it is an incredibly utilitarian ERP system as well as a powerful platform. The purpose of this book is, quite simply, to help new developers and keen consultants to explore the platform side of AX.

Erlend Dalen, the author of the first edition (*Microsoft Dynamics AX 2009 Programming: Getting Started*), and I have tried to make it easier for the reader to understand AX concepts by providing real-world examples of focusing our energy on elements that matter the most. For example, AX has a useful metadata-based development that enables developers to activate most of their goals without actually writing any code.

I thank you for your interest in Microsoft Dynamics AX and I hope you enjoy reading this book as much as I have enjoyed writing it.

What this book covers

Chapter 1, *Understanding Dynamics AX 2012*, takes you through the development environment in AX and explains some of the development tools that are included in AX. You will also be able to write your first AX program, if you have never done so before.

Chapter 2, *The X++ Language*, covers the basics of the AX programming language that is X++ and explains in brief how data types, statements and loops, operators, classes, methods, and macros work.

Chapter 3, *Storing Data*, takes you through the process of creating extended data types, tables, and relations.

Chapter 4, Data User Interaction, shows you how to create forms where users can read, update, insert, and delete data. You will also learn how to create reports, menu items, navigation pages, and menus.

Chapter 5, Searching for Data, explains different options that you can use when you need to search and retrieve a set of data from the database. It shows you how to create a query, how to create a view, and how to write different `select` statements.

Chapter 6, Manipulating Data, explains how to insert, update, and delete data using table methods to manipulate one record at a time and discusses set-based manipulation to manipulate a set of data.

Chapter 7, Integrating Data, explains how to read and write data to and from different kind of files and to and from a database using ODBC. It also provides an example of how to write a generic import/export program in AX.

Chapter 8, Integrating with Standard AX, explains how some of the main modules in AX (Inventory, Ledger, Account Receivable, and Accounts Payable) are built by discussing their entity schemas. You will also see examples of how to achieve typical tasks within these modules.

Chapter 9, Creating a New Module, explains how to create a new module in AX by creating number sequences, parameter tables, license codes, configuration keys, and security keys.

Chapter 10, Working with .NET and AX, explains how you can use .NET classes in AX with the Common Language Runtime and how you can write .NET code that use AX classes by using .NET Business Connector for AX.

Chapter 11, Web Services, explains how to create a web service that exposes the AX logic, how to publish the web service to Internet Information Services, and how to make AX consume a web service.

Chapter 12, Enterprise Portal, explains how to expose AX data to web by using the Enterprise Portal and SharePoint.

Appendix A, Links, provides useful links related to Dynamics AX.

Appendix B, Debugger, gives you a quick guide on how to use the debugger.

What you need for this book

All of the examples in this book are created using the Virtual PC (VPC) image called Pre-Sales Demonstration Toolkit for Microsoft Dynamics AX 2012.

I recommend that you either use the VPC or to use an AX installation that is not in use by anyone else when you follow the examples in this book so that you don't step on anyone's toes.

VPC can be downloaded from PartnerSource (for partners) or Customer Source (for AX customers).

If you prefer to install MS SQL Server, Dynamics AX 2012, Visual Studio 2008, and all other required software to follow all the examples in this book, you should take a look at the following link to find the standard system requirements for Dynamics AX 2012: http://technet.microsoft.com/en-us/library/dd361989.aspx

Who this book is for

This book is for developers who are new to Microsoft Dynamics AX and consultants who know the functional side of AX, but would like to learn how AX works behind the scenes. Experienced AX developers might also pick up some good pointers here and there.

Conventions

In this book, you will find a number of styles of text that distinguish between different kinds of information. Here are some examples of these styles, and an explanation of their meaning.

Code words in text are shown as follows: "Your label-file will then be named AxXXXen-gb.ald, where XXX is a 3-letter abbreviation chosen when walking through the wizard."

A block of code is set as follows:

```
@SYS390 Quantity that is not yet cost accounted in the BOM unit.
@SYS400 Create and compose serial numbers automatically.
@SYS403 Finish must be greater than start.
@SYS418 Transfer customer information?
```

Preface

New terms and **important words** are shown in bold. Words that you see on the screen, in menus or dialog boxes for example, appear in the text like this: "clicking on the **Next** button moves you to the next screen."

> Warnings or important notes appear in a box like this.

> Tips and tricks appear like this.

Reader feedback

Feedback from our readers is always welcome. Let us know what you think about this book—what you liked or may have disliked. Reader feedback is important for us to develop titles that you really get the most out of.

To send us general feedback, simply send an e-mail to feedback@packtpub.com, and mention the book title via the subject of your message.

If there is a topic that you have expertise in and you are interested in either writing or contributing to a book, see our author guide on www.packtpub.com/authors.

Customer support

Now that you are the proud owner of a Packt book, we have a number of things to help you to get the most from your purchase.

Downloading the example code

You can download the example code files for all Packt books you have purchased from your account at http://www.packtpub.com. If you purchased this book elsewhere, you can visit http://www.packtpub.com/support and register to have the files e-mailed directly to you.

Errata

Although we have taken every care to ensure the accuracy of our content, mistakes do happen. If you find a mistake in one of our books—maybe a mistake in the text or the code—we would be grateful if you would report this to us. By doing so, you can save other readers from frustration and help us improve subsequent versions of this book. If you find any errata, please report them by visiting http://www.packtpub.com/submit-errata, selecting your book, clicking on the **errata submission form** link, and entering the details of your errata. Once your errata are verified, your submission will be accepted and the errata will be uploaded on our website, or added to any list of existing errata, under the Errata section of that title. Any existing errata can be viewed by selecting your title from http://www.packtpub.com/support.

Piracy

Piracy of copyright material on the Internet is an ongoing problem across all media. At Packt, we take the protection of our copyright and licenses very seriously. If you come across any illegal copies of our works, in any form, on the Internet, please provide us with the location address or website name immediately so that we can pursue a remedy.

Please contact us at copyright@packtpub.com with a link to the suspected pirated material.

We appreciate your help in protecting our authors, and our ability to bring you valuable content.

Questions

You can contact us at questions@packtpub.com if you are having a problem with any aspect of the book, and we will do our best to address it.

1
Understanding Dynamics AX 2012

In this chapter, you will learn how the development environment is structured and what tools are accessible to the developer in Microsoft Dynamics AX. The famous **Hello World** code will be a piece of a cake for you to understand after the first step-by-step walkthrough in this book, and you will know what the different nodes in the application object tree represent.

Here are some of the topics you will learn in this chapter:

- A tour of the development environment
- A look at the tools available
- Creating a job that prints something on the screen
- An overview of the AX architecture

Understanding the development environment

Let's have a look at the main features of the Dynamics AX development model:

- The AX programming language
- The Application Object Tree
- The X++ code editor
- The compiler
- Labels

Understanding Dynamics AX 2012

Programming language

The programming language in AX is called X++ and its syntax is similar to Java and C#. In addition to being an object oriented programming language, it also includes embedded SQL. This means that writing SQL statements in AX is very easy, because as a developer, you don't need to create a connection to the database, then create a statement that is executed on the connection, and so on. Instead, you can write the SQL statements directly into the X++ code, much like you now can with **language-integrated query (LINQ)** for .NET.

You will get to know the syntax, features, and how the X++ language works in *Chapter 2, The X++ Language*.

MorphX

In addition to the programming language, Dynamics AX provides an integrated development environment called MorphX. It is all about visual development in AX and it lets the developer create code elements in a graphical way, much like Visual Studio, by dragging-and-dropping and setting properties on an element. This also is the recommended approach to development in most cases. Most of the AX elements can be edited using MorphX.

Application Object Tree

The **Application Object Tree (AOT)** is where you find all code elements in AX.

You can open it by clicking on the AOT icon, shown in the following screenshot, from the top menu or by pressing *Ctrl + D* from anywhere in AX; this will launch the development workspace.

Chapter 1

You will then see the AOT presented in a tree view, as shown on the right-hand side in the following screenshot:

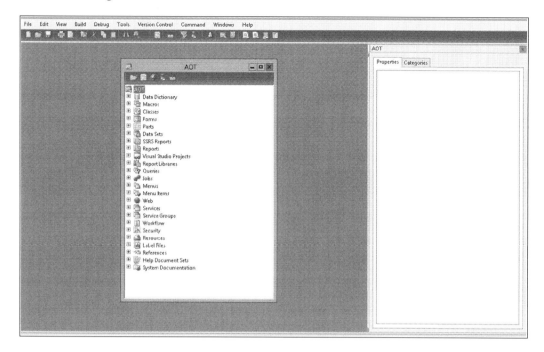

Data Dictionary

The AOT is organized to have all elements that relate to how the data is stored in the database and those that relate to security, such as **Security Keys**, **Configuration Keys**, and **License Codes**, under a node called **Data Dictionary**. Under this node, you will find **Tables**, **Maps**, **Views**, **Extended Datatypes**, **Base Enums**, **License Codes**, **Configuration Keys**, **Security Keys**, **Table Collections**, and **Perspectives**.

Macros

Macros are predefined values used throughout the solution, and they are just mechanisms by which a value (a bit of string) can be defaulted within your code, so that you won't have to **hardcode** values.

Classes

In the development world, an object is a self-contained component that contains properties and methods needed to make a certain type of data useful. An object's properties are what it knows and its methods are what it can do.

Objects are the fundamental building blocks of applications from an object-oriented perspective. You will use many objects of many different types in any AX function you develop. Each different type of object comes from a specific class of that type.

A class is a blueprint, template, or a set of instructions to build a specific type of object, and every object is built from a class.

Forms

Forms are UI elements of Dynamics AX. They can open windows to search for data, view data, change data, create new records, or delete records. In addition, forms very often contain buttons that link to other forms, reports, and classes that execute business-logic (it is not recommended to write business logic within forms; classes are the right place for this).

Datasets

Datasets are used by Visual Studio components such as Reporting Services reports and AX User Controls, as you will see in later chapters. The datasets define which tables are used by these Visual Studio components by adding the tables to the datasets, much like you would do with a table in a data source.

SSRS Reports

All AX 2012 reports are executed and rendered using SQL Server Reporting Services. This node holds all the SSRS reports that will be used within AX.

Reports

Reports are the standard AX reports that display data in the form of reports to the users or write the data to a printer or file. This is available as a node to manage legacy reports only and is not the recommended approach to create new reports.

Report Libraries

Report libraries are links to reporting projects in Visual Studio. You can't create a report library directly from AX. You have to create a report project in VS first and import it into AX. Then it becomes a report library. This is available as a node only to manage legacy reports and is not the recommended approach to create new reports.

Queries

Queries in the AOT are predefined static queries that can be reused throughout the whole application. A query contains a hierarchy of data sources that defines which data should be available for the query. Queries can also be used by other elements in AX, such as forms, reports, and classes.

Jobs

Jobs are static methods intended to directly execute a small piece of code. They work fine for code that is supposed to execute just once, but are not intended to be part of a solution. Jobs are typically used to correct/update a particular table/record that might have been incorrectly modified in the data migration process.

Menus

Menus present the end users with options to open the most used forms and reports and to start periodic tasks. Menus are effectively groupings of forms; end users typically view menus as modules (that is, functional area).

Menu Items

Menu items are pointers to forms, reports, and classes. There are three different types of menu items, namely, **Display**, **Output**, and **Action**. The display menu items are used to open forms, the output is used to open reports, and the action is used to execute a class with a main method (`startpoint`).

Web

The **Web** node consists of subnodes that in turn hold different types of elements relevant for the development of web applications such as the **Enterprise Portal** (**EP**).

Services

Services are used to set up web services that let other applications use AX classes through the **Application Integration Framework** (**AIF**). The AIF is used for electronic communication with trading partners or applications.

Workflow

The workflow framework in AX lets developers create workflows that define certain execution flows, depending on certain events. The typical scenario for using a workflow in AX is the purchase requisition where one employee enters a purchase order. If the purchase order is over a certain limit, it has to be approved by a manager. If denied by the manager, a message is sent to the employee who created the order. If approved, the order is automatically sent to the vendor.

Resources

Resources are files that are imported into the AX database and can be referenced in the code from the resources node in the AOT rather than using a directory and filename from the disk. These files are typically images, icons, cascaded stylesheets, and XML files. You can preview the files by selecting a **Resources** node in the AOT, right-clicking it, and selecting **Open**.

System Documentation

At the bottom of the AOT, you can find help in the form of system documentation. It consists of documentation about the AX core. The elements found here are not open source. This means that you, as a developer, have to relate to these elements as black boxes. This means that only you know what to put into methods and what you can expect to get back. You can find information about global functions here, such as `strlen()`. This function and most other functions are documented with an explanation of the input parameters, return value, and an example of how to use the function.

The same goes for core classes and their methods. Typical core classes are `Map`, `Array`, `AsciiIo`, `FormRun`, and `XppCompiler`, just to mention a few.

Application Developer Documentation

Application Developer Documentation consists of documentation regarding standard AX tables and classes. This documentation is basically just another way of displaying information that you as a developer should be able to find by browsing the AOT, reading code, and looking at properties.

Chapter 1

Properties

So, how do I look at properties, you might ask. Well, at any time while you are in the AOT, you can hit *Alt + Enter* or right-click and select properties to open the **Properties** window, as shown in the following screenshot:

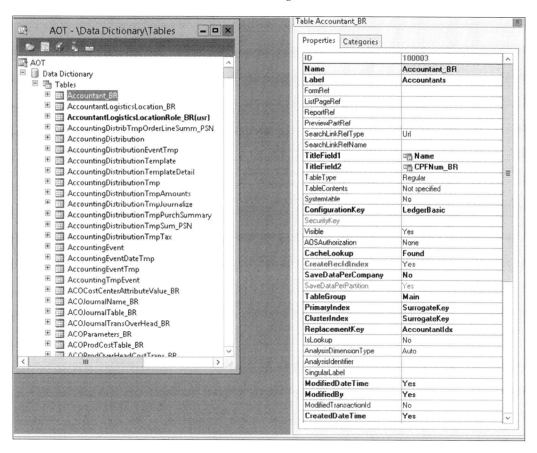

Each element type in the AOT will have a fixed set of properties that can be changed by the developers. The properties marked with bold text have been changed specifically for the selected element. The pink background you can see in the **Name** property in the preceding screenshot means that it is mandatory. The yellow background means that it is best practice to have something in that property. The rest of the properties are defaulted by the system.

Understanding Dynamics AX 2012

The properties are by default organized by relevance, relative to the element they represent. This sorting can, however, be set to alphabetical order from the user options form. Click on the Microsoft Dynamics AX button (*Alt + F*) and navigate to **Tools | Options**, to open the user options form. Under the **Development** tab, you can enable the **Sort alphabetically** checkbox to sort the properties alphabetically, as shown in the following screenshot:

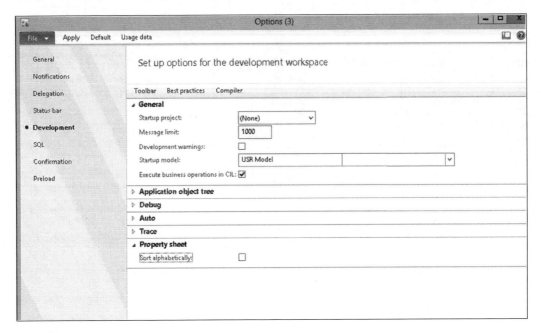

X++ code editor

The X++ code editor that ships with AX 2012 is based on Visual Studio's code editor and hence, it supports color coding, word completion, automatic indenting, scripting, zoom, multiline editing, and many other features that are available in Visual Studio. This is where all the X++ code will be written.

X++ code editor consists of three sections; method list, menu bar, and code window.

The method list shows all the methods in the selected element if you double-click an element. If you double-click a method within an element, you will only see that method in the method list. If you then double-click another method in the same element, you can see both the selected methods in the method list. When you change a method, it displays an asterisk after the method name in the method list, to show you a changed method that has not yet been saved.

The code window obviously shows the X++ code for the selected method in the method list:

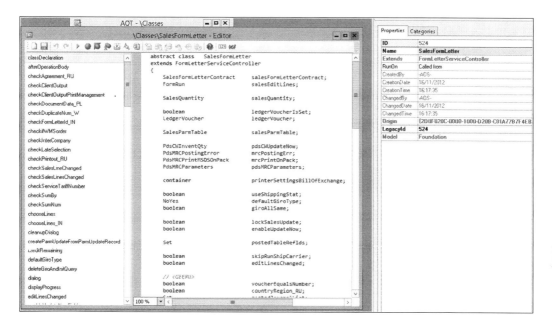

The menu bar shown in the preceding screenshot has the following options, listed from left to right:

The available options are explained as follows:

- **New**: This option creates a new method within the selected element.
- **Save**: This option saves all the methods open in the method list.
- **Run**: This option executes the method/class if it is executable.
- **Breakpoint**: This option sets a breakpoint at the line where the cursor has been placed.
- **Enable/Disable breakpoint**: This option enables or disable a breakpoint.
- **Remove all breakpoints**: This option removes all breakpoints for the current user.
- **Compile**: This option compiles and checks for errors in the code.

- **Lookup properties/methods**: This option displays help for the selected text if the cursor is placed over a core function/method; for example, list methods for a class, available values for enums, and so on.
- **Lookup label/text**: This option opens the label editor and searches for the selected text.
- **Scripts**: This option opens a context menu, which consists of small code snippets such as the do-while loop, header comments, and so on. You can also create your own scripts by creating new methods in the `EditorScripts` class.
- **Source Code Controls**: The following five options are to manage source code (version control):
    - **Add to Source control**: This option enables version control for the object
    - **Check Out**
    - **Check In**
    - **Undo Check Out**
    - **History**
- **Help**: This option displays the help file for the selected text in the code window, if such a help file exists. If not, it displays the help file for the X++ code editor.
- **Display Changes**: This option is similar to Visual Studio's option with the same name, wherein changes will be color coded in the editor.
- **Display Line numbers**: This option displays line numbers on the left-hand side of the code editor.

Compiler

The compiler in AX is in many ways just like any other compiler; it checks for syntax errors and presents the developer with error messages if there are any syntax errors. It can also give warnings if it sees any code that it finds misplaced or not written according to rules followed as best practices.

One of the major differences between the AX compiler and other compilers (such as the Visual Studio's .NET compiler) is that the AX compiler only requires you to compile the code that you have changed. The problem with this is that the code you have changed can make classes that consume your changed code to stop compiling. If they are not recompiled, and probably changed as well, users will experience a runtime error.

To decide how the compiler should act when compiling the code, you can look into some options provided to you when you change the compiler parameters.

First of all, to change the compiler parameters, you have to open the user options form (click the Microsoft Dynamics AX button (*Alt + F*) and select **Tools | Options**). From the **Development** tab in the user options form, click on the **Compiler** option to open the **Compiler setup** form, as shown in the following screenshot:

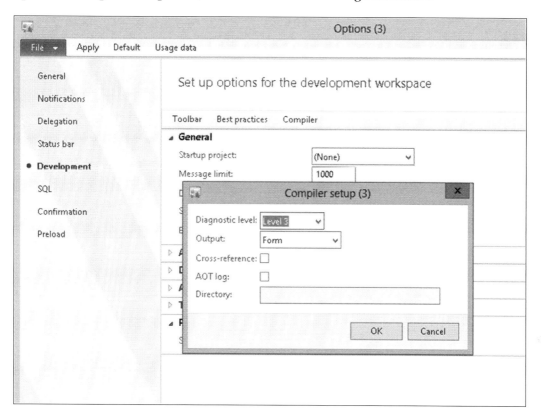

Here you check the **Cross-reference** flag and you are good to go. Remember that compiling code in AX will take a lot more time when it has to update the cross-references as well. Refer to the *Cross-references* section for more information regarding the cross-references. The fields in this form control how the X++ compiler should act. The code can be set to give compiler warnings at different levels, by changing the **Diagnostic level** option. You can choose not to receive any warnings about strange looking code (such as having a line of code after a return statement in a method). Compiler errors will, of course, still show. **Level 4** means that the compiler will also run checks for best practices.

The output defines where the compiler messages should appear. They can appear in a compiler output form such as the one shown in the following screenshot:

Alternatively, messages can appear in a print window:

```
Message window
Compiling Job HelloWorld
HelloWorld: line 5, pos 1 : *** Error: -1, Syntax error.
```

The compiler output form is set as the default because it contains more information and has a more standardized look and feel with division into the following tab pages:

- **Status**: This page lets you see the overall status of what you have compiled
- **Errors and warnings**: This page displays any errors or warnings, depending on the diagnostics level set in the compiler setup form
- **Best practices**: This page shows the best practice warnings as specified in the best practice parameters form
- **Tasks**: Tasks are added in the code by writing a comment that has the TODO statement:

  ```
  // TODO: Remember to fix the for-loop
  ```

Labels

The labels in Dynamics AX are a way of translating all user-visible text by only referencing to a label ID in the code. Each language is represented by a language-specific label file, and the file itself is stored in a database along with the AX models. These label files consist of the label ID and the text for that label in that specific language. When opening a label file in a text editor, you can see labels listed, such as the following:

```
@SYS390 Quantity that is not yet cost accounted in the BOM unit.
@SYS400 Create and compose serial numbers automatically.
@SYS403 Finish must be greater than start.
@SYS418 Transfer customer information?
```

This means that if you write `@SYS403` in the label property of a field in AX, it will display **Finish must be greater than start** to the users who are viewing that field in a form or report if they are using the language code `en-gb` (as this was taken from the label file `AxSYSen-gb.ald`).

To create a new label file, simply start the label file wizard from the Microsoft Dynamics AX button (*Alt* + *M*) and navigate to **Tools | Development tools | Label file wizard** and run through the three self-explanatory steps of the Wizard.

Your label file will then be named `AxXXXen-gb.ald`, where XXX is a three letter abbreviation chosen when walking through the Wizard.

Creating your first AX program

To make the Hello World example, we simply open the AOT by pressing *Ctrl* + *D* from anywhere in the main Dynamics AX window, or pressing the AOT button in the top menu, as shown in the first screenshot of this chapter. Then perform the following steps:

1. Go to the **Jobs** node in the AOT, right-click on it and select **New job**.
2. Check if the job opens automatically.
3. A new X++ editor window will open, showing a new job:

   ```
   static void Job1(Args _args)
   {
   }
   ```

As a job is static and has an input parameter of the `Args` class, it can be run directly. Obviously, the preceding example doesn't do anything, but simply editing the job as shown in the following code will display a **HelloWorld** message in the print window, after running the job by clicking on the **Go** button or pressing *F5*.

```
static void HelloWorld(Args _args)
{
    print "HelloWorld";
    pause;
}
```

The `pause` statement will halt the execution of the program and ask you if you would like to proceed. It is used in this example so that you will see what's in the print window. If the `pause` statement hadn't been put here, the print window would print `HelloWorld` and just close again in the blink of an eye.

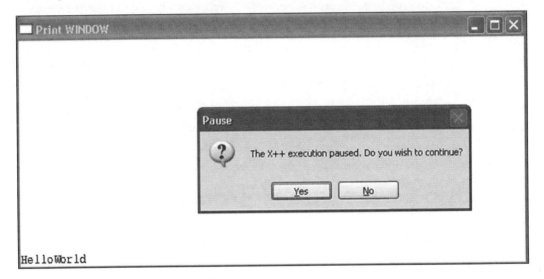

Utilizing the different development tools

AX comes with many different tools that can help developers in doing their job more efficiently. Some of these tools are however rarely used because they have little value. We will now have a look at some of the tools you will use on a day-to-day basis when programming in AX. Some of the tools you need to know about are as follows:

- Cross-references
- MorphX version control
- Debugger

Cross-references

Cross-references let developers select an element in the AOT and ask the system where the element is used. The result is listed in a form and shows if the element is used for read or write, the names of the elements it is called from, the methods using it, and where it is used in the methods (line/column). Cross-references also enable developers to see all elements used by the selected element. Of course, the best use of the cross-reference tool is to be able to see where a particular element is used.

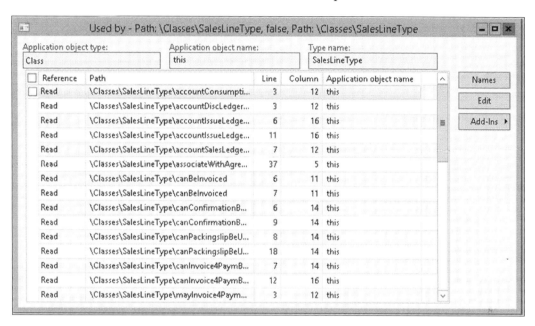

To be able to see the cross-referenced data, you need to update cross-references on a regular basis, at least if you want to see it in a development environment at a point in time where changes are being made. This can be done by setting up the cross-reference update to run in a batch, or you can set cross-references to update each time you change an element. To set it up to update every time you change an element, you need to change the compile parameters.

First of all though, you have to run a full cross-reference update. This is done by selecting the Microsoft Dynamics AX button (*Alt + F*) and navigating to **Tools | Development tools | Cross Reference | Periodic | Update**. You will see the following window:

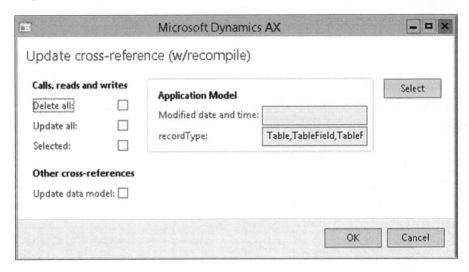

You can choose to delete all existing cross-references before creating them again, update cross-references for all elements in the AOT, or select which elements you would like to have updated by selecting **Selected** and clicking on the **Select** button. You will then get a query where you can filter what kind of elements you would like to update cross-references for.

In addition, there are two other useful types of cross-references that can be updated from this form. Updating the data model will enable end users to filter queries not only for the fields in the query that they are running, but also for fields from other related tables. An example of this is when the end user wants to print the report Cust, which lists customers. Let's say they would like to limit the report to show only the customers who have ever created an order. He would then have to add the SalesTable to the structure of the report so that it would create an inner joint between the CustTable and the SalesTable.

Updating the type hierarchy will enable developers to look at a class or an extended datatype and see if it belongs to a hierarchy, as seen in the following screenshot:

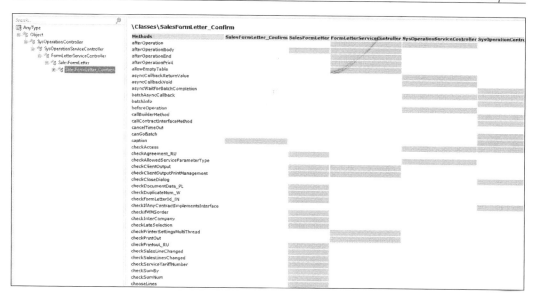

The left side of the application hierarchy tree shows which class hierarchy the `SalesFormLetter_Confirm` class belongs to. All classes in AX automatically extend the `Object` class, as you can see at the top of the tree. The right part of the form will show you all the methods of `SalesFormLetter_Confirm` and where they are implemented in the class hierarchy.

MorphX version control

If you have done development in Visual Studio on projects with multiple developers, you have most likely used a version control tool and know the essentials of it. Basically, it is a repository where you can check elements in and out, and track changes done to an element over time. If for some reason you would like to use an older version of an element, the version control enables you to do that as well.

When you check an element out, it is locked for other developers, so only you can make changes to it. When you have made your changes to the element, simply check it in and comment on what kind of changes you have made. It will then be available for other developers to change again. If for some reason one of the changes made to the element creates an unwanted situation, you can simply revert the element to the state in which it was before the particular change was made.

Setting up the MorphX version control

To set up the MorphX **Version Control System** (**VCS**) in AX, simply click on the Microsoft Dynamics AX button (*Alt + F*) and navigate to **Tools** | **Development tools** | **Version Control** | **Setup** | **Parameters**.

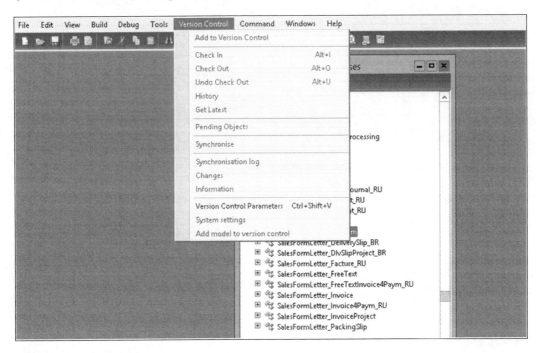

You should then set up this form, as shown in the preceding screenshot. First of all, you have to select **Enable** in the source control status. Then you need to select the version control type you would like to use. This book only covers the MorphX VCS as it is the best option for a small-sized project with five or less developers. The main reason for this is that it doesn't require each developer to have a full AX installation locally like the Visual Source Safe and Team Foundation Server do.

If you are creating a new module for AX, or if you are already using the Team Foundation Server, selecting the Team Foundation Server as the version control for AX might be a better option.

Chapter 1

> When using the MorphX VCS, the repository is actually inside the AX database, so you will always have access to it as long as you are logged on to your AX solution.

You can also choose to have the AOT elements color coded, depending on the VCS status, and to receive a warning when reverting objects, as shown in the following screenshot:

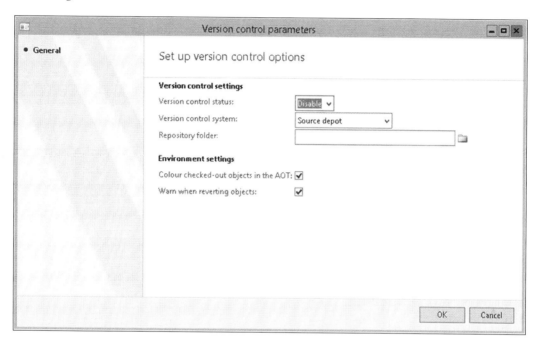

After setting these parameters, you can choose to create a repository by clicking on the Microsoft Dynamics AX button (*Alt + F*) and navigate to **Tools | Development tools | Version Control | Setup | Create repository**.

This will basically check in all elements in the AOT with a shared comment at that point in time. If you have a new solution without any modifications to the standard AX, this is not needed as you always have the option to go back to the original version in the system layers.

You can also set some rules as to what should be allowed or denied when trying to check in an element into the VCS, by clicking on the Microsoft Dynamics AX button (*Alt + F*) and navigate to **Tools** | **Development tools** | **Version Control** | **Setup** | **System settings**.

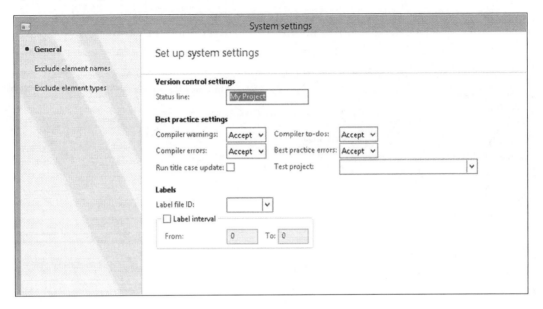

In this form, you can select to set rules so that the developers can't check the code that doesn't compile or have best practice errors.

You can also set up a test project and run the code through that test project successfully before being able to check in code.

Using the MorphX version control

When you have set up the MorphX VCS, you can start adding elements to the VCS as you start working on them.

To add an element to the VCS, simply select the element in the AOT and click on the **Add to version control** button from the AOT menu bar or by right-clicking the element and selecting **Add to version control**.

When an element has been added to the version control, you will be able to check in the element to add your changes to the repository. This is done by clicking on the **Check-In** button from the AOT menu bar, hitting *Alt + I*, or right-clicking the element and selecting **Check-In**.

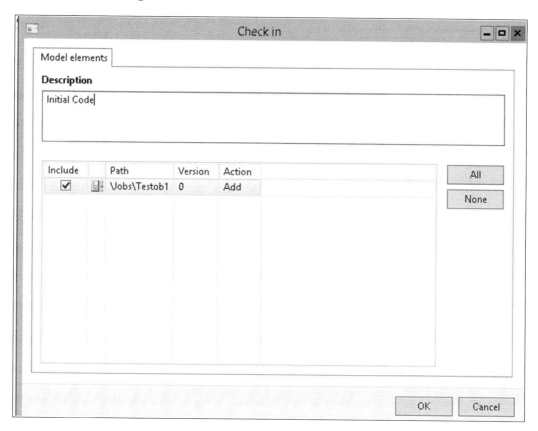

You will then see a form consisting of all elements that are checked out (or added to the VCS but not yet checked in). You have to type a description of what you have done to the element before clicking on **OK**. The element will then be checked into the repository.

To see the history of what has been done to this element over time, you can select the element in the AOT and click on the **History** button, or right-click the element and select **History**.

The **History** form will show the history of a specific element in the AOT. The history consists of all the check ins with comments, user ID, date, time, and version ID.

You can also open the .xpo file from the history form by clicking on the **View File** button.

 XPO is the export format that is used by AX to export and import code. It can be used to transfer code from one AX solution to another. The .xpo files are in text format and can be opened in a text editor for verification.

To open the selected version of the element in an AOT window, click on the **Open new window** button. If you open a version other than the current one or one that is checked out by someone else, you will only be able to read the code (no changes allowed).

Selecting two versions of the same element enables the **Compare** button, where you can compare the two different versions to track the changes.

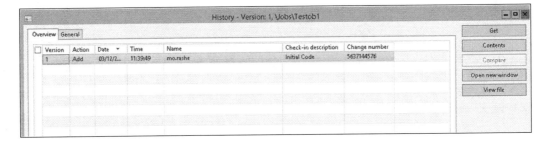

The debugger

The most important developer tool is the debugger. This tool helps you in your search to find what is wrong with your code, if you are one of those developers who write code that doesn't work as expected. Even if you never write code with bugs, you might be lucky enough to find other developers' bugs, and the debugger will then hopefully make you curse and swear a little less.

The debugger contains two main sections, the code section at the top and the information section at the bottom.

The code section is where you see the active code being executed. You can execute the code step-by-step, run it from where you are, stop the code's execution, step into, step over (and even go backwards) in the active method, set breakpoints, toggle breakpoints, and remove breakpoints.

The information section contains separate windows for the call stack, local, global, and class variables, as well as breakpoints, output, and the variable watch.

Dissecting the AX architecture

Now that you have seen some of the development tools in AX, let's have a look at how AX is built from a technical perspective.

We will look at the following concepts:

- Application object layers
- Network tiers

Application object layers

Dynamics AX 2012 consists of 16 application object layers that contain all the elements you see in the AOT. These 16 layers are basically formed out of eight core application layers and a patch layer for each core layer.

These layers can be looked at as an onion with multiple layers; the lowest layer or core application layer being the SYS layer and the outermost layer being the user layer USR.

So when any application element is being executed, the system will look at the outermost code layer first, to see if there is any code for that element. If there isn't, it peels a layer off the onion and tries the next layer. When it hits a layer where the element exists, it will use the code from this layer and will not continue to peel off layers to find code for that element in the innermost layers. The 16 layers of Dynamics AX 2012 are shown here:

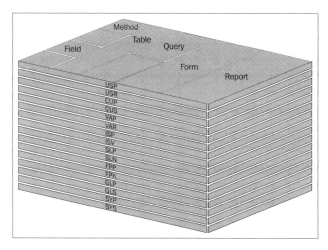

The following list is taken from the Dynamics AX 2012 MSDN site and provides an explanation for each layer:

Layer	Description
USR	The user layer is for user modifications, such as reports.
CUS	The customer layer is for modifications that are specific to a company.
VAR	**Value Added Resellers** (**VAR**) can make modifications or new developments to the VAR layer as specified by the customers, or as a strategy of creating an industry-specific solution.
ISV	When an **Independent Software Vendor** (**ISV**) creates its own solution, the resultant modifications are saved in the ISV layer.
SLN	The solution layer is used by distributors to implement vertical partner solutions.
FPK	The FPK layer is an application object patch layer reserved by Microsoft for future patching or other updates.
GLS	When the application is modified to match country- or region-specific legal demands, the modifications are saved in the GLS layer.
SYS	The standard application is implemented at the lowest level, the SYS layer. The application objects in the standard application can never be deleted.

Network tiers

AX 2012 is built as a three-tier solution. This means that it has a data tier, in which the data is stored, a logic tier, where all business logic is executed, and a presentation layer, which presents information to the user and receives input from the user.

As an AX developer, you can choose to have the piece of code you are writing to run on the client or the server. The client will represent the presentation tier and the server will represent the logic tier. The AX server is also called the **Application Object Server** (**AOS**). The data tier is hosted on MS SQL Server.

There are also two completely different clients available in AX. The regular Windows client, also known as the rich client, is the one most users think of when we talk about the AX client; but there is also a business connector client. The business connector client can be used by a third-party application to integrate with AX, and it is also used by the enterprise portal.

In addition to these three layers, we also often talk about a fourth component in the tier model, which is the file server. The file server is not really a tier itself, as it does not execute any code but only stores the code.

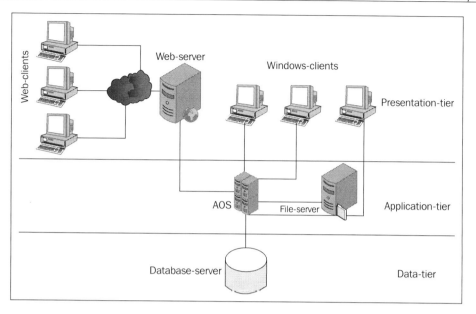

Case study – Carz Inc.

Most of the examples in this book are related to a case study where you have been assigned with the task of developing a module in AX for Carz Inc., a car rental company.

Carz Inc. rents out cars and sells them after they have reached a certain mileage.

The company needs to store information about their cars and their customers, and they need a booking system within Dynamics AX that enables them to see which cars are available/rented out within different car groups.

The customers should also be able to see availability from an enterprise portal site.

The examples will show you step-by-step how to create extended data types, tables, forms, reports, and everything you need to make the whole module work according to the best practice rules and according to the requirements set by Carz Inc.

Summary

Now that you have made it through the first chapter of this book, you have hopefully gained a good foundation to learn more on how to program in AX.

This chapter has shown you how to write the famous Hello World program in AX. It has taken you through the development environment, where you learned about the different elements in the AOT.

You have seen some of the most important development tools that you will get to know very well once you get going with the AX development.

The application object layers and network tiers have shown you the main concepts behind the technical architecture of AX and you have read a little bit about the case study that we will continue to use throughout the book.

In the next chapter, you will learn the syntax of the X++ language by looking at the different data types you can use in X++, how to write statements and loops (such as if/else and while loops), how different operators are used, and how to create and use classes and methods.

The X++ Language

X++ is the programming language used to build Dynamics AX functionalities. X++ is an object-oriented programming language like C++.

After finishing this chapter, you will be able to understand the X++ language; you will know what kind of datatypes are available, how to create all kinds of loops, how to compare and manipulate variables, where to find predefined functions, and how to use them.

The chapter will cover:

- Comments
- Datatypes
- Statements and loops
- Operators
- Classes and methods
- Macros
- Events

Introduction

You have already seen the Hello World example and probably thought that this looks pretty easy and yes, it is. The X++ syntax is not very strict, as it is case insensitive. However, you should try to follow the naming conventions used in the rest of AX.

Some, but not all, of these naming conventions are listed here:

- Application object names are in mixed case (the first letter of the name is uppercase and so is the first letter of each word in the name). This is called Camel casing, for example, `SalesFormLetter`.
- Methods, variables, and functions have mixed case names with lowercase first letter. This is called Pascal casing, for example, `initFromSalesTable`.
- Primitive variable types use lowercase names, for example, `str`.
- All names should be in US English.
- Be consistent while naming.
- Only tables, base enums, and extended datatypes should have the prefix `DEL_`. This prefix is used to indicate that the element will be removed in the next version and is used by the data upgrade scripts in AX.

To learn more about the different best practices in AX, please check out the developers' help file or MSDN for Dynamics AX.

When writing comments in the code, you can either use a one-line comment or a multiline comment. The one-line comment is written as follows:

```
// This is a one line comment
```

A multiline comment is written as follows:

```
/* This comment spans over
   multiple lines.

   This is the last line of this comment */
```

Comments are colored green in the editor window.

Datatypes

We will now take a look at the different kind of datatypes you can use in AX. They can be separated into two main groups:

- Primitive datatypes
- Composite datatypes

Primitive datatypes

Primitive datatypes are the building blocks of the programming language. They are used to store a single value based on the type in runtime code. The values that can be stored for each datatype varies depending on the datatype that is used. If you want to store a text string, you can use the string datatype. If you want to store a date value, you can use the `date` datatype or perhaps `utcdatetime`. You can also use the datatype `anytype` if the type of data read into the variable is decided at runtime.

In the next chapter, we will create extended datatypes and see how they can be used to easily create fields in a table. All of the extended datatypes extend primitive datatypes. The different primitive datatypes available in AX are as follows:

- String
- Integer
- Real
- Boolean
- Date
- Enum
- timeofday
- utcdatetime
- anytype

String

The string datatype is probably one of the most frequently used datatypes. It is used to hold text information and the length can either be set while declaring the variable or it can be dynamic. When using fixed length, simply add the number of characters you would like to limit the variable to between the variable type and the name of the variable, as shown in the following example (note that the variable type keyword is `str` and not `string`):

```
static void Datatypes_string1(Args _args)
{
    str 7   fixedLengthString;
    str     dynamicLengthString;


    fixedLengthString = "Welcome to Carz Inc";
    dynamicLengthString = "Welcome to Carz Inc";
```

```
        print fixedLengthString;
        print dynamicLengthString;
        pause;
}
```

The `print` statements in the preceding code will display the following window:

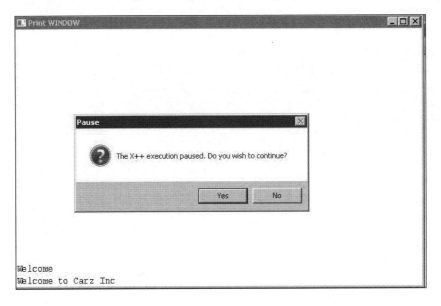

When working with strings, there are some nice functions that will help you manipulate strings, search for text inside a string, and so on. These functions can be found in AOT by navigating to **System Documentation | Functions** and some can be found by navigating to **Classes | Global**. Some of these functions are covered in this chapter, but you should get familiar with more functions by browsing AOT and trying them out yourself.

The strfmt method

The `strfmt` method is used to format a string and change any occurrences of `%n` with the parameter n:

```
Syntax: str strFmt(str _string, ...)
```

To illustrate this, the following job will print **100: Welcome to Carz Inc**:

```
static void Datatypes_string_strmft(Args _args)
{
    str     name;
    int     a;
```

```
        name = "Carz Inc";
        a = 100;

        print strfmt("%1: Welcome to %2", a, name);
        pause;
    }
```

Notice that the `strfmt` method also converts other datatypes into string.

The substr method

The `substr` method returns a part of a string. The first parameter is the original string, the second is the start position, and the third is the number of characters to read. Here is an example:

```
    Syntax: str subStr(str _text, int _position, int _number)
    static void Datatypes_string_substr(Args _args)
    {
        str     carBrand;

        carBrand = "Volkswagen";

        print substr(carBrand, 6, 5);
        pause;
    }
```

The `print` statement from the preceding method will display **wagen** as the substring starts at position 6 of the value of the first parameter, which is **Volkswagen**, and reads five characters ahead.

Integer

Integers are numbers without decimals, and in AX, they are divided into two separate datatypes: `Int32` is a 32-bit integer and `Int64` is a 64-bit integer.

The `Int32` datatype ranges from -2,147,483,647 to 2,147,483,647. The `Int64` datatype ranges from -9,223,372,036,854,775,808 to 9,223,372,036,854,775,808, which should be enough for most of us.

You can do any kind of arithmetic operation with the integers directly in the code, for example, a multiplication operation as shown in the following example that will print **Carz Inc have 24 cars in total**:

```
    static void Datatypes_integer1(Args _args)
    {
        int     carsInEachOffice;
```

```
    int     offices;

    carsInEachOffice = 6;
    offices = 4;

    print strfmt("Carz Inc have %1 cars in total", carsInEachOffice *
offices);
    pause;
}
```

Dividing two integers will result in a real number, unless you are returning the value to an integer. This means that dividing 24 by 4 gives the result 6.00, but returning the result to an integer and printing the integer returns 6 as the output, as you can see from the following example:

```
static void Datatypes_integer2(Args _args)
{
    int     x = 24;
    int     y = 4;
    int     res = x/y;
    ;
    // Prints a real value
    print strfmt("%1 / %2 = %3", x, y, x/y);
    // Automatically type casted to int
    // to print the integer value
    print strfmt("%1 / %2 = %3", x, y, res);
    pause;
}
```

Real

A real variable can consist of decimal numbers and integers. It spans a range of $-(10)^{127}$ to $(10)^{127}$ with a precision of 16 significant digits. It is worth mentioning that in a few European countries, even though the system language setting might use commas as the decimal separator, the code in AX accepts only periods as the decimal separator.

When the code is executed, the `print` statement will show the decimal separator that is set in your regional settings.

In a Norwegian locale, the following job will print **The car has used an average of 3,61 gallons gas**:

```
static void Datatypes_real1(Args _args)
{
    real    mileage;
```

```
    real    mpg;

    mileage = 127.32;
    mpg = 35.24;

    print strfmt("The car has used an average of %1 gallons gas",
mileage/mpg);
    pause;
}
```

There are also some useful functions to use with the `real` datatype in AX. Some of the frequently used datatypes are `str2num` and `num2str`.

The str2num function

If you have a string variable representing a number, you can convert the value into a real variable by using the `str2num` function:

```
Syntax: real str2Num(str _text)
static void Datatypes_str2num(Args _args)
{
    str     mileage;
    real    mileageNum;

    mileage = "388272.23";
    mileageNum = str2num(mileage);

    print strfmt("The car has run %1 miles", mileageNum);
    pause;
}
```

The num2str function

You can also go the other way around by converting the value of a real variable into a string. However, this operation demands to know more about how you would like the number to be represented. The code is as follows:

```
Syntax: str num2Str( real number, int character, int decimals,
   int separator1, int separator2)
```

Look at the comments in the following example for an explanation of the parameters:

```
static void Datatypes_num2str(Args _args)
{
    str     mileage;
    real    mileageNum;
```

The X++ Language

```
        mileageNum = 388272.23;
        // num2str(number to be converted,
        //         minimum characters required,
        //         required number of decimals,
        //         decimal separator <1=point, 2=comma>,
        //         thousand separator <0=none, 1=point,
        //         2=comma, 3=space>)
        mileage = num2str(mileageNum,0,2,2,0);
        print strfmt("The car has run %1 miles", mileage);
        pause;
    }
```

The preceding job will print **The car has run 388272,23 miles**.

Boolean

The Boolean datatype is just a representation of an integer that can only have the values 0 (false) or 1 (true):

```
    boolean    isAvailable = true;
```

Date

The Date datatype obviously holds date values. The dates are system formatted as dd\mm\yyyy:

```
    date birthday = 29\01\2008
```

The variable of type date can hold values from 1\1\1900 to 31\12\2154 and you can use integers to add or subtract to a date.

To get the session date set in AX, you can use the systemdateget() function. The session date in AX is automatically set to be equal to the machine date on the computer running your AX client when you start the AX client. You can change the session date by pressing *Alt + F* and going to **Tools | Session Date**. In the form that opens, you can change both the session date and time. This is typically done to post a journal as if it were posted on a different date than the actual one.

To retrieve the local machine's date, use the today() function.

Enum

Enum datatypes are represented in AOT by navigating to **Data Dictionary | Base Enums**. You can use these enums in the code as a list of literals as it is much more convenient to read and understand than a list of integers. Each enum can have a maximum of 251 literals.

The first literal in an enum is indexed by the integer 0, the next one is indexed by 1, and so on; each of these integers represent a more understandable value as shown in the following example. Here, you can see how you can assign an enum value to an enum variable of type `Weekdays`:

```
Weekdays day = Weekdays::Monday;
```

The value that is stored in the variable day will be the integer 1 since the enum `Weekdays` also has a value 0 that represents the enum `None`, but it's a lot easier to read this code instead of the following that does the exact same thing:

```
Weekdays day = 1;
```

The enum2str function

To get the label for one specific enum value, simply use the `enum2str` function as shown in the following example:

```
static void Datatypes_enum2str(Args _args)
{
    SalesType        salesType; // a standard enum in AX

    salesType = SalesType::Sales;
    info(strfmt("The name of the current sales type is '%1'",
enum2str(salesType)));
}
```

This example will display an output as shown in the following screenshot:

Actually, in the preceding example, you don't have to use `enum2str` as the enum value is automatically converted to a string, as it is used in the `strfmt()` function. However, trying to use the enum variable directly in the info like the line below instead, will result in a compilation error because you cannot add an enum variable to a string. So, in this example, the `enum2str` function would come in handy:

```
info("The name of the current sales type is " + salesType);
```

> Note that we used the `info` method in this example instead of the `print` statement. The `info` method is a more user-friendly way of displaying information to the end users. It is defined as a static method in the `Global` class and simply adds a new message of type info to the AX information log. Other types that can be put into the information log (also known as the infolog) are error and warning. Try them out by using `error()` and `warning()` instead of `info()`.

The enum2int function

In the same way as you get the label of the enum value, you can also get the integer that it represents by using the `enum2int` function. This is shown in the following example:

```
static void Datatypes_enum2int(Args _args)
{
    SalesType       salesType;

    salesType = SalesType::Sales;
    info(strfmt("The value of the current sales type element is %1",enum2int(salesType)));
}
```

The `info` statement will print the following output:

The timeofday datatype

The variable type `timeofday` is an integer representing the number of seconds since midnight. It can have a value from 0 to 86400, which is stored in the database. When used in a report or a form, it is automatically converted to values from 12:00:00 a.m. to 11:59:59 p.m.

The str2time function

The `str2time` function converts a string representation of time to the `timeofday` value as long as the string is a valid time. If it's not a valid time, the function returns -1. This is shown in the following code:

```
static void Datatypes_str2time(Args _arg)
{
```

```
    str timeStr;
    timeofday time;
    ;
    timeStr = "09:45";
    time = str2Time(timeStr);
    info(strfmt("%1 seconds have passed since midnight when the clock
is %2", time, timeStr));
}
```

The preceding example will print the following output to the infolog:

35100 seconds have passed since midnight when the clock is 09:45

The utcdatetime datatype

The `utcdatetime` datatype holds date, time, and the timezone information (although the timezone part cannot be used within an X++ query).

One of the really nice things about `utcdatetime` is that you can store a value in an `utcdatetime` variable and have it displayed to users around the world in their local time zone and time format.

UTC is an abbreviation for Coordinated Universal Time.

The anytype datatype

The `anytype` datatype can contain any of the other primitive datatypes. The type of the variable data is decided by the first value that is set for the variable.

In the following example, the `any` variable will work as a string variable at runtime because the first value is a string. As the second value is an integer, it is actually converted at runtime to a string, so the `print` statement will show 33 when executing the job. The code is as follows:

```
static void Datatypes_anytype1(Args _args)
{
    anytype any;

    any = "test";
    any = 33;

    print any;
    pause;
}
```

There has to be a catch with a datatype like this, right? Consider the following code:

```
static void Datatypes_anytype2(Args _args)
{
    anytype any;

    any = systemdateget();
    any = "test";

    print any;
    pause;
}
```

The compiler will not give any errors here because we can assign any value to the variable, as we are using the `anytype` datatype. However, trying to set a string value to a variable of type `date` will give a runtime error.

As you probably understand, you should try to avoid using the `anytype` datatype. The only exception where the `anytype` datatype can be useful is for parameters or return values for methods that can take different datatypes as input or output. Consider the example where a method can be called from different places and with different input. In one situation, the method will be called with a string and in another situation, the method will be called with an integer. Instead of creating two methods or one method with two different input parameters, you can use the `anytype` datatype as the input parameter to the method and have the method check if it's an integer or a string that was passed to it.

Composite datatypes

Composite datatypes are datatypes where each variable can have multiple other variables. The different kinds of composite datatypes are:

- Container
- Class
- Table
- Array

Container

A container can consist of multiple values of any primitive datatypes mixed together. You can store containers as fields in tables by using the container field.

Containers are immutable and adding or deleting a value in the container requires the system to actually create a new container, copy the value before and after the new value, and remove the deleted value.

The container functions

In the following example, you can see some of the container functions that you will be using to insert values into containers, delete values from containers, read values from containers, and get the number of elements in a container.

 Check out the Global class to find other methods.

```
static void Datatypes_container_functions(Args _args)
{
    container    con;

    // conins - Insert values to the container
    con = conins(con, 1, "Toyota");
    con = conins(con, 2, 20);
    con = conins(con, 3, 2200.20);
    con = conins(con, 4, "BMW");
    con = conins(con, 5, 12);
    con = conins(con, 6, 3210.44);

    // condel - Delete the third and the fourth element
    // from the container
    con = condel(con, 3, 2);

    // conpeek - Read values from the container
    info(conpeek(con,1));
    info(conpeek(con,2));
    info(conpeek(con,3));
    info(conpeek(con,4));

    // connull - Reset the container
    con = connull();

    // conlen - Get the length of the container
    info(strfmt("Length: %1",conlen(con)));
}
```

The X++ Language

Class

Classes in Dynamics AX are mostly similar to classes in other languages; they are blueprints that define the application logic.

When you create an object of a class, you also want to be able to reference that object throughout the scope where you are using the class methods and the data stored within the object.

See the following example to get a hint on how an object is created from a class and how the object is referenced by a class variable:

```
static void Datatypes_class_variable(Args _args)
{
    // Declare a class variable from the RentalInfo class
    RentalInfo    rentalInfo;

    // An object is created and referenced by the
    // class variable rentalInfo
    rentalInfo = new RentalInfo();

    // Call methods to set/get data to/from the object
    rentalInfo.setCar("BMW 320");
    info(strfmt("The car is a %1", rentalInfo.getCar()));
}
```

The `RentalInfo` class is implemented as follows:

```
public class RentalInfo
{
    str    car;
}
void setCar(str _car)
{
    car = _car;
}
str getCar()
{
    return car;
}
```

Classes and methods have been described in greater detail in the following sections.

Table

A table can be used in X++ by creating a table object. This technique of referencing data elements as objects is fairly unique to Dynamics AX (LINQ in C# has a similar concept).

This means that you can easily insert, update, delete, search, and perform other actions against the table data directly, without creating a connection and a statement.

In the code, you can simply write a `select` statement, as shown in the following example:

```
static void Datatypes_table(Args _args)
{
    CustTable       custTable;   // This is the table variable
    CustAccount     custAccount;

    custAccount = "1000";
    select Name from custTable
        where custTable.AccountNum == custAccount;

    info(strfmt("The name of the customer with AccountNum %1 is %2",
custAccount, custTable.Name));
}
```

All tables in the data dictionary are actually classes that extend the system class `common`. They can be seen as wrappers for their corresponding tables in the database, as they have all the necessary functionality to read, create, modify, and delete the data stored in the table that they wrap. In addition, the developer can of course add more methods than what are inherited by the common class. In the following subsections, you can find some of the frequently used table methods.

The find method

All tables should have at least one `find` method that selects and returns one record from the table that matches the unique index specified by the input parameters. The last input parameter in a `find` method should be a Boolean variable called `forupdate` or `update` that defaults to `false`. When it is set to `true`, the caller object can update the record that is returned by the `find` method.

See the following example from the `InventTable` class:

```
static InventTable find(ItemId    itemId,
                        boolean   update = false)
{
    InventTable   inventTable;

    inventTable.selectForUpdate(update);

    if (itemId)
    {
        select firstonly inventTable
            index hint ItemIdx
            where inventTable.ItemId == itemId;
    }

    return inventTable;
}
```

The exist method

As with the `find` method, there should also exist an `exist` method. It is basically the same as the `find` method, except that it just returns true if a record with the unique index specified by the input parameter(s) is found.

In the following example, also from the `InventTable` class, you can see that the `exist` method returns true if the input parameter has a value and the `select` statement returns a value:

```
static boolean exist(ItemId   itemId)
{
    return itemId && (select RecId from inventTable
            index hint ItemIdx
            where inventTable.ItemId == itemId
        ).RecId != 0;
}
```

The initFrom method

Tables that are related to each other share the data that makes up the relationship and other information as well. When creating new records in the many table in a one-to-many relationship, you can create the `initFrom` methods that set the common fields in the table.

The `initFrom` method can also be used to default the values in fields in a table from another table.

The following example is taken from the `BOMTable` class and shows how it initiates the `ItemId` and `ItemGroupId` fields in `BOMTable` from the corresponding fields in the `InventTable` class:

```
void initFromInventTable(InventTable table)
{
    this.bomId        = table.ItemId;
    this.ItemGroupId  = table.ItemGroupId;
}
```

Array

An array is a list of values that are all of the same type as opposed to the container that can consist of values of different types. The list of values starts with element 1. If you set a value to index number 0 of an array, the array is reset.

There are two different ways of using an array. You can either use a fixed length array if you know how many elements (maximum) you will have in the array. If you don't know how many elements can be stored in the array at runtime, you can use a dynamic array.

In addition to this, you can also specify something called *partly on disk arrays* that specifies how many elements should be loaded into memory when the array is referenced. This might be a good performance optimization if you have arrays with a lot of data.

The following example explains the different uses of arrays:

```
static void Datatypes_array(Args _args)
{
    // Fixed length array
    str licenceNumber[10];

    // Fixed length array partly on disk.
    // 200 elements will be read into memory when this array
    // is accessed.
    int serviceMilage[1000,200];

    // Dynamic array
    str customers[];

    // Dynamic length array partly on disk.
    // 50 elements will be read into memory when this array
    // is accessed.
    Amount prices[,50];
}
```

Statements and loops

Statements and loops are used to control the execution flow of a program and most programming tasks would be impossible without them.

In AX, you have access to the following statements and loops:

- The `for` loop
- The `continue` statement
- The `break` statement
- The `while` loop
- The `do-while` loop
- The `if-else if-else` loop
- The `switch` statement

The for loop

A `for` loop can be used if the code at runtime knows how many times it should loop through a piece of code before the loop starts. The pseudocode of a `for` loop in AX is the same as any `for` loop in most programming languages derived from the C programming language. It is actually called a three-expression `for` loop, since it is made up of three steps:

1. Initialization of the variable used to increment the `for` loop.
2. Initialization of the test statement.
3. Setting the increment or decrement values for the variable.

As the following example shows, the variable `i` is initiated to `1`, then it tells the `for` loop to keep on looping as long as `i` is less than or equal to `10`. Then, it increments `i` by one for each loop:

```
int i;
for (i=1; i <= 10; i++)
{
    info (strfmt("This is the %1 Toyota", i));
}
```

The continue statement

If you would like the code to jump straight to the next iteration of the code, you can use the `continue` statement inside any loop.

The break statement

The `break` statement can be used to jump out of the loop even when there are more iterations to execute as per the loop condition.

In the preceding example, the `info` function was used rather than the `print` function from the Hello World example. The `info` function is much more convenient and looks much better from a user point of view. The print window should only be used to display messages to the developers when executing a test job or something similar.

The while loop

You can use the `while` loop to execute a piece of code many times until a certain condition is met. The `while` loop will only execute if the while condition is met. Here is an example:

```
int carsAvailable=10;
while (carsAvailable != 0)
{
    info (strfmt("Available cars at the moment is %1",
      carsAvailable));
    carsAvailable --;
}
```

The do-while loop

The `do-while` loop is pretty much the same as the `while` loop, except that it will execute once even though the while condition is not met. In a `do-while` loop, the loop is executed at least once, as the `while` expression is evaluated after the first iteration. Here is an example:

```
int carsAvailable=10;
do
{
    info (strfmt("Available cars at the moment is %1",
      carsAvailable));
    i--;

} while (carsAvailable != 0);
```

The if-else if-else loop

The execution flow of an `if-else if-else` loop is as follows:

1. The `if` statement checks to see if the condition used in the statement returns true. If it does, the system executes the body of the `if` statement.
2. If the `if` statement returns false, it is checked if the condition inside the `else-if` statement returns true. If it does, the system executes the body of the `else-if` statement.
3. The last `else` statement can be used directly with the `if` statement or after an `else-if` statement. The system will execute the body inside the last `else` statement only if the `if` statement and all the `else-if` statements return false.

The following is an example of the `if-else if-else` loop:

```
if (carGroup == CarGroup::Economy)
{
    info("Kia Picanto");
}
else if (carGroup == CarGroup::Compact)
{
    info("Toyota Auris");
}
else if (carGroup == CarGroup::MidSize)
{
    info("Toyota Rav4");
}
else if (carGroup == CarGroup::Luxury)
{
    info("BMW 520");
}
else
{
    info("Standard cars");
}
```

You can of course add as many `else-if` statements as you'd like and you can also nest them to have another `if` statement inside the body of an `if` statement, but this might not be the best way of getting things done. Instead, you should consider using the `switch` statement. The reason for this is that the condition has to be evaluated for each `if` and `else-if` statement, while the `switch` statement evaluates the condition once and then finds the correct hit.

The switch statement

The `switch` statement is similar in function to the `if` statement; however, the `switch` statement syntax makes the code far more legible. Note that you have to use the `break` statement at the bottom of each case. If it is not used, the system will continue to execute the next case as well.

The `default` statement can be used in similar way as the `else` statement to say that if none of the other cases contained the correct value, execute the default instead. Here is an example:

```
switch (carGroup)
{
    case CarGroup::Economy :
        info("Kia Picanto");
        break;
    case CarGroup::Compact :
    info("Toyota Auris");
        break;
    case CarGroup::MidSize :
        info("Toyota Rav4");
        break;
    case CarGroup::Luxury :
        info("BMW 520");
        break;
    default
        info("Standard cars");
        break;
}
```

Exception handling

As a developer it is always important to expect the unexpected. One way of making sure that your program can handle abnormal situations is using exception handling. In AX, that means using the following statements: `try`, `catch`, `throw`, and `retry`.

The `try` and `catch` statements should always go together. Using a `try` statement without a `catch` statement or vice versa will result in a compiler error.

When you use the `try` statement, you are indicating that whatever code is inside the `try` block, it might generate an abnormal situation that should be handled. The situation is handled in the `catch` block by specifying what kind of exception the `catch` block is taking care of. The following example shows how to catch an error exception and a deadlock exception. A deadlock will never occur in this example, but it is here just to show you how you can use the `retry` statement:

```
static void ExceptionHandling(Args _args)
{
    try
    {
        // Do something
        info("Now I'm here");
        // A situation that causes an error occur and you would
        // like to stop the execution flow
        if (true)
            throw error("Oops! Something happened");

        info("Now I'm there");
    }
    catch (Exception::Error)
    {
        // Handle the error exception
        info ("I would like to inform you that an error
           occurred");
    }
    catch (Exception::Deadlock)
    {
        // Handle the deadlock exception
        // Wait for 10 seconds and try again
        sleep(10000);
        retry;
    }
    info ("This is the end");
}
```

Operators

Operators are used to manipulate or check the values of variables. There are three different types of operators that we use when developing AX:

- Assignment operators
- Relational operators
- Arithmetic operators

Assignment operators

In order to assign values to variables, you have to use an assignment operator in X++. The most obvious operator is, of course, the = operator that will assign the value to the right of the = operator to the variable on the left. This means that the car variable in the following example will be assigned the value BMW.

```
str   car = "BMW";
```

Other assignment operators include ++, --, +=, and -= as you already know if you have been programming in C#, C++, Java, and so on. Refer to the following example for an explanation:

```
static void AssignmentOperators(Args args)
{
int carsInStock = 10;

carsInStock++; // carsInStock is now 11
carsInStock+=2; // carsInStock is now 13
carsInStock--; // carsInStock is now 12
carsInStock-=3; // carsInStock is now 9
}
```

The increment and decrement operators can also be prefixed instead of postfixed as shown in the preceding example, but there is no difference in their usage in X++ and it is best to use them as postfixed.

Relational operators

As you have seen already in the loops and if statements, the two frequently used relational operators are == and !=. These are used to find out if a variable is equal or not equal to the value to their right side.

This means that relational operators are used in statements that return true or false. Let's see the various relational operators available to us:

- The == operator returns true if both expressions are equal
- The != operator returns true if the first expression is not equal to the second expression
- The && operator returns true if the first expression *and* the second expression are true
- The || operator returns true if the first expression *or* the second expression *or* both are true

- The `!` operator returns true if the expression is false (can only be used with one expression)
- The `>=` operator returns true if the first expression is greater than or equal to the second expression
- The `<=` operator returns true if the first expression is less than or equal to the second expression
- The `>` operator returns true if the first expression is greater than the second expression
- The `<` operator returns true if the first expression is less than the second expression
- The last relational operator is the `like` operator, which I have explained in the following example:

```
static void RelationalOperatorLike(Args _args)
{
    str     carBrand = "Toyota";


    // use the * wildcard for zero or more characters
    if (carBrand like "Toy*")
    {
        info ("The car brand starts with 'Toy'");
    }
    // use the ? wildcard for one character
    if (carBrand like "Toy??a")
    {
        info ("The car brand starts with 'Toy' and the last character is 'a'");
    }
}
```

Arithmetic operators

The last type of operators is the arithmetic operators. These are used to perform mathematical calculations on variables, such as multiplication, division, addition, and subtraction and binary arithmetic as well.

As binary arithmetic is rarely used in standard AX, I won't go into its details here, but you can learn more about it in the SDK.

The following code shows examples of arithmetic operators:

```
static void ArithmeticOperators(Args _args)
{
    int x, y;

    x = 10;
    y = 5;

    info(strfmt("Addition: %1 + %2 = %3", x, y, x+y));
    info(strfmt("Subtraction: %1 - %2 = %3", x, y, x-y));
    info(strfmt("Multiplication: %1 * %2 = %3", x, y, x*y));
    info(strfmt("Division: %1 / %2 = %3", x, y, x/y));
}
```

This will print the following output to the infolog:

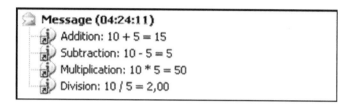

Classes and methods

One of the core components of an object-oriented programming language is a class. Classes are blueprints for objects and are used to define what an object of a certain type can do and what kind of attributes it has.

Classes in AX are similar to classes in C#, but you don't specify the methods of a class within its curly brackets; instead, you create new nodes under the class in AOT for each method.

The class declaration is used to hold variables that are global in the class. These variables are always protected as opposed to private and public. This means that objects of that class or objects of a subclass have direct access to these variables.

During development, you write classes and the classes are instantiated as objects at runtime. So, if Car is a class that defines the characteristics and behaviors of a car, the specific car with license number DE2223ED is an object (instance) of the Car class.

Method access

One can use the access modifiers or keywords such as public, protected, and private to control whether the methods in a class can call methods in another class. One can architect a class in such a way that methods that perform rudimentary tasks and are of use only within the class can be hidden. This makes the class safer to use as only deliberately exposed methods can be called by outside classes. This concept is referred to as encapsulation and is a key principle of object-oriented programming.

Encapsulation ensures that objects protect and handle their own information. Changes to an object's state can only be done from safe methods. This is done by using the access modifiers in the beginning of the method definitions:

- **Public**: These methods can be used from any methods where the class is accessible and can also be overridden by classes that extend the parent class (subclasses). If no access modifiers are explicitly written in the code, the compiler assumes that they are public and handles them accordingly.
- **Protected**: These methods can be used from any of the methods in the same class or its subclasses.
- **Private**: These methods can only be used from any of the methods in the same class.

The RunOn property

The code in AX can run on either the client or the server. The server here will be the AOS server. There are two ways of controlling where objects of a certain class should execute. When developing static methods, you can select to use the client or server modifier in the method header, as shown in the following example:

```
// This method will execute on the client.
static client void clientMethod()
{

}

// This method will execute on the server.
static server void serverMethod()
{

}
```

You can also set the RunOn property on a certain class to make all objects of that class run on either the client or the server. You can also set the RunOn property on the class to `CalledFrom`. This will make objects of that class execute on the same layer as the method that created the object.

One example of making sure that a method runs on the server or client is when you try to import a file from disk. When referencing to a fixed file location, the C drive is obviously the server's C drive when the code is executing on the server and the C drive on the client when the method is executing on the client.

Static methods

In AX, you will see that some methods have a method modifier named `static`. Actually, all the jobs we have looked at so far have been using the `static` modifier. This means that the method can be called directly without creating an object. Of course, this also means that the static classes can't access the protected data defined in the class declaration of the class.

The access modifier is used at the beginning of the method definition right after the method access modifier and before the return value, as shown in the following example:

```
public static void main(Args args)
{
}
```

To call a static method, you use a double colon instead of a period as you do in object methods:

```
SomeClass::staticMethod()
```

The default parameter

To set a default value for an input parameter in a method, simply add = <default value> as shown in the following example:

```
void defaultParameterExample(boolean test=true)
```

In this example, the variable test will default to true if no parameter is given when the method is called. This also means that the parameter is optional. If the method is called with the parameter set to false, it will be false when this method executes. However, if it's not called with any parameters, the test variable will automatically be set to true.

The Args class

The Args class is used extensively in AX in order to create a pointer to a caller object for the executing method.

It is used in forms, queries, and reports as the first argument in the constructor. This means that for any form, query, and report, you can get the Args class that has been passed to it by using the args() method. The Args class is also used to pass additional information by using the following methods:

- record: This will pass a record from a table
- parm: This will pass a string value
- parmEnum (along with parmEnumType): This will pass an enum value
- parmObject: This will pass an object of any type

This example demonstrates the effect of using Args when calling the main method in a class from a method in another element. The RentalInfoCaller is the calling class that calls the main method of the RentalInfo class:

```
public class RentalInfoCaller
{
}

// The main method here is just used
// to be able to execute the class
// directly and show the example.
```

```
public static void main(Args args)
{
    RentalInfoCaller      rentalInfoCaller;

    rentalInfoCaller = new RentalInfoCaller();
    rentalInfoCaller.callRentalInfo();
}

// This is the class that calls the
// main method if the RentalInfo class
void callRentalInfo()
{
    Args           args;

    args = new Args(this);

    RentalInfo::main(args);
}

// This method is just used as
// a proof that you are able
// to call methods in the calling
// object from the "destination" object
void callBackMethod()
{

    info ("This is the callBackMethod in an object of the RentalInfoCaller class");
}
```

 AX has a built-in reference to the current object called, which is used in the preceding example inside Args (this).

The following code shows the main method of the RentalInfo class:

```
public static void main(Args args)
{
    RentalInfoCaller       rentalInfoCaller;

    rentalInfoCaller = args.caller();
    rentalInfoCaller.callBackMethod();
}
```

The X++ Language

When executing the `RentalInfoCaller` class, the program will start in the `main` method and a new object of `RentalInfoCaller` is created followed by calling the `callRentalInfo` method. The `callRentalInfo` method will then create a new `args` object and pass the `rentalInfoCaller` object executing it as a parameter. This can be done either by passing the `rentalInfoCaller` object as the first parameter in the constructor or by calling the `args.caller()` method after the `args` object has been created. Then, the main method of the `RentalInfo` class is called with the newly created `args` object as parameter.

When the `main` method in the `RentalInfo` class starts, it uses the `args.caller()` method to get a reference to the object that called `RentalInfo`. This enables a callback to the caller object and executes its methods.

So, when executing the `RentalInfoCaller` class, the following result will be printed in the info window:

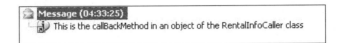

Inheritance

One of the central concepts of object-oriented programming is the possibility to inherit functionality defined at a higher level in the system. This can be done by having a class hierarchy where a method in a subclass overrides a method in the superclass (higher level). The method in the subclass can still use the functionality of the same method in the superclass by using the super function, as shown in the following example:

```
public void sellCar()
{
    super();
}
```

This method implies that the current class that the method belongs to extends another class where the functionality in the `sellCar` method is already written or that the `sellCar` method is defined at a higher level in the class hierarchy to which the current class belongs.

In our example, we have a superclass called `Car` that extends `Object` and we have the `Car_Economy`, `Car_Compact`, `Car_MidSize`, and `Car_Luxury` classes that extend the `Car` class. We have also overridden the `toString` method for all of these classes. An example for the `Car_Economy` class is shown here:

```
public str toString()
{
    str ret;

    ret = "Economy";

    return ret;
}
```

To make sure that all of the subclasses have the updated information about the superclass it is a good idea to compile forward when modifying the class hierarchy. This is done by right-clicking on the superclass, selecting **Add-Ins**, and clicking on **Compile Forward**. To see the methods that your class can use from the parent classes, simply right-click on the class in AOT and select **Override method**. You will get a list of methods that you can override in this class, as shown in the following screenshot:

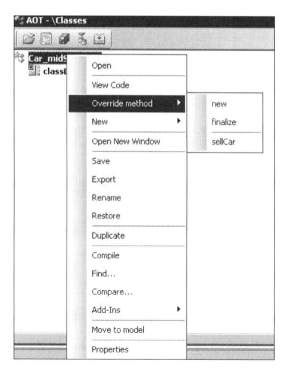

The construct method

As you saw earlier in this chapter, you can create an object of a class by using the reserved word `new`. AX has taken the creation of objects to the next level and created a method called `construct`. It is one of the best practices to create all the objects from the construct method.

The `construct` method should consider any parameters sent to it and based on those parameters, create and then return the correct object. The reason I say *the correct object* here is that a superclass should have a `construct` method that can create objects for all its subclasses and create the correct object based on the parameters sent to it.

Construct methods should always be static, public, and named `construct`, as shown in the following example:

```
public static Car construct(CarGroup carGroup)
{
    Car     car;

    switch (carGroup)
    {
        case CarGroup::Economy :
            car = new Car_Economy();
            break;
        case CarGroup::Compact :
            car = new Car_Compact();
            break;
        case CarGroup::MidSize :
            car = new Car_MidSize();
            break;
        case CarGroup::Luxury :
            car = new Car_Luxury();
            break;
    }
    return car;
}
```

The main method

Classes that should be able to start with the use of a menu item (a button in a form or an element in a menu) need a starting point.

In AX, this is achieved with a static method called `main`. The `main` method always takes one parameter of the `Args` type. This is done to be able to tell where the `main` method was called from. An example could be that a class is called in a form and you need to know which record the user had selected when pressing the button. This information can be passed on to the class in the `args` object.

The task of the `main` method is to create an instance of the class by calling the `construct` method (or in some cases where the `construct` method doesn't exist, calling the `new` method), prompting the user for information if needed (the `prompt` method), and then calling the method that controls the flow of the class (typically, the `run` method).

This is a typical example of a `main` method taken from the standard AX class `CustExchAdj`:

```
    public static void main(Args args)
    {
        CustExchAdj custExchAdj = new CustExchAdj();

        if (custExchAdj.prompt())
        {
            custExchAdj.run();
        }
    }
```

The RunBase framework

Whenever you write a class that typically asks a user for input and then starts a process based on that input, you use the RunBase framework. This is because most of the typical methods needed for such a job are already implemented in the `RunBase` class.

The RunBase framework is used either by directly extending `RunBase` or by extending a class that extends `RunBase`.

Some of the features implemented in the RunBase framework are as follows:

- **Run**: This feature follows the main flow of the operation
- **Dialog**: This feature prompts the user for input and storing that input
- **Batch execution**: This feature schedules the job for later execution
- **Query**: This feature is used to select data

- **Progress bar**: This feature is used to see current operation's progress
- **Pack/unpack with versioning**: This feature is used to store the variable's state (so that previously selected options can be restored when the user opens the form)

> Take a look at `tutorial_RunbaseForm` to see an example of how the `RunBaseBatch` class can be extended and how all of the preceding features are used.

The SysOperation framework

At a very high level, the SysOperation framework might seem similar to the RunBase framework, that is, the SysOperation framework allows code to be executed in batch mode and also query/parameterization potentially through a dialog. However, the SysOperation framework couldn't be more different. SysOperation is based on the **Windows Communication Foundation** (**WCF**) and uses a development pattern similar to **Model View Controller** (**MVC**).

Code written using the SysOperation framework can be exposed as a (web) service and can be executed within the .NET **Common Language Runtime** (**CLR**) environment (thereby performing significantly better than X++ (the RunBase framework code)). As one would expect, the SysOperation framework is the recommended method to develop batch-based operations in Dynamics AX 2012.

The SysOperation framework can be as simple or as complex as needed, for example, developers do not need to design complex dialogs if they are simply looking to develop a function that can execute in batch mode.

Let's develop a simple batch. In this example, we will create a batch process that loops through the customer call records and logs those that have the statistics group set to `Car` (or any other value specified as a parameter).

To begin with, we need a contract. A data contract is an effective class that contains the fields (called data members) that will be displayed on the batch dialog.

The data contract class must have the attribute `DataContractAttribute`, and the member functions should have the attribute `DataMemberAttribute`:

```
[DataContractAttribute]
public class CarDataContract
{
    CustAccount custaccount;
```

```
    NoYes           selectQuery;

    str             salesQuery;

}

[DataMemberAttribute
,SysOperationLabelAttribute(literalStr(@SYS96450))
,AifQueryTypeAttribute('_salesQuery', querystr(SalesTableSelect))
]
public str parmQuery(str _salesQuery = salesQuery)
{
    salesQuery = _salesQuery;

    return salesQuery;
}
```

The hierarchy of classes is shown in the following screenshot:

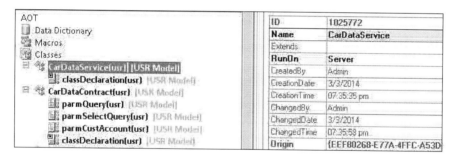

Notice the `SysOperationLabelAttribute` attribute in the preceding screenshot. Dynamics AX 2012 enables developers to decorate member functions with additional attributes. These attributes effectively function as metadata on a table field, for example, they can be used to change the label displayed on the dialog. The following are some of the key attributes used on member functions:

- `SysOperationLabelAttribute`: This attribute is used to specify the label that should be displayed on the dialog for the field represented by the member function

- `SysOperationHelpTextAttribute`: This attribute is used to display help text for the field linked with the member function

- `AifQueryTypeAttribute`: This attribute is used if the member function represents a query

The X++ Language

Next, we will create a service that is effectively the last function that will be called by the batch process.

We will create a method called `checkCustomer` and decorate it with the attribute `SysEntryPointAttribute`. This attribute indicates that function is a service operation. We will also pass the contract as a parameter. The code is as follows:

```
[SysEntryPointAttribute]
public void checkCustomer(CarDataContract _carDataContract)
{
    CustTable custtable;

    QueryRun   salesQueryRun;

    if(_carDataContract.parmSelectQuery())
    {
        salesQueryRun = new QueryRun(_carDataContract.parmQuery());

        while(salesQueryRun.next())
        {
            custtable = salesQueryRun.get(tableNum(CustTable));

            if(custtable.StatisticsGroup == "CAR")
                info(custtable.AccountNum);
        }
    }
    else
    {
        select custtable where custtable.AccountNum == _
carDataContract.parmCustAccount();

        if(custtable.StatisticsGroup == "CAR")
            info("Yes");

    }
}
```

Key Points
- Make sure that the parameter signature is as follows: _dataContract. Hence, in our example, it will be _CarDataContract.
- Make sure that the class property is set to execute on the server.

[68]

Chapter 2

Now we have two options:

- We can add the preceding operation directly to a service, which allows us to quickly deploy the batch function.
- We can create a custom controller class (by extending `SysOperationServiceController`), which will give us more flexibility. For example, we might want to call our service from the vendor form and have the vendor account prefilled in the query.

Let's run through the first option.

Using a standard instance of `SysOperationServiceController`, we will create a new service:

1. Create a new service and call it `CarDataService`.
2. Change the class property to `CarDataService`.
3. Right-click on the **Operations** node and select the **Add** operation.
4. Add the **checkVendor** operation.

Now we will add a menu item with the following steps:

1. Create a new action menu item and call it `CarDataService`.
2. Set the `ObjectType` property to `Class`.
3. Set the `Object` property to `SysOperationServiceController`.
4. Set the `Parameter` property to `CarDataService.checkCustomer`. Note that a dropdown is not available.

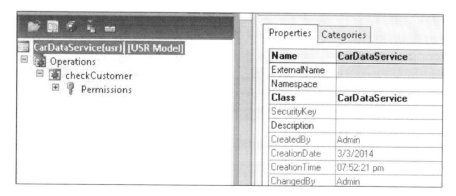

Before we can run the menu item, we must compile our code in the **common intermediate language** (CIL).

[69]

The X++ Language

The collection classes

In addition to the composite datatypes we looked at earlier in this chapter, there are also some classes that you can use to store multiple values and even objects in a given way.

These classes are called collection classes and were earlier known as foundation classes. They are system classes, so you can't change them; however, you can extend them to create your own collection classes. The following collection classes are found in standard AX:

- Array
- List
- Map
- Set
- Struct

Array

I know that this is a bit confusing since there is a composite datatype called array as well, but the collection class for array is a bit different, as you can see in the following example. It can also store objects which the array datatype can't. The example code is as follows:

```
static void Collection_Array(Args _args)
{
    // Create a new Array where the
    // elements are objects
    Array   cars = new Array(Types::Class);
    Car   car;
    int i;

    // Set new elements to the car Array
    // at the given index positions
    cars.value(1, new Car_Economy());
    cars.value(2, new Car_Luxury());
    cars.value(3, new Car_Compact());

    // Display the content of the Array
    info (cars.toString());

    // Loop through the Array to display
    // each element
```

```
        for (i=1; i<=cars.lastIndex(); i++)
        {
            car = cars.value(i);
            info(strfmt("Class: %1", car.toString()));
        }
    }
```

List

A list contains elements of one given type that are accessed sequentially. As you can see from the following example, you can store elements by using `addStart` or `addEnd` any time. However, when you loop through the list using `ListEnumerator`, the elements are accessed in the correct sequence. The example code is as follows:

```
    static void Collection_List(Args _args)
    {
        // Create a new list of type string
        List names = new List(Types::String);
        ListEnumerator    listE;

        // Add elements to the list
        names.addEnd("Lucas");
        names.addEnd("Jennifer");
        names.addStart("Peter");

        // Display the content of the list
        info (names.toString());

        // Get the enumerator of the list
        // to loop through it
        listE = names.getEnumerator();
        while (listE.moveNext())
        {
            info (strfmt("Name: %1", listE.current()));
        }
    }
```

Map

A map is used to index a value using a key value. Both the key and the value can be of any type specified in the `Types` enum. The example code is as follows:

```
    static void Collection_Map(Args _args)
    {
        // Create a new map with a key and value type
```

The X++ Language

```
    Map cars = new Map(Types::Integer, Types::String);
    MapEnumerator    mapE;

    // Insert values to the map
    cars.insert (1, "Volvo");
    cars.insert (2, "BMW");
    cars.insert (3, "Chrysler");

    // Display the content of the map
    info (cars.toString());

    // Get the enumerator to loop
    // through the elements of the map
    mapE = cars.getEnumerator();
    while (mapE.moveNext())
    {
         info(strfmt("Car %1: %2", mapE.currentKey(), mapE.currentValue()));
    }
}
```

Set

A set can contain one of the valid types of the `Types` enum. The values in the set are unique and they are sorted automatically. As you can see after executing the following example, the values will be stored in the following order: `Ford`, `Mazda`, and `Toyota`. The example code is as follows:

```
static void Collection_Set(Args _args)
{
    // Create a new set of type String
    Set cars = new Set(Types::String);
    SetEnumerator    setE;

    // Add elements to the set
    cars.add("Toyota");
    cars.add("Ford");
    cars.add("Mazda");
    // Check to see if an element
    // exists in the set
    if (cars.in("Toyota"))
        info ("Toyota is part of the set");
```

```
        // Display the content of the set
        info (cars.toString());

        // Get the enumerator of the set
        // to loop through it
        setE = cars.getEnumerator();
        while (setE.moveNext())
        {
            info(setE.current());
        }
    }
```

Struct

A struct can be viewed upon as a class with only attributes and no methods. It can store several values of different datatypes, but one struct can only hold one set of values. Here is an example:

```
    static void Collection_Struct(Args _args)
    {
        // Create a struct with two fields
        Struct myCar = new struct ("int ModelYear; str Carbrand");
        int i;

        // Set values to the fields
        myCar.value("ModelYear", 2000);
        myCar.value("Carbrand", "BMW");

        // Add a new field and give it a value
        myCar.add("Model", "316");

        // Loop through the fields of the struct
        for (i=1; i<=myCar.fields(); i++)
        {
            info(strfmt("FieldType: %1, FieldName: %2, Value: %3",
                     myCar.fieldType(i),
                     myCar.fieldName(i),
                     myCar.value(myCar.fieldName(i))));
        }
    }
```

The X++ Language

Macros

Macros are constants or pieces of code that are being taken care of by the compiler before the rest of the code in order to replace the code where the macro is used with the content of the macro. There are three different types of macros: standalone macros, local macros, and macro libraries.

Macros are typically constant values that are only changed by developers. They are used so that developers don't have to hardcode these kind of values in the X++ code.

The macro libraries can be found in AOT under **Macros**. Each of them can contain multiple macros that can be used throughout the rest of AX.

To use the macros from a macro library in AX, simply include them in the scope that you would like to use them. The following example shows how to use two different macros from the same macro library in a job.

First, we create a macro library that consists of two macros:

```
#define.Text('This is a test of macros')
#define.Number(200)
```

Then, we use these macros from within a job:

```
static void Datatypes_macro_library(Args _args)
{
// Referencing macro library has to be done in the class declaration
// or in the  declaration like in this example
    #MacroTest

    info(strfmt("Text: %1.  Number: %2", #Text, #Number));

}
```

This job will print the following output in the infolog:

> Message (12:42:27 pm)
> Text: This is a test of macros. Number: 200

A local macro is defined in the class declaration of a class or in the variable declaration of a method, as shown in the following example:

```
static void Local_Macro(Args _args)
{
    // Define the local macro
```

[74]

```
        #localmacro.WelcomeMessage
        {
            info("Welcome to Carz Inc.");
            info("We have the best offers for rental cars");
        }
        #endmacro;

        // Use the local macro
        #WelcomeMessage

    }
```

Standalone macros are the same as the macros used in macro libraries, except that they are defined in the declaration of one of the variables of the method or in the class declaration of a class.

Events

Events are probably one of the most powerful technical features that was introduced in Dynamics AX 2012. In previous versions (and in Dynamics AX 2012), when a developer changes any standard code (code in a lower layer), a copy of the code (method) is created in the layer that the developers are using—thus making it possible to extend the application without ever deleting or overwriting any of the code that Microsoft has developed. However, if the application has been significantly extended on a project, then it becomes very hard to merge code with future versions (or service packs / fixes) of Dynamics AX. Events help solve this problem, that is, they allow the application to be extended and yet be simple to upgrade to a future version.

Key terms

- **Event**: A key occurrence in a program module where additional modules must process the occurrence
- **Event handler**: A method that subscribes to an event

In AOT, one can assign a method as an event handler for the pre-method event or the post-method event of another method. In either case, we say the event handler subscribes to an event of the host method.

An event handler that is underneath a method node can run either before or after the method runs. One can control the timing by setting the `CalledWhen` property on the event handler node. The `CalledWhen` property has the following options:

- **Pre**: The event handler runs before the method
- **Post**: The event handler runs after the method ends

The event handler method can manipulate parameters (pre handler) and/or return objects (post handler) using an `XppPrePostArgs` object.

Summary

In this chapter, you learned about the basic building blocks of AX programming. You read about the different datatypes you can use to store data and also saw some of the functions you can use to manipulate the variables.

You have also seen how you can use conditional statements and loops to control the flow of the code and how to use operators to analyze, assign, and manipulate data.

In the section that explained how classes and methods work, you learned about RunBase frameworks and also learned how to create an object of a class, how inheritance works in AX, and how static methods work.

At the end of the chapter, you saw how the different types of macros can be used to replace the X++ code.

In the next chapter, we will discuss how to create tables, fields, and relations so that we get a data model in the third normal form that can store the data in the AX database.

3
Storing Data

You should always try to store data and relate it to other data in the best possible way, as it will reduce the time spent on coding. It will also make sure that the solution you are building will be more stable and perform better.

This chapter will show you how to create tables where you can store data, how one can create relations between tables, and how to enforce referential integrity by creating unique indexes and delete actions.

You will learn about the following topics in this chapter:

- Tables
- Extended datatypes
- Relations

Extended datatypes

In order to understand how data is stored in Dynamics AX 2012, you need to get an understanding of the extended datatypes.

As you have read in the previous chapter, there are certain primitive datatypes you can use when programming in AX. Primitive datatypes can be extended and with more information to help you when you program in AX. A real datatype can be extended to create a `quantity` or an `amount` field, and each extended version can have its own set of properties, for example, four decimal places might be allowed for the `amount` field, but `quantity` might be restricted to zero decimal places. If one does not use an extended datatype for quantity, one would have to set the label, help text, number of decimals, and other relevant information on all the tables where the field is used.

Storing Data

Extended datatypes can be extended any number of times, for example, the type `quantity` can be created from `Real` and `quantity` can be further extended to create `PurchQuantity` and `SalesQuantity`.

Creating an extended datatype

To create an **extended datatype** (**EDT**), open the AOT and expand the node **Data Dictionary | Extended Data Types**. Then right-click **Extended Data Types** and select **New**. You will then get a submenu as shown in the following screenshot:

The following are the different types of which you can use one as the base for your extended datatype:

Datatype	Information
String	A string can contain all kinds of characters and the length is decided in the properties of the EDT.
Integer	An integer can contain integer values from -2,147,483,647 to 2,147,483,647.
Date	A date can hold a date value and the value will be stored in the form 3/23/2009.
Time	A time value can hold the time of a day from 12:00:00 am to 11:59:59 pm. The value stored in the database is, however, an integer specifying the seconds after midnight, where the range spans from 0 to 86400.
UtcDateTime	This datatype combines the date and time types into one datatype. In addition, it also holds information regarding the time zone. Its value ranges from 1900-01-01T00:00:00 to 2154-12-31T23:59:59.
Enum	This datatype should always be linked to a base enum by the enum property `Type`.
Container	This datatype contains a list of values with different datatypes.
GUID	This datatype is a Global Unique Identifier—a number that consists of 16 bytes. It is written in text as a sequence of hexadecimal digits, for example, {5EFB37A3-FEB5-467A-BE2D-DCE2479F5211}. An example of its use in AX is the `WebGUID` field in the `SysCompanyGUIDUsers` table.
Int64	This datatype is a 64-bit integer that can contain integer values from 9,223,372,036,854,775,808 to 9,223,372,036,854,775,808.

In this example, we will use a string. To open the property window, right-click on **String** and select **Properties**.

The property window will appear as follows:

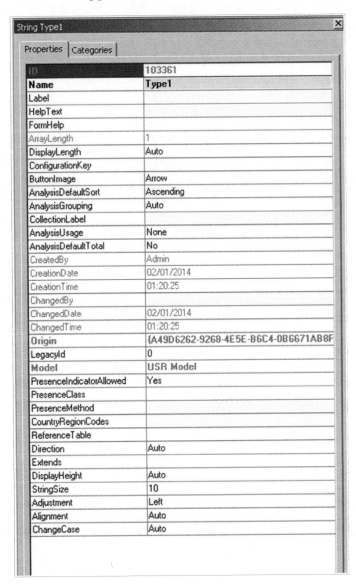

As you can see, some of the properties have a yellow background. This means that it is a best practice to have these properties filled out.

Also notice that if you change any of the properties that have a default value, the value entered will be bold. This is only done to make changes more visible. If you see properties with a red background, they are mandatory.

You can also see a categorized list of properties, in all property windows, by pressing the **Categories** tab. The categories will vary depending on what kind of element is active. The following screenshot shows the categories for the extended datatype we have created:

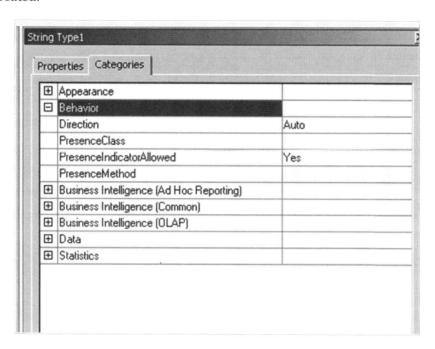

The first thing you would want to change is the name of the EDT. In our example we will call it `CarId`. You should also give the EDT a label that users see throughout the solution. So open the label editor by clicking on the square to the right in the **Label** field. Create a label with text `Car Id`. Do the same in the **HelpText** field and create a label with text `Unique identifier for a record in the CarTable`. The last thing you want to check now is the length of the field. By default, a string is set to `10` characters, which is fine for our example.

There will be times where you will want to check more properties as well, and if you are creating an EDT of type integer, it obviously has a different set of properties than a string, but these are just the basics.

Storing Data

Here is a list of some of the most used properties for all kinds of extended datatypes. Not all of the properties are explained here as that is beyond the scope of this book, so if there are properties you want to know more about that haven't been explained in this book, take a look in the developers' help file.

Property	Information
ID	ID is set by the AX core according to a number sequence for each object layer and cannot be changed by the developer.
Name	Name is the system name that you will use when writing code that references to this extended datatype.
Label	Label is the name of the field that the users will see in forms and reports.
HelpText	Help text is shown in the lower-left corner of a window when the field is active in a form.
FormHelp	FormHelp can be used to specify a specialized lookup form when the user does a lookup action on this field.
DisplayLength	DisplayLength is the maximum number of characters shown in a form or report.
Extends	Extends is used to inherit another extended datatype.

Tables

The **Tables** node under **Data Dictionary** in the AOT corresponds to tables in the database. When a table is created in the AOT, it is automatically synchronized with the SQL server. The synchronization process runs scripts in the background to make sure that the SQL table is created/updated to reflect the table in the AOT.

> A table in AX should *always* be created from the AOT and never by running a SQL script or by creating a new table using the SQL Server Management Studio as AX also creates additional system fields in the tables and also keeps references to the tables and its fields in system tables.

Creating a table

To create a new table, open the AOT, expand the **Data Dictionary** node, and then the **Tables** node. Right-click on the **Tables** node and select **New Table** as shown in the following screenshot:

Chapter 3

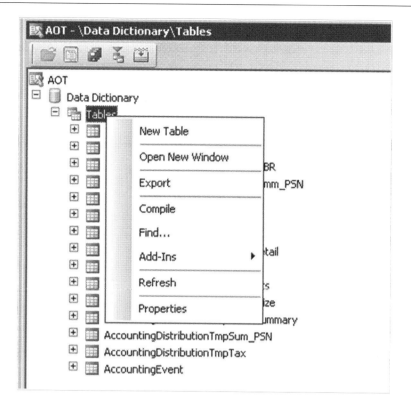

Now that a table has been created, the first thing you want to do is to give the table a descriptive name. Let's call our table `CarTable`.

To change the name of the table, right-click on the table and select **Properties**. Then change the **Name** property to `CarTable`.

You will now see a red line to the left of the name of the node in the AOT:

[83]

Storing Data

This red line indicates that an element has been changed but not saved. Select **CarTable** in the AOT and press *Ctrl + S* to save the element. Notice that the red line disappears.

Before we start adding fields, indexes, relations, and so on, let's have a look at the properties of our table:

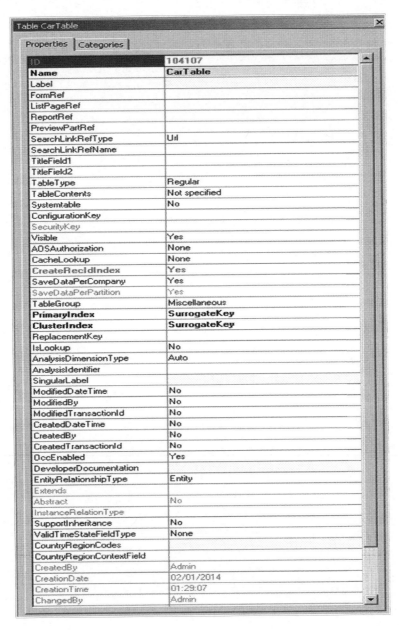

The properties of importance here are as follows:

Property	Information
ID	ID is set by the AX core according to a number sequence for each object layer and cannot be changed by the developer.
Name	Name is the system name that you will use when writing code that references to this extended datatype.
Label	Label is the name of the table that the users will see in forms and reports.
FormRef	This is a link to a display the menu item to be executed when a reference is done to the current table by the "go to main table" functionality in AX. It is also used in reports that have a primary index field from the table in the report to link to the form.
ReportRef	This is a link to an output menu item to be executed when the main table report is being created. Typically, when clicking on the **print** button in a form, the table referenced by the active datasource will have a link to a report in **ReportRef**. If not, the default report is created using the fields in the autoreport field group.
TitleField	**TitleField1** and **TitleField2** are used in the title bar in the main form to give a brief information regarding the selected record.
TableType	The types of tables that can be defined are: • **Regular**: These are standard tables that are stored on the SQL server and can be displayed/edited on an AX client. • **In Memory**: These tables will not be created on the SQL server. The data inserted into a temporary table will only exist in memory in the tier and the programming scope in which it was inserted. • **TempDB**: These are SQL temporary tables (that is, they are created on the SQL server) and can be queried as regular tables. However, **TempDB** tables cannot be directly displayed on an AX client.
ConfigurationKey	This is the configuration key that the table is connected to. If the configuration key is switched off, the table and all its data will be removed from the database.
SecurityKey	This property is not editable. It is present to assist with upgrades from AX 2009.

Property	Information
TableGroup	Grouping of tables in AX is done by selecting one of the table groups, namely, **Miscellaneous**, **Parameter**, **Group**, **Main**, **Transaction**, **Worksheet Header**, and **Worksheet Line**. See the following link for more details on **TableGroup** options: `http://msdn.microsoft.com/en-us/library/aa623733.aspx`
PrimaryIndex	When you have set up multiple indexes for a table, you should specify which one is the primary one. This is done to optimize the data fetching done towards this table.
ClusteredIndex	This specifies which index needs to be clustered. Clustered indexes should always be set on tables that have the **TableGroup** property set to **Group** or **Main**.
SupportInheritance	It is used to specify if the table supports the inheritance functionality in AX 2012. By default, this property is set to **No**. When changed to **Yes**, the **Abstract** and **Extends** properties are enabled and can be changed.
Abstract	If the value is **Yes**, the table cannot be a direct target of X++ SQL statements such as `select` or `update`.
Extends	A table is derived from another table that is selected in this property. For more information, refer to the *Table inheritance* section.
ModifiedDateTime, CreatedDateTime, ModifiedTransactionId, and CreatedTransactionId	These properties are used to store information about who created the record, when it was created, who modified it last, and when it was modified last. A transaction ID can also be attached to create a transaction and another one for the modification of a transaction.

There are other properties available and you can find out more about them in the developers' help section. Here we've described only the most commonly used properties.

Adding fields to a table

A table without any fields doesn't do any good, so let's look at how we can add fields to our newly created table.

To add fields to a table, you can open two AOT windows and drag an extended datatype into the **Fields** node of a table. You can also add a new field by right-clicking the **Fields** node in a table and selecting **New**. Under **New**, you will get a submenu where you can select what kind of field you would like to create.

1. First, we create the `CarId` field. In the following example, we will use the extended datatype called `CarId`, which we created in the previous section of this chapter.

    To add it to the table, just drag-and-drop it in the **Fields** node of the **CarTable**.

    Your result should look as follows:

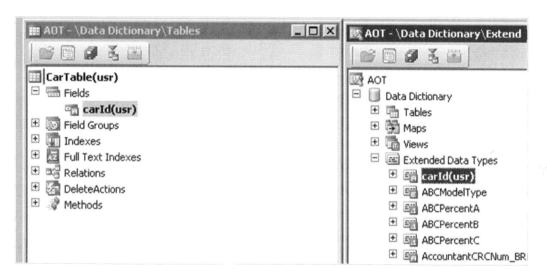

Storing Data

2. Next, we create the `ModelYear` field. We will create a new Integer field directly. Simply right-click the **Fields** node under the table and select **New | Integer**:

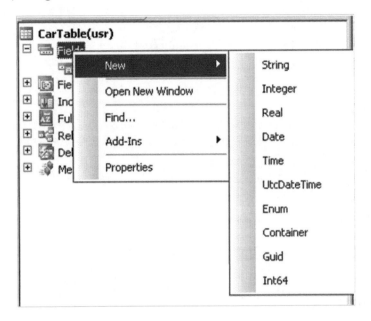

3. Now, we set properties for the `ModelYear` field. Right-click on the new field and select properties. Change the name of the field to `ModelYear`. Also, set the property **Extended Data Type** to `Yr`, which is the standard AX datatype for year. The label and form help will now be inherited from the extended datatype `Yr`, so we don't have to fill out anything here (unless we are not satisfied with the standard label and form help).

4. Create the rest of the fields. We will also add two other fields in the `CarTable` so that the table contains the following fields:

Field	Extended datatype	Label	Key
CarId	CarId		PK, UIdx
ModelYear	Yr	Model Year	
CarBrand	Name	Brand	
Model	Name	Model	

Here, PK means that the field should be a primary key and UIdx means that the field is included in the unique index. You will learn how to create the primary key and unique index later in this chapter.

[88]

5. Create the `RentalTable` table. We will also create another table called `RentalTable` that will have the following fields:

Field	Extended datatype	Label	Key
RentalId	RentalId		PK, UIdx
CustAccount	CustAccount		
CarId	CarId		
FromDate	FromDate	From date	
ToDate	ToDate	To date	

Adding fields to a field group

In all standard AX forms, fields are grouped into collections of fields that are related to each other and it is best practice that all fields exist in at least one field group.

To add a field to a field group, simply drag the field from the **Fields** node and drop it into the **Field Group** node that you want to add the field to.

All tables in AX have five system-created field groups called **AutoLookup**, **AutoReport**, **AutoIdentification**, **AutoSummary**, and **AutoBrowse**, as shown in the following screenshot:

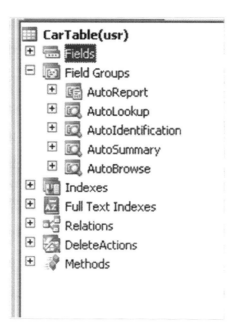

Storing Data

The **AutoLookup** field group is used when the user wants to select a value in a foreign key field. We will look into more of this in the next chapter.

The **AutoReport** field group is used to automatically create a report based on a standard report template in AX containing the fields in the **AutoReport** field group. The report is generated when the users click the print icon ▣, or press *Ctrl + P* in a form where the table is used as the main datasource.

By default, when a new table is created, the primary key on the table is set as the surrogate key (RecId). RecIds are system-generated numbers (`Int64`) that are unique per table, per company, per partition. Surrogate keys can be used as foreign keys on other tables and can be displayed on the forms. The group **AutoIdentification** is a mechanism used by AX to replace surrogate key field with the fields within this group when the surrogate key is present on a form.

AutoSummary is used to set the default summary field on the fast tab. Summary fields are key fields that are displayed when a fast tab is collapsed.

▷ **Manage costs**　　　　　　　　　　　　　　　　　　　　　　　0.00

Creating an index

Indexes in AX are used to maintain uniqueness and to speed up table searches. Dynamics AX 2012 automatically creates a primary index called the surrogate key (RecId). This field is not visible in the indexes section but can be seen on the table properties.

When a `select` statement in AX executes, it is sent to the database query optimizer that analyzes the statement and decides which index will be the best to use for the statement before it is executed in the database and records are returned to AX.

To find out which other index a table should have and which fields they should be made up of, you need to look at the `select` statements that use the table and look at how they select data. Fields that are often used in ranges, in joining tables, and in grouping or sorting are candidates for indexing. You should, however, limit the number of indexes in a table as each index will have to be updated whenever a record is inserted, updated, or deleted from the table. This can become a performance bottleneck especially for transactional tables.

You can create an index for a table by right-clicking on the index node under the table in the AOT and selecting **New Index**. A new index called **Index1** will then be created. Right-click the index, select **Properties**, and change the name of the index. The best practice to name indexes is to use the name of the fields in the index postfixed with `Idx`, unless the last field ends with **Id**. In that case, we just add an x at the end, so in our example, we have created an index called `CarIdx`.

The next thing to do is to add a field to the index. This is done by dragging the field from the **Fields** node in the table and dropping it onto the newly created index.

As the `CarId` is the primary key in the table, it is also the obvious candidate for the unique index. To make the index unique, simply set the property **AllowDuplicates** on the index to **No**.

The **CarTable** should now appear as follows:

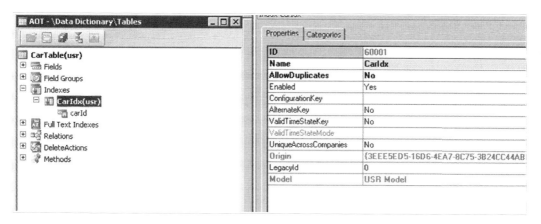

Now you can try to add a unique index on the **RentalTable** on your own. It should consist only of the `RentalId` field.

The property **AlternateKey** indicates that other tables can create foreign key relations that reference this key as an alternative to referencing the primary key. A table can have several alternative keys. Any one alternative key can switch to being the primary key (provided the alternative key comprises only one field).

Alternative keys can also be set as replacement keys. This will automatically add the fields that are present in the **AlternateKey** index to the **AutoIdentification** field group.

Storing Data

Creating a relation

One of the ways of creating a relation between two tables is to do this directly on the foreign key table.

You can see an example of how a table relation looks, by taking a look at the table `SalesTable` in the AOT and expanding the **Relations** node. Open the relation called **Agreement** and look at the fields used in the relation. These are the same fields that make up the primary key in the table that the relation points at. Look at the property called table in the relation to see which table the relation points to (select the relation and right-click on it to open the **Properties** window). Then find that table in the AOT and notice that the same fields make up the unique index in that table.

Each of the fields that make up the relation can be put into the relation as two different types. So far, we have only seen the type called normal. The other type is called conditional relations. These relations are used together with normal relations to add a condition on the related data. To better understand how this works, here is an example.

Take a look at the relation `CustMarkupGroup` on `SalesTable`:

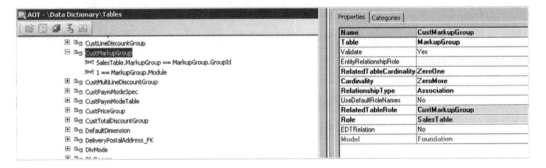

One of the fields in the relation is the `MarkupGroup`, which holds a reference to an ID in the table that it relates to. In this case, the `GroupId` in the `MarkupGroup` table.

The other field is the module, which is a related fixed enum. This relation type (`FixedField`) implies that the conditional value must be present in the related table. In this example, the value for each relation is **1**. The base enum used in this case is the **MarkupModuleType** and its value **1** indicates the enumeration customer:

Chapter 3

You can also create relations that are used for navigation purposes between forms. These kinds of relations are called navigational relations. These relations are used for tables where there are no constraints on integrity, such as the one we have between foreign and primary keys.

  Cardinality and relation type properties in AX 2012 do not control the behavior of the relation. Rather, those properties are available as a reference for developers.

Creating a delete action

To enforce referential integrity, it is crucial to add a delete action for all tables that have a foreign key pointing to the current table.

This will make sure that we delete any references to any record being deleted so that we are not left with records that point at other records that no longer exist.

To illustrate this, let's say you have a table called `RentalTable` and another table called `CarTable`. A record in `RentalTable` will always have a link to one (and only one) record in `CarTable`, and a record in `CarTable` can exist in many records in `RentalTable`.

This scenario is visualized in the simple data model here:

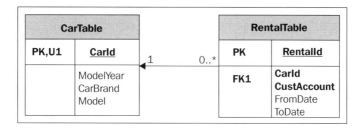

Storing Data

We then have a one-to-many relationship between the `RentalTable` and the `CarTable`. It is then important that if a record in the `CarTable` is about to be deleted, that either one of two actions take place. Either all the records in the `RentalTable` with a link to the record in `CarTable` are also deleted or the user is not allowed to delete the record in `CarTable` because it has referencing records in `RentalTable`.

Perform the following steps to create a delete action in **CarTable**:

1. Open the delete actions under the **CarTable**.
2. Right-click and navigate to **New | DeleteAction**.
3. Select the new delete action.
4. Open the **Properties** window.
5. Change the table that it should point to, in our case, the **RentalTable**.
6. Decide which action should take place when a record in the **CarTable** is deleted according to options in the following list:

Delete action	Information
None	No action will take place on related records in the `RentalTable` when you delete a record in the `CarTable`.
Cascade	All records in `RentalTable` related to the record being deleted in `CarTable` will also be deleted.
Restricted	The user will get a warning saying that the record in the `CarTable` cannot be deleted because transactions exist in the `RentalTable`. The user will not be able to delete the record in `CarTable` if one or more related records exist in the `RentalTable`.
Cascade+Restricted	This option is used when deleting records through more than two levels. Let's say that another table existed that had a cascade delete action against `CarTable` and the `CarTable` had a Cascade+Restricted delete action against `RentalTable`. If the record in the top level table was about to be deleted, it would also delete the related records in `CarTable`. In turn, all the records in `RentalTable` related to the records being deleted from `CarTable` would also be deleted. If only a record in `CarTable` was about to be deleted, the user would get the same message as when using the Restricted action.

Table browser

If you want to see all the data that exists for all fields in a table, you can open the table browser. To launch the table browser in AX 2012, simply select the table in the AOT and press *Ctrl + O* or the open button.

Chapter 3

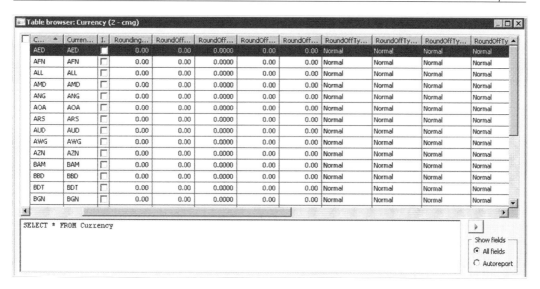

You will also notice that it lists certain fields that you haven't added. These are system fields.

Field name	Information	Optional
Partition	This field defines the partition that the record is associated with.	No
dataAreaId	This field will store the company account the record was created in.	No
recVersion	The first time a record is created, it will have the record version as 1. Any changes done to the record will cause the recVersion to get a random new integer value. The field is used to make sure that two processes cannot overwrite the same record.	No
RecId	The RecId is a system-set unique identifier for each table in AX. In older versions, the RecId was unique per company account, but from version 4.0, it was changed to be unique per table.	No
ModifiedDateTime, CreatedDateTime, ModifiedTransactionId, and CreatedTransactionId	As described in the *Creating a table* section, these system fields can be added to a table to see when a record was created/modified and who created/modified it. A transaction ID can also be added for both, the creation and modification. Only the last change to the record will be stored by the modified fields.	Yes

[95]

Table inheritance

The concept of table inheritance (base-derived tables) from an ER structure perspective, has been used in Dynamics AX since the earliest versions. However, in AX 2012, table inheritance has been baked into the core framework and hence, it is supported throughout the application (modeling, runtime, and execution).

A derived table can extend from or derive from another table (base). Each table has the `SupportInheritance` property and the `Extends` property, which together control table inheritance.

Terminology is important here. Microsoft prefers to use the terms derived and base tables, rather than parent or child tables in an inheritance relationship, as the terms parent and child can be used to describe foreign key relationships between tables.

Consider the following scenario. As a developer, say you have to design and build a data structure that can hold data for multiple `CarType` instances, for example SUV, Coupe, and so on. Though all types share a number of common properties (such as engine size and average miles per gallon (mpg)), the cars can have unique properties based on the type. For example:

- SUV:
    - Bicycle storage (yes/no)
    - Dog friendly (yes/no)
- Coupe:
    - Golf bag storage (yes/no)

The preceding structure can be architected in Dynamics AX using table inheritance in the following way:

1. Create a new enum called `CarType` and add `SUV`, `Coupe`, and `Sedan` as elements, as shown here:

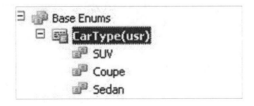

2. Create a base table called `CarType` and change the **SupportInheritance** property to **Yes**.

Chapter 3

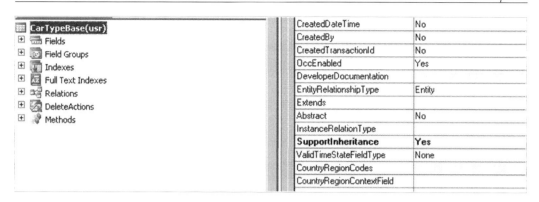

3. Create a new `Int64` field called `InstanceRelationType` and set the field's `ExtendedDataType` property to `RelationType`.

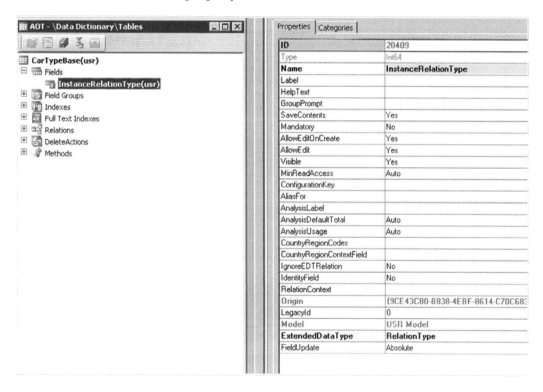

The **InstanceRelationType** field is used to hold the `RecId` of the derived table. This way, when a user queries the derived table, AX will automatically add a join to the base table on the **InstanceRelationType** field.

Storing Data

If we do not manually add this field, then AX will automatically create a field called **RelationType** and use it for the purpose described before. However, this field will not be available in the AOT (it will be present on SQL server though).

4. Navigate back to table properties, change the **InstanceRelationType** property, and set the **Abstract** property to **Yes**.

Abstract	No
InstanceRelationType	InstanceRelationType
SupportInheritance	Yes

By setting the **Abstract** property we are disallowing users/developers to query the base table directly as we would like them to query the derived table (which in turn will hold the field from the base table)

5. Add the enum `CarType` to this table along with two real fields, `EngineSize` and `AvgMPG`.

6. Create a new table called `CarTypeSUV` and set the **SupportInheritance** property to **Yes** and set **Extends** to **CarTypeBase**.

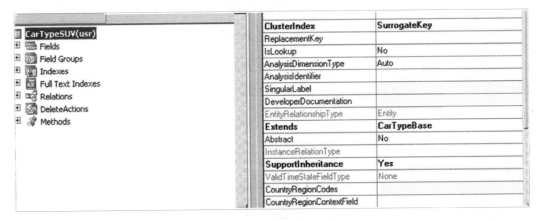

[98]

Chapter 3

7. Add two enum fields(**NoYes**) called `BicycleStorage` and `PetFriendly`:

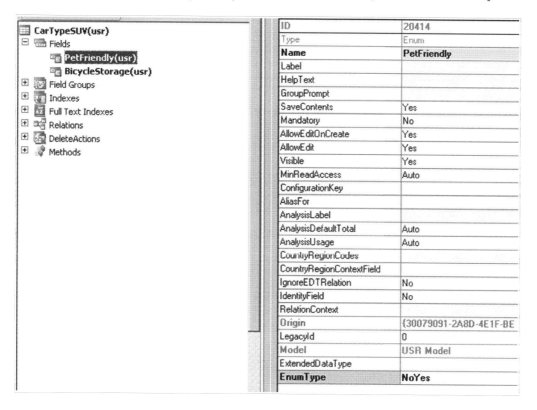

Querying data on inherited tables

Like regular tables, all tables in the inheritance hierarchy are synchronized and hence, physical tables are created on the database. Dynamics AX automatically creates the relationship between the base and derived tables, and will automatically apply the join condition when the derived table is queried. For example, consider we write the following code within X++:

```
Select * from CarTypeSUV
```

The AX will automatically add a join to `CarTypeBase` and hence, AX will retrieve fields from both tables.

Storing Data

As Dynamics AX permits the tables to be derived from other derived tables, calls to the database without specifying the list of fields that need to be fetched can cause performance issues. Hence, it's recommended that when querying a table (especially if the table supports inheritance), the list of fields to be fetched must be specified, for example, when the following statement is executed, the system will only fetch the `CarTypeSUV` table form the database:

```
Select PetFriendly from CarTypeSUV
```

Valid time state tables

Date-effective tables (also called valid time state tables) allow the Dynamics AX to associate valid from and to dates (and time) with the application artifacts, for example, a purchase pricing agreement can be valid between a range of dates.

Dynamics AX uses the valid time state table framework to simplify the maintenance of data for which changes must be tracked at different points in time. For example, the discount rate on a sales price agreement can be 5 percent for the first year and 6 percent for the second year. During the second year, one might still want to know that the rate was 5 percent in the previous year.

The date effectiveness feature is a central framework. It enables developers to write less code and to create forms that manage viewing and editing of current, past, and future records.

On a table in the AOT, one can set the `ValidTimeStateFieldType` property to make it a valid time state table. That causes the system to automatically add the `ValidFrom` and `ValidTo` columns, which track a date (and time) range in each row. The system guarantees that the values in these date or date-time fields remain valid by automatically preventing overlap among date ranges.

Execute the following steps to create a date-effective table that can be used to record the mileage of a given car over a date range:

1. Create a new table called `CarMileageTable`.
2. Add a new real field to the table called `Mileage`.
3. Add a relation to `CarTable` (based on the primary key `carId`) as shown in the following screenshot:

Chapter 3

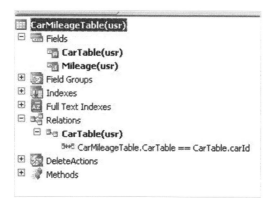

4. Change the **ValidTimeStateFieldType** property of the table to **Date**.
5. The system will now automatically add two date fields to the table (**ValidFrom** and **ValidTo**).

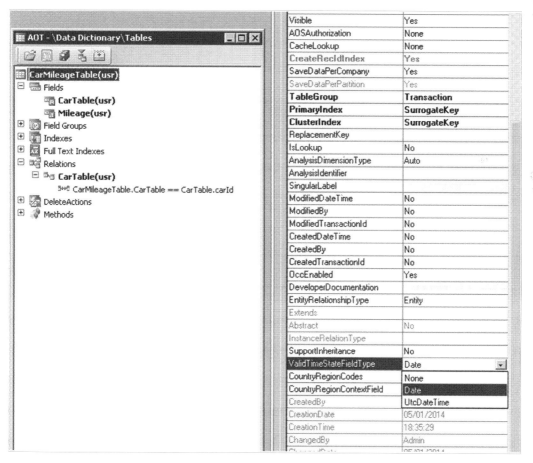

[101]

Storing Data

 If the property is changed to UtcDateTime, then the framework will add two `utcdatetime` fields (these can be used to define date ranges that include time).

6. Create a new index with the **Fields** as `CarTable`, `ValidFrom`, and `ValidTo`. The **Properties** will be as follows:

    - **Allow Duplicates** set to **No**.
    - **AlternateKey** set to **Yes**.
    - **ValidTimeStateKey** set to **Yes**. This enables the **ValidTimeStateMode** field.
    - **ValidTimeStateMode** set to **Gap**. Use this field to allow and prohibit gaps within the date range entered. If gaps are not allowed, and if multiple records are created for the same key field (car in this example), then the system will ensure that there is no gap between `ValidTo` of the first record and `ValidFrom` of the second record.

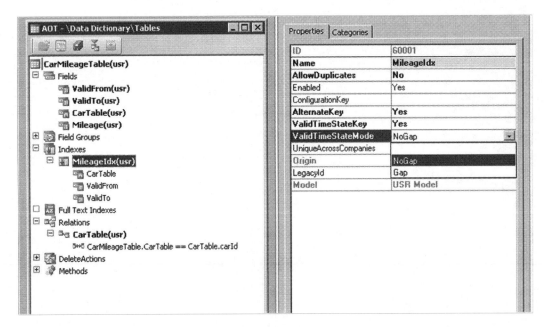

[102]

When selecting data in X++, a keyword `validTimeState` can be used to specify dates so that the data returned is valid for those dates. There can be one or two dates specified. If one is specified, all records that are valid on that date are returned. If two are specified, all records that are valid within the date range are returned, for example:

```
select validTimeState(asAtDate) from CarMileageTable;
select validTimeState(fromDate, toDate) from CarMileageTable;
```

The key points to note are as follows:

- The `ValidTimeStateFieldType` property cannot be set for any table that inherits from another table
- The `ValidFrom` and `ValidTo` columns can both be of the date datatype or both can be of the `utcDateTime` datatype
- The `Query` class also has methods that provide filtering by date range, such as `validTimeStateAsOfDateTimeRange`

Summary

In this chapter, you have read about how to create tables in AX, how to set up an extended datatype, and how to create fields in tables, based on extended datatypes.

You have also read how to enforce referential integrity by adding delete actions, how to create indexes to ensure uniqueness of data, and how to create relations between tables to link related information.

You should now be ready to create data storage for your tables in AX and set them up as per best practices.

In the next chapter, you will learn how to create forms that enable users to see data from tables, and enter and update data and navigation pages that are used to display data. You will also learn how to create menu items to be used as buttons in forms and as items in menus and to create new menus.

4
Data User Interaction

Data is no good unless it can be entered by and shown to the users. In this chapter, you will learn how to create tools for user interaction by creating a form that has both one data source and two data sources related to each other. It shows data from both data sources and links the report to the selected record in the form by using menu items. You will also be able to create a menu and a navigation page consisting of menu items that will open the form and the report.

This chapter will also show you how to create Reporting Services reports in Visual Studio using the new Reporting Services extensions.

We will go through the following topics in this chapter:

- Forms
- Reports
- Menu items
- Navigation pages
- Menus

Forms

Forms are used for basic user interaction to display data to users and to retrieve data from users. In addition, users can also start actions from a form. Starting an action from a form compared to starting the same action from a menu can be very different as the user can have a record active when inside a form. Hence, the user can open a new form or report with data related to the record selected.

This function to link records across forms is incredibly simple to implement in AX when the tables used in the two forms relate to each other. This functionality is achieved through the `Args` class that we discussed in *Chapter 2, The X++ Language*, and through relations as you learned in the previous chapter.

Main components of a form

A form has five subnodes that we will discuss in more detail:

- **Methods**: Methods enable the developer to write code that is relevant only to the current form.
- **Data Sources**: Data sources are links to tables and are used to fetch data from the database and make that data available to the form.
- **Parts**: Parts are the special, informative, and actionable sections that appear on the right-hand side of the form. Parts are seen as miniforms that are embedded within a form.
- **Designs**: Design options specify the look and feel of the form.
- **Permissions**: Permissions enable the developer to specify the tables that can be modified on the form and the processes that can modify them.

Methods

All forms in AX extend the system class `FormRun`. This means that they all have standard methods that they use when being executed. These methods can be overridden in the **Methods** subnode. To override a standard method, right-click on the **Methods** subnode and select **Override** method; you will get a list of all the methods that can be overridden in the root of the form. Once you override them, you can see that they all call a method known as `super`. This is basically just a call to the method with the same name in the class that the form extends (`FormRun`).

 Executing a parent method by using the `super()` call can be done in any method that is overridden from an extended class. It is a standard feature in many object-oriented languages.

The most common methods to override in a form are listed in the following table. A complete list of the form methods can be found in the SDK.

Method	Comment
init	This method is executed when a user opens the form. It creates the runtime object of the form and is used to initialize variables and form controls that are used by other methods in the form.
run	This method is executed immediately after the init method. The super call in run method opens the form and runs the data selection defined by the data sources in the form.
close	This method is executed by closeOk or closeCancel. It closes the form and writes any data in the form that hasn't been updated yet if the closeOk flag is set.
closeCancel	This method is executed when the user clicks on the *Esc* key or the cancel button. It also makes sure that data is not updated when entering the close method.
closeOk	This method is executed when the user clicks on the **OK** button. This method will set the closeOk flag to true so that the close method will actually close the form.

These methods enable you to write code in forms to control their behavior. You are, of course, free to write any kind of code in the form methods, but you should bear in mind that all forms execute on the client. Writing code in forms that call methods on the server will generate client server traffic that leads to decreased performance.

It is considered best practice to write code in classes and tables so that the code can be reused in other elements.

Data sources

The easiest way to display data from the AX database in a form is to add at least one data source to the form. The data source is actually a table variable that is used to fetch data from the database and hold the data in the table variable as long as the form is active or until an action in the form forces the data source to refresh the data from the database.

Data User Interaction

Here is a list of some of the properties you will change when adding a data source in a form. The complete list of properties can be found in the SDK:

Property	Comment
Name	The name of the data source should be the same as the table used by the data source.
Table	The name of the table used by the data source.
Index	This property sets the index defined on the table to be used as the default sorting for the data source.
AllowEdit	If this is set to `false`, none of the fields from this data source will be editable in the form.
AllowCreate	If this is set to `false`, users are not allowed to create new records in the table used by this data source.
AllowDelete	If this is set to `false`, users are not allowed to delete records from the table used by this data source.
JoinSource	This is used to link two related tables to each other in the form. It can only be used if two or more data sources exist in the form. This should be set on the secondary data source.
LinkType	It maintains the link between the joined data sources. See the SDK for the different options.
DelayActive	If this is set to `Yes`, it will delay the execution of the active method so that scrolling down a grid will cause the active method to execute only for the final record selected.

Each data source also has some standard methods that you can override. The methods are defined by the `FormDataSource` system class. Some of the commonly overridden methods are listed in the following table. A complete list of data source methods can be found in the SDK.

Method	Comment
`init`	This method is executed by `super()` in the form's `init` method. It creates the query specified by the properties on the data source. This is where you initialize any variables you want to use to override the default query.
`executeQuery`	This method is executed when the form opens and every time the data is sorted, filtered, or refreshed. This method is used to fetch data from the table and make it available for the form. If you want to use a dynamic query in the form that changes the records fetched that are based on a user input, you should remove the call to `super()` in this method and write your own query.

Method	Comment
`create`	This method is called when the user creates a new record by pressing *Ctrl + N* or pressing the **New** button from the menu.
`active`	This method is executed when the user selects a record in the form. It fetches data from the joined data sources (if any) when the user selects a new record.
`write`	This method is executed when a record is either inserted or updated in the form. It will call the `validateWrite` method to make sure that the `insert/update` operation has been properly constructed before passing the command to the server to actually execute the `insert` or `update` operation in the database.
`delete`	This method is executed when a user deletes a record in the form. It passes the handle to the server, which in turn will delete the actual record from the database.
`validateWrite`	This method is executed by the `write` method to make sure that all data is valid (mandatory fields are filled out) and no keys are violated.
`validateDelete`	This method is executed by the `delete` method. It asks the user to confirm the deletion.
`reread`	This method rereads the active record from the database.
`refresh`	This method refreshes the view of all the records currently held in the data source.
`research`	This method refreshes the complete query defined in the data source, while maintaining any filters applied by the user.

Designs

Here is a list of some of the properties that you find under the **Designs** node. You can find the complete list of these properties in the SDK.

Property	Comment
Left/top	Defines the *x* and *y* coordinates where the form will open on the screen.
Width/Height	This defines the width and height of the form. If you want the users to be able to resize the form, set these parameters to the column width and column height of the form.
Caption	This is the name of the form that you want to present to the users. The caption is shown at the top line of the form.
TitleDatasource	The **TitleField1** and **TitleField2** values of the selected table in this property will be displayed to the left of the caption.
WindowType	This should be set to **Standard**, except for lookup forms where this property should be set to **Popup**.

Data User Interaction

Each of the visual components that you can use within a form also has a set of properties and methods, so you have a lot of options as a developer. Most of the time, you won't have to change any of these properties, at least as long as you have done a good job defining the elements in the data dictionary.

Creating a form with one data source

We will now create a form that enables the users to create, read, update, and delete data from the `CarTable` that we created in the previous chapter.

Form templates

Although a user can start creating forms from scratch as described in the following sections, it is actually a lot more convenient and recommended to start from a template.

Forms templates are effectively very basic forms (skeleton forms) that implement standard form design patterns as described by Microsoft. When a user selects a template, the system effectively creates a copy of a base form the template is linked with.

To create a form with a template, right-click on **Forms** in AOT, click on **New Form from template**, and then click on the template that specifies the type of form you want to create.

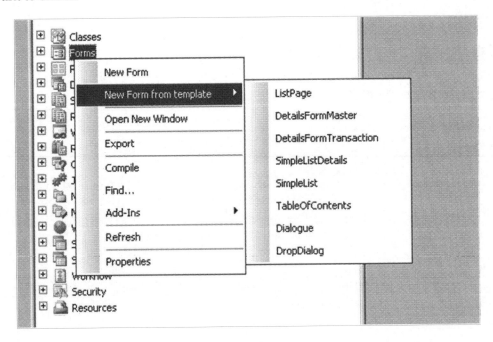

The following extract from MSDN describes the various templates:

Template	Purpose
DetailsFormMaster	Use this template to create a details form to view, edit, and act on the master data
DetailsFormTransaction	Use this template to create a details form with lines to view, edit, and act on master data that has line items
Dialogue	Use this template to create a dialog window that provides a response to a question
DropDialog	Use this template to create a drop dialog form to perform an action with the data, for example, selecting dimensions on the **Released Products** form
ListPage	Use this template to create a list page you can use to find, analyze, and perform actions on master data, for example, the **Customer List** page
SimpleList	Use this template to create a simple list form to view, edit, and act on dependent or reference data
SimpleListDetails	Use this template to create a simple list and details form to view, edit, and act on dependent and reference data, for example, the **Released Product Detail** form
TableOfContents	Use this template to create a table of contents form to view and edit configuration or setup data, for example, the **Sales & Marketing Parameter** form

Creating the form

Perform the following steps to create a form:

1. Open AOT and select the **Forms** node.
2. Right-click on the **Forms** node and select **New Form**. A new form called **Form1** will be created. Change the name of the form to `CarTable` so that the name of the form will be the same as the table it will represent.

> It is best practice to name the form the same as the data source if it represents a main form for the table used.

Adding the data source

Now, we need to add the data source. This can be done either by dragging and dropping the `CarTable` into the **Data Dictionary** node in the form or by right-clicking on the **Data Sources** node and selecting **New Data Source**. If you choose the latter, you will have to change the table property of the data source to `CarTable`. The name of the data source will automatically be the same as the table it is representing, and it is also best practice to keep it that way as long as you don't have multiple data sources using the same table.

Creating a form design

Forms in AX that consist of one data source where the table used as the data source is not a parameter table are mainly built by navigating to **Design | Tab | TabPage | Grid | Fields**.

If the form has any buttons that open other related/unrelated forms, reports, or start classes, these buttons should be put into a button group, so that the schema is extended by navigating to **Design | ButtonGroup | Buttons**.

In our example, we created a form that looks like this:

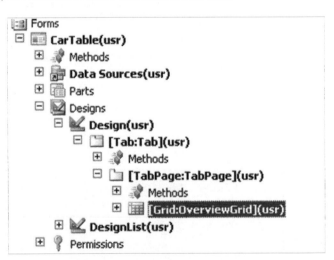

The parameters we have changed are highlighted in the following code:

```
TabPage:Overview:
Name=Overview
Caption=Overview (Use the label find tool to find a label with this
text).
Grid:Grid:
DataSource=CarTable
```

To add the fields, we simply drag them from the **Fields** node under the data source `CarTable` and drop them onto the grid.

Once this is done, you can take a look at the form in design mode by double-clicking on the **Design** node.

You will then see the form in design mode and also have a toolbar that you can use to add other fields or graphical components. It should look something like this for the `CarTable` form:

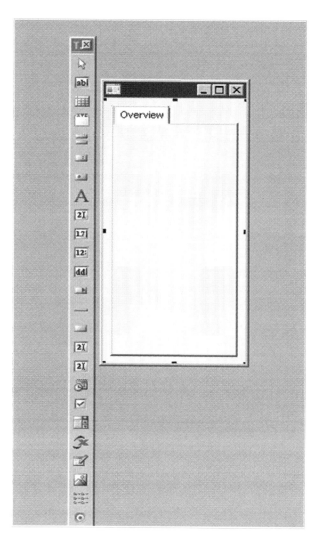

To get a full list of all the different graphical components that you can add to a form, check out the SDK.

Data User Interaction

> Take a look at the tutorial forms located under the **Forms** node in AOT. Search for forms starting with **Tutorial_Form**. These forms will show you how to set up forms and all kinds of form controls.

To test the form and see if it holds any data, simply select the form in the AOT and press *Ctrl + O* or click on the **Open** button in the toolbar.

The form should then look something like this:

You should also create a similar form for the `RentalTable` that we will use later in this book.

Creating a form with two data sources

Now, we would like to create one form with two data sources. The basics are the same as when we use one data source, but under the data source node we obviously add two data sources instead of one. In our example, and in most cases in AX, these two data sources are linked together through a relation either in the extended datatype or in the table.

Either way, you will need to change the **JoinSource** property in the data source that is the "many" node in the one-to-many relationship.

Take a look at the **tutorial_Form_Join** form to see an example of how to use the **JoinSource** property.

In our example, we will use the `CarTable` as the main data source and join `RentalTable` to `CarTable`, since `RentalTable` is the "many" node in this relationship. It should look like the following screenshot when the data sources are joined together in the form:

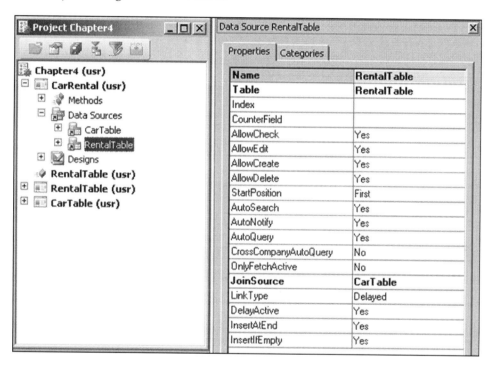

We will now take a look at the design of this form.

Separating the design using a form splitter

Since the meaning of this form is to show data from both tables, we will divide the form into two parts in the same way that the `SalesTable`, `PurchTable`, and other standard AX forms are built when showing a parent/child relationship.

Data User Interaction

This means that under the design node, we will add a group node for the car information and another group node for the rental information. In addition, we will add a group that will work as a form splitter. The purpose of the form splitter is to enable the users to resize the different parts of the form.

To make the form splitter work, we need to add some code in the form. First of all, we will add a variable in the class declaration as follows:

```
public class FormRun extends ObjectRun
{
    SysFormSplitter_Y              _formSplitterVertical;
}
```

Also, we have to initialize this variable to point to the `formSplitter` in the form and link it to the first group in the design. This means that when you move the form splitter, the first group in the design will resize accordingly. We do this in the `init` method as shown here:

```
public void init()
{
    super();
    _formSplitterVertical  = new SysFormSplitter_Y(ctrlSplitVertical, CarGroup, this);
}
```

Note that the variables `ctrlSplitVertical` and `CarGroup` will give a compilation error here because they don't exist. To make it work, we will change the **AutoDeclaration** property on both the splitter group itself and on the first group (the group that holds the car's information; I have called this group `CarGroup` in our example) in the **Design** node to **Yes**.

We also need to override three methods under the `ctrlSplitVertical` group in the design. The code is as follows:

```
int mouseUp(int x, int y, int button, boolean ctrl, boolean shift)
{
    int ret;

    ret = super(x, y, button, ctrl, shift);
```

```
        return _formSplitterVertical.mouseUp(x, y, button, ctrl, shift);
    }
    int mouseMove(int x, int y, int button, boolean ctrl, boolean shift)
    {
        int ret;

        ret = super(x, y, button, ctrl, shift);

        return _formSplitterVertical.mouseMove(x,y,button,ctrl,shift);
    }

    int mouseDown(int x, int y, int button, boolean ctrl, boolean shift)
    {
        int ret;

        ret = super(x, y, button, ctrl, shift);

        return _formSplitterVertical.mouseDown(x, y, button, ctrl, shift);
    }
```

This is done to make sure that the variable we declared in the `Declaration` class and initialized in the `init` method is changed when the user moves the form splitter in the form up or down. To understand why we have to do this, simply remove all the code in the form and see what happens when you open the form and try to drag the form splitter up or down.

In addition to creating a form splitter, we will also change the width and length on the groups, tabs, tab pages, and grids in the form to column width and column height (except from the form splitter which will be set to a fixed height).

Another important thing to remember is to change the data source property on the grid that will hold the records from `RentalTable` from `CarTable` (which is the default as it is the first data source in the form) to `RentalTable`.

Then, you add fields to the grid the same way you did in the first form by dragging the fields from the data source and dropping them under the grid.

Data User Interaction

The form should now look like this in AOT:

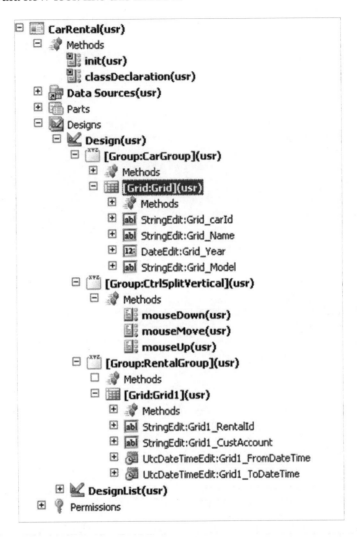

Chapter 4

When you open the form, it should look like the following screenshot:

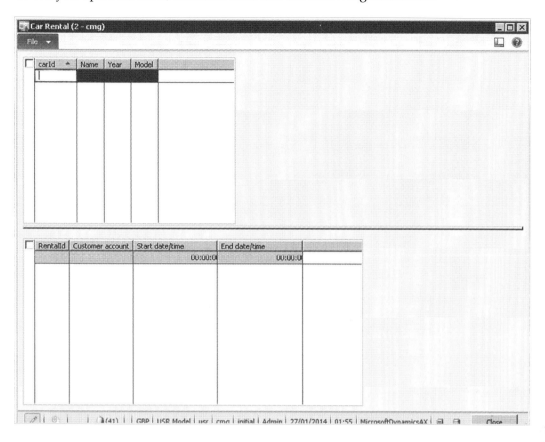

The rental part of the form will now only show records related to the record selected in the car part of the form. The `CarId` field in the `RentalTable` was not added to the grid, since the information is obsolete (the `CarId` already shows in the cars part of the form).

Data User Interaction

Display and edit methods

Sometimes, you want to present data from two different data sources in one grid in a form. Let's say you have a form that only shows the records in the rental table. The grid in the form will look like this:

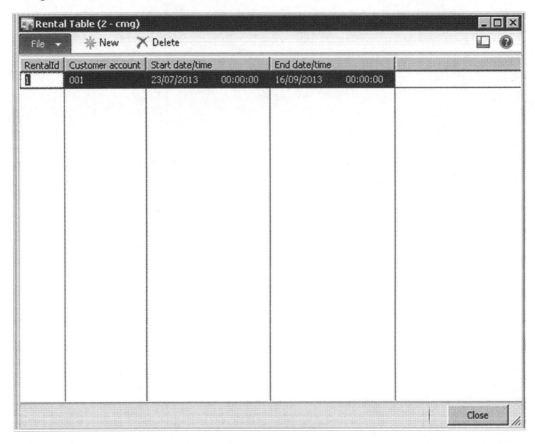

The end users though will say that the `CarId` field doesn't tell them anything and they would like to be able to see the brand and model from the `CarTable` in the grid as well.

This is not a problem since one record in the `RentalTable` will always only point to one record in the `CarTable`.

What you need to do then is to create two display methods in the `RentalTable`.

 Display and edit methods should preferably be written on tables and not in data sources or elsewhere in forms or reports, although it is possible to do so.

The display methods should be written as follows:

```
display carbrand brand()
{
    Name        ret;

    ret = CarTable::find(this.CarId).CarBrand;
    return ret;
}

display carmodel model()
{
    Name        ret;

    ret = CarTable::find(this.CarId).Model;
    return ret;
}
```

The display modifier at the beginning of the method will make the fields read-only in the forms and will enable you to drag-and-drop the method from the table to the grid in the form. So, the next thing to do is to drag these methods from the `RentalTable` and drop them under the grid in the `RentalTable` form. They will then become fields in the grid. You will also have to set the data source property on these fields to `RentalTable` as they are defaulted empty.

The form will now look like this:

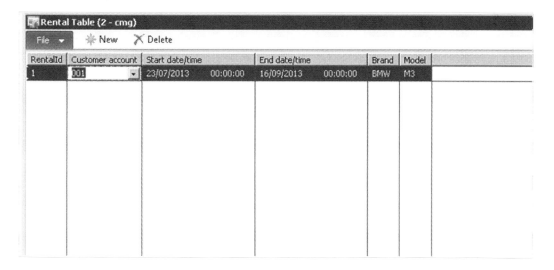

Data User Interaction

Note that we used new extended datatypes for `CarBrand` and `CarModel` in the display methods; this way the right label is displayed in the fields of the form. Ideally, we would have used these extended datatypes when we created the fields themselves.

Edit methods

Edit methods are basically the same as display methods, except that users can also write data to the fields. Instead of using the `display` modifier in the method header, you use the `edit` modifier. In addition, the first input variable should be of type Boolean and called `set`. This variable will be set to `true` if the user changes the value in the field in the form. The second input parameter should hold the value that the user types in the field in the form.

To give an example of an edit method, we will create a new field in the `CarTable` to hold the mileage of the car and have an edit method in `RentalTable` that enables the users to be in the `RentalTable` form and still edit the field in `CarTable`.

We'll create an extended datatype of type integer for the new field and call it `Mileage`. Then we'll add the field to the `CarTable`.

The `edit` method in `RentalTable` will then look like this:

```
edit Mileage mileage(boolean set, Mileage value)
{
    CarTable        carTable;
    Mileage         ret;

    carTable = CarTable::find(this.CarId, set);
    if (set)
    {
        ttsbegin;
        carTable.Mileage = value;
        carTable.update();
        ttscommit;
    }
    else
    {
        ret = carTable.Mileage;
    }
    return ret;
}
```

The first thing we do in this method is that we find the record in `CarTable` by using the `carId` in the record that is selected in the form. If the field is edited, the `set` parameter is true and we can use that parameter to decide if the record we select from `CarTable` should be selected for update or not.

If the `set` parameter is true, we then tell the server to lock the record so that only this process can update the record by using the `ttsbegin` statement. You will learn more about manipulating data later in the book so I won't go into details here, but the `Mileage` field in `CarTable` is set to be equal to the value that the user entered and the `carTable` record is then updated. The `ttscommit` keyword will make sure that the record is written to the database and also unlock the record so that it can be updated by other processes.

If the `set` parameter is false, we simply return the `Mileage` value from the selected `CarTable` record.

Considerations

There are a few things to consider when using display and edit methods:

- When a display or edit method from one table returns data from another table, then it is best practice to write code to check record-level security in this method.
- In a grid within a form, users usually click on the field's title to sort the form. If a field is bound to use a display or edit method, then sorting will not work.
- Using display/edit methods in a grid has performance implications. Caching display methods will, however, help in optimizing performance.

Caching display methods

In order to speed up the performance of display methods, we can add it to the cache. Data retrieved by the display method is then put into the cache and fetched from the cache in consequent requests until the `reread` method on the data source is called.

Follow these steps to add the display method brand to the `init` method of the `RentalTable` form:

1. Find the `RentalTable` form in AOT.
2. Right-click on the `RentalTable` data source and go to **Override method | init**.
3. Add the following code after `super()` in the `init` method:
   ```
   RentalTable_ds.cacheAddMethod("brand");
   ```

Data User Interaction

The `cacheAddMethod` also has a second parameter that is defaulted to `true`. If it's set to `false`, the value of the display method will not be refreshed when a record is written to the database.

 You cannot add edit methods to the cache.

Creating a lookup form

In the previous chapter, you learned that there are two standard table groups in all tables in AX. One of these table groups is `AutoLookup`. This table group is used to create a lookup form when users click on the lookup button in a form.

However, sometimes you need a lookup that has extended functionality. Maybe it only shows a limited set of records from the table based on some logic, or maybe in some cases you have to present additional fields in the lookup form.

In these cases, you have to create a customized lookup form. This can be achieved in two different ways:

Creating a lookup form by adding a new form in AOT

To create a lookup form by adding a new form in the AOT, simply create a form the way you want your lookup form to look like and then set the **WindowType** property to **Popup** in the **Design** node. Before `super()` in the `run` method (or after `super()` in the `init` method) of the form, use the `selectMode()` method to set the field that should return a value to the form that opened the lookup form.

In the form that you want to use this new specialized lookup, change the lookup method of the lookup field in the data source.

We will create a lookup form like this for the `CarTable` so that the lookup can sort by the mileage when the user is in the `RentalTable` form.

First, we create the new form in the AOT and call it `CarIdLookup`. We add the `CarTable` in the data sources and add a piece of code in the `init` method of the data source to make sure that the form will sort by mileage:

```
public void init()
{
    super();
        this.query().dataSourceTable(tablenum(CarTable)).
addSortField(fieldnum(CarTable, Mileage), SortOrder::Ascending);
}
```

This method basically uses the standard `addSortField()` method on the data source table in the current query to set the mileage as the sort field and tells it to sort the mileage in an ascending order.

The next thing we do is to create a grid under the design node of the form and add the fields we would like to display in the lookup form of the grid.

The last thing we have to do with the form is to tell the form to return `CarId` to its calling form. To do this, first you have to set the property **AutoDeclaration** to **true** on the `CarTable_CarId` field in the grid. Then, you have to add the `selectMode()` call in the `run` or `init` method of the form:

```
public void init()
{
    super();
    this.selectMode(CarTable_CarId);
}
```

Now, we have to change the `RentalTable` form and add this code to the `lookup` method on the `CarId` field in the `RentalTable` data source:

```
public void lookup(FormControl _formControl, str _filterStr)
{
    Args      args;
    FormRun formRun;

    args = new Args(formstr(CarIdLookup));
    formRun = classfactory.formRunClass(args);
    formRun.init();
    this.performFormLookup(formRun, _formControl);
}
```

This code creates a new `FormRun` class and uses the `Args` class to point to the new lookup form we just created. It then calls the form's `init` method and finally calls a method on the field called `performFormLookup` with the `FormRun` object as parameter. It will then open the `CarIdLookup` form and wait for the user to select a record in the lookup form and return the value set in the field set by the `selectMode` method.

Creating a lookup in the lookup method

You can also create a lookup on a field by using the `lookup` method. You can override this method to implement your own lookup on the form.

```
public void lookup(FormControl _formControl, str _filterStr)
{
    SysTableLookup   sysTableLookup;
    Query                    query = new Query();
```

Data User Interaction

```
        QueryBuildDataSource    queryBuildDataSource;

    //Create an instance of SysTableLookup with the form control passed in
        sysTableLookup = SysTableLookup::newParameters(tablenum(CarTable),
 _formControl);

        //Add the fields to be shown in the lookup form
        sysTableLookup.addLookupfield(fieldnum(CarTable, CarId));
        sysTableLookup.addLookupfield(fieldnum(CarTable, CarBrand));
        sysTableLookup.addLookupfield(fieldnum(CarTable, Model));
        sysTableLookup.addLookupfield(fieldnum(CarTable, Mileage));

        //create the query datasource
        queryBuildDataSource = query.addDataSource(tablenum(CarTable));

        // Clear any existing sort fields and add the new sort field
        queryBuildDataSource.sortClear();
        queryBuildDataSource.addSortField(fieldnum(CarTable, Mileage),
 SortOrder::Ascending);

        //add the query to the lookup form
        sysTableLookup.parmQuery(query);

        // Do the lookup
        sysTableLookup.performFormLookup();
}
```

In some versions of AX, I have noticed that there is a bug that will make the sorting fail in this example, because the first field set using the `addLookupfield` will always have the sort priority of one. You would then have to put the mileage field first instead to make the sorting work.

Parts

A part is a special type of control that can show additional information linked to a form or record. Generally, a part is used to retrieve the data that appears in the **FactBox** pane of a form; however, parts can also be used in the **Preview** pane of a list page or the enhanced preview of a control.

There are effectively three types of parts:

Type	Description
Info	A part that shows a collection of data fields from a specified query. This part uses metadata to describe how the data appears. This can be used in both the AX client and the enterprise portal.
Form	This is as effective as a form that appears in the **FactBox** section. This makes them immensely powerful, as developers can add buttons links and other functions to them. However, unlike info parts, form parts cannot be deployed to enterprise portal.
Cue	This is effectively a representation of a query. Cues are displayed on a user's home page and typically provide some indication of the query result (such as count of records or sum of a field). When a user clicks on a cue, they are taken straight into the associated form.

Reports

In AX, reports are used to display data to users in a format that is suitable for the way that the information is read. Reports is a commonly used word to describe all predefined outputs that are printed on paper. So, this can be picking list, invoices (that is, business documents), cash flow statements, and so on.

All reports in AX use **SQL Server Reporting Services** (**SSRS**) to render reports. This effectively means that all the functionalities available in SSRS are now available to AX report developers.

In the previous versions of Dynamics AX, reports were built using a native MorphX report designer. This reports designer is still available in AX 2012; however, it is scheduled to be deprecated in the next release and none of the start reports leverage this technology—instead, all reports are executed using SSRS.

The SQL Server reports are more flexible and can use diagrams, pivot and key performance indicators, as well as standard two dimensional report layouts. It is also very easy to use data from cubes instead of directly from the AX database using Reporting Services.

Dynamics AX 2012 integrates Reporting Services in such a way that developers can write code in Visual Studio that accesses the business logic within AX.

Reporting Services

Microsoft SSRS is a report generation software that is a part of Microsoft SQL Server. It enables users to execute reports using a web interface or even as embedded reports in applications by using a web services interface.

Developers typically use Microsoft Visual Studio with the Business Intelligence Projects plugin installed to develop reports for Reporting Services. Very basic reports (reports created by end users) can also be created using the Report Builder tool that is included.

The Reporting Services reports are stored as XML files following a standard called **Report Definition Language** (RDL). When executed, the files can be transformed into Excel, PDF, XML, and even as images like TIFF.

Dynamics AX comes with extensions for Reporting Services and Visual Studio reporting tools for AX that integrates Dynamics AX with Reporting Services and Visual Studio. This enables developers to create Reporting Services reports in Visual Studio that display data from Dynamics AX. The developers can also call business logic inside AX from the Reporting project in Visual Studio.

Creating an AX report using Visual Studio

We will now go through the steps needed to create a simple Reporting Services report in Visual Studio that displays AX data.

1. Open Visual Studio and go to **New | Project**.
2. In the **Project types** window, select **Visual C#** (or **Visual Basic** under **Other Languages** if you prefer to write the code in Visual Basic).
3. Then, select the **Dynamics** type and **Dynamics AX Reporting Project** from **Visual Studio installed templates**.
4. Name the project `CarRentalReports`.
5. Click on **OK** to create the project.

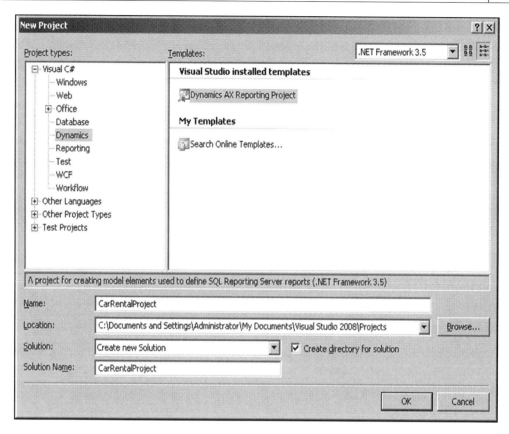

6. When the project opens, a new report named **Report1** (the filename is named Report1.moxl) is ready. We will rename this report and call it CarList instead. This can be done by right-clicking on the report, selecting **Properties**, and changing the **Name** property to CarList.

7. Also, set the **Title** of the report to Car List.

The next step is to create a dataset to use in the report. A dataset can have either one of two different data source types in the report, that is, either a query defined in the AOT in AX or the business logic which is data returned from a method written in the current project.

Data User Interaction

We will only use a query in our example and the query is defined in the next chapter and called `CarList`. So jump to the next chapter if you would like to see how it's created.

1. Right-click on **Datasets** in the report and select **Add Dataset**. Name the dataset `Cars` and open its properties. Go to the query property and click on the lookup button to the right in the field.

2. In the window that opens, select the `CarList` query (if you have jumped to the next chapter and created the query in AX). Then click on **OK** to go back to the report again. Notice that the query property now has the value:

   `SELECT * FROM CarList`

   This means that this dataset will select all records that the `CarList` query returns.

3. If you now expand the **Cars** dataset, you will see all the fields from the query that you now can use in the report. The Visual Studio window should now look like this:

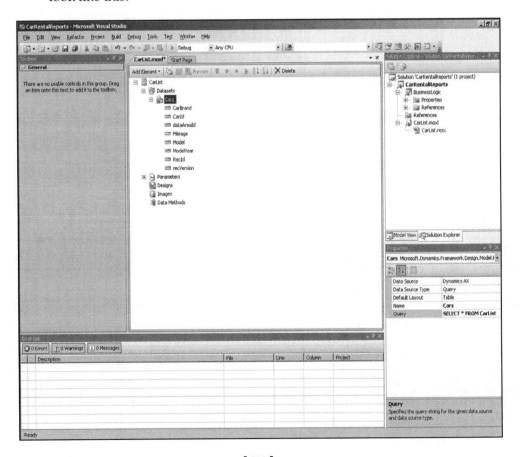

[130]

Chapter 4

We will also create a parameter for our report where the user can enter a maximum mileage. We will use this parameter as a filter in the design of the report later, so that the report only will show cars with less mileage than selected in this parameter.

1. Right-click on the **Parameters** node and select **Add parameter** to add the parameter. Rename it `MaximumMileage`. Also, change the datatype of the property from **System.String** to **System.Int32**, as this is the datatype of the mileage field that we will compare it to later.

2. Now add an auto design element to the report by right-clicking on the **Designs** node and navigating to **New | Auto Design**. An auto design element named **AutoDesign1** will be created. Right-click on **AutoDesign1** and go to **Add | Table**.

3. To add fields from the dataset to the table in the design, just drag-and-drop them onto the **Data** node in the table like this:

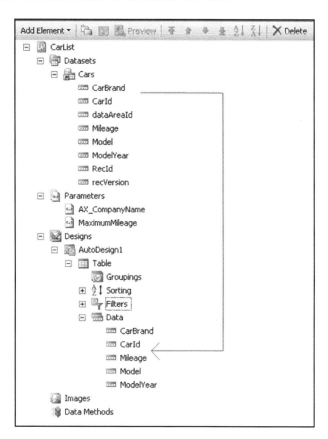

4. You can now have the report sort by mileage by dragging the **Mileage** field from the **Data** node in the table and dropping it in the **Sorting** node.

5. Repeat the same procedure to add the filter. Also, to make the filter work against the parameter you just created, you have to modify its parameters to look like this:

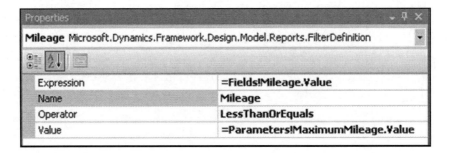

6. You can now preview the report by right-clicking on the **AutoDesign1** node and selecting **Preview**. Enter a value in the **MaximumMileage** parameter and select the **Report** tab to view the report. The report should now look like this:

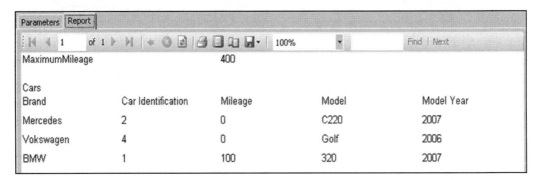

7. If you want to change the layout of the report to have bold labels, other fonts, and so on, you have to create a precision design instead of an auto design.

8. Now that your report project is ready to be used in AX, you should send it to AOT. This is done by right-clicking on the **CarRentalReports** project in the solution explorer in Visual Studio and selecting **Save to AOD**.

9. To be able to run the report from AX though, it must be deployed to the Reporting Services server. Again, right-click on the **CarRentalReports** project in the solution explorer and select **Deploy**.

The report will then be compiled and sent to the Report Services server and can now be executed from AX by adding a menu item that points to it as shown in the following section.

Menu items

Menu items are basically classes that are used to start forms, reports, and classes. They can be used as visual components in forms as buttons or in menus as links.

There are three types of menu items:

- **Display**: This is used to start forms
- **Output**: This is used to start reports
- **Action**: This is used to start classes that have a `main` method

Creating a menu item

The easiest way to create a menu item is to drag a form into the **Display** node, a report into the output node, or a class into the actions node under menu items in the AOT.

After the drag-and-drop operation, you have to add a label to the menu item.

You can also create output menu items that point to SSRS Reports. You will then have to create an output menu item by right-clicking on the output node under menu items and selecting **New Menu Item**. The next thing to do is to change the object type property to SSRS Report and select the report from the drop down list in the object property. Add an output menu item for the report you created in Visual Studio by right-clicking on the output node under menu items in the AOT and navigating to **New** | **Menu Item**. Change the name of the menu item to `CarList` and label to `Car List`. Then set the object type to `SQLReportLibraryReport` and the object to `CarRentalReports.CarList.AutoDesign1` (`<ReportLibrary>.<ReportName>.<DesignName>`).

Now create menu items for the `CarTable`, `RentalTable`, and `CarRentals` forms and the `CarsTimesRented` report by dragging them into the **Display** and **Output** nodes under **MenuItems** in AOT. Set the label for all of them.

Now that you have created menu items for these objects, you should also go back to the tables you created in the previous chapter and set the **FormRef** property so that the table `CarTable` points to the form `CarTable` in the **FormRef** property and the `RentalTable` points to the `RentalTable` form.

Using a menu item as a button in a form

You can also add a menu item to a form and make it open another form. This is done simply by dragging the menu item and dropping it onto a form design.

To do this, in our example, you should first add an action pane to create the MS Office ribbon-like button structure at the top of the window. In this example, we change the action pane's **Style** property to **Strip**, which reduces the size of the buttons. Then just drag the **RentalTable** menu item from one AOT window and drag it onto the button group that is automatically added under the **ActionPane** tab.

A new button will then be created that will open the RentalTable form. However, to get only rentals for the selected car in the CarTable form, you have to set the data source property on the button to CarTable.

The form will then look like this:

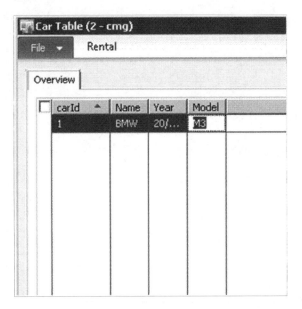

The form in AOT with the properties of the button should look something like this:

Navigation pages

Navigation pages are a new feature in Dynamics AX 2012 used to provide links to the most common operations, reports, and forms that users need for each area in the solution.

There are three different kinds of navigation pages:

- **List page**: This contains a list of records in the content pane and has buttons that start actions on one or many of the records.
- **Content page**: This is used for navigation and is placed inside the content pane. It can contain records in another format than a list. An example is the organization view, which can be found in the main menu by navigating to **Administration | Organization View**).
- **Area page**: The content of a menu defined in the AOT under **Menus** is displayed as area pages. The area pages open inside the client content page.

Data User Interaction

List pages

We will look more into how list pages work as they are the most advanced and interesting of these three. List pages typically contain a collection of other user interface elements to display data and to perform actions against those data.

This is an example of a list page and the different UI elements used:

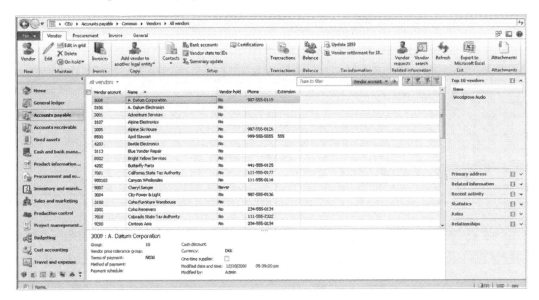

The window shown in the preceding screenshot is divided into following sections:

- **Action pane**: The action pane is like a tab with tab pages that contains different kind of actions. Changing to another action pane tab will only change the actions inside the action pane and not the rest of the list page.

- **Filter pane**: The filter pane is used to filter the data in the content pane. The filter pane will appear automatically in your list page.

- **Content pane**: The content pane consists of a grid with fields from the data source of the list page.

- **Preview pane**: The preview pane is a HTML component that is generated at runtime based on fields in certain groups in the form design and is an optional component in the list pages.

Creating a list page

Before we start creating a list page, we need to create a query that will be used to display data and a list page interaction class.

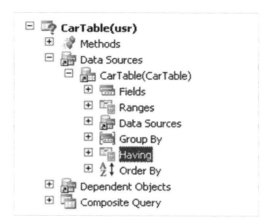

1. Right-click on the **Query** node and create new query. Rename the query `CarTable`.
2. Drag-and-drop the `CarTable` as a data source.
3. Select the **Fields** node and change the **Dynamic** property to **Yes**.

Using the following steps, we will create a basic interaction class. The class is a simple shell that can later be extended to add logic to control form interaction. For example, certain buttons can be hidden based on how the user launches the form. For now, we will keep it simple.

1. Create a new class called `CarListPageInteraction`.
2. Ensure the class extends `ListPageInteraction`:

   ```
   public class CarListPageInteraction extends ListPageInteraction
   {
   }
   ```

Data User Interaction

We will now create a list page that shows records in the CarTable and add an action in this list page that opens the RentalTable form:

1. Right-click on the forms node in AOT and select **New** by navigating to **Template | List Page**.
2. Change the name of the form to CarsListPage (check out the following information box).
3. On the **Design** node (under the **Designs** node) you must change the **WindowType** property to **ListPage**. This will make the rest of the form understand that this is a list page and treat it accordingly. Also, set a caption for the form, for example, Cars in our example.
4. Now, click on the **Data Source** node and select the CarTable query.
5. Scroll down to the grid and change the **DataSource** property to CarTable and change the **DataGroup** property to **Overview** (or drag-and-drop the required fields).

 It is best practice to postfix the name of a list page with **ListPage** to make it easier to find in AOT.

6. Open a new AOT window and find the display menu item RentalTable that we created earlier in this chapter. Drag this menu item and drop it onto the Button group. A new menu item button is now created that will open the **RentalTable** form.
7. Right-click on the new menu item's button in the form and change the **ButtonDisplay** property to **Text & Image**.
8. Change the **Big** property to **Yes**.
9. Set the **DataSource** property to **CarTable** and also add an image to the button by setting the **NormalImage** property to an image/icon on your hard drive that you think fit for the **RentalTable** button.

If you open the form now, it should look like this:

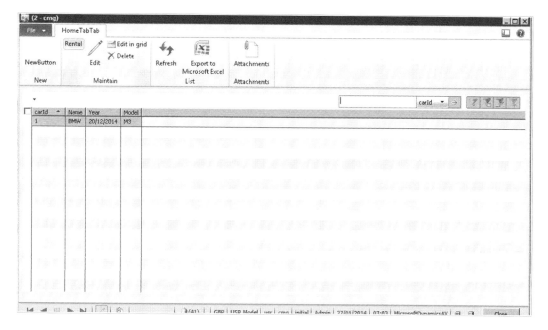

Try out the functionalities by clicking on the buttons and filtering the records.

Menus

Menus are listed as modules in the navigation pane to the left in a standard AX installation. When selecting a module, the content pane will change to show the contents of the selected menu.

Now that you have created menu items for the forms and reports you have created earlier in this chapter, you are ready to add them to a menu.

Create a new menu by right-clicking on **Menus** in the AOT and select **New Menu**. Open the **Properties** window for the menu and change the name to `CarRental` and the label to `Car Rental`.

Data User Interaction

Save the menu. Then right-click on it and go to **New | Submenu**. Open its **Properties** window and change the name and label to Reports.

Open another AOT window and find the display menu items that you created earlier in this chapter. Drag them from the AOT window and drop them onto the **CarRental** menu in the other AOT window. Do the same for the output menu items you created, but put these menu items in the **Reports** submenu.

You have now created a new menu in AX, but in order to get the menu to show in the main menu, you also have to change the main menu.

1. Go to **MainMenu** under **Menus** in AOT, right-click on it, and go to **New | Menu reference**. A new AOT window with all the menus in the AOT will appear.
2. Find the **CarRental** menu in this new AOT window and drag-and-drop it into the **MainMenu** node in the original AOT window so that it looks like this:

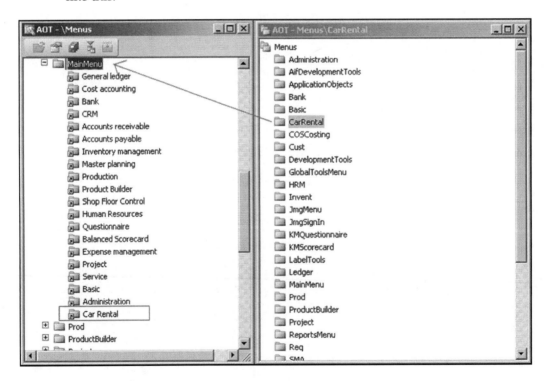

3. Restart AX to view the new menu.

[140]

Summary

This chapter should have given you an overview of how to create a basic user interface according to best practices and you also learned about some of the major new development features in Dynamics AX 2012.

You should now be able to create forms, reports, menu items, menus, and navigation pages. Although the examples I have showed you so far are very simple, I hope that they trigger your curiosity to play around and try to change parameters in order to see how they affect the result. Basically, this is how you will broaden your knowledge with the possibilities and hopefully few limitations of AX.

In the next chapter, we will look at how to retrieve data using views, queries, and select statements.

5
Searching for Data

In this chapter, you will learn about different mechanisms for retrieving data from the database:

- Queries that are reusable and are often used in reports and periodic jobs
- Views that are created in AOT and translated to optimized `select` statements at runtime
- The `select` statements that are used in X++ to fetch data from the database to the application

After reading this chapter, you will know how to use these mechanisms and which one of them to use in different cases.

Queries

Queries are typically used to ask users about ranges and sorting and selecting data based on the feedback from the users. A query can consist of one or multiple data sources and can be created both as static queries in AOT or as dynamic queries using X++. Most commonly, they are used when the ranges or values are not known until runtime. Static queries are defined in AOT and dynamic queries are defined in the X++ code.

Creating a static query using AOT

Follow these steps to create a static query in AOT:

1. Open AOT, expand the **Queries** node, right-click on **Queries**, and select **New Query**. A new query is created in AOT.
2. Right-click on the query, select **Properties**, and change the **Name** to `CarList` (or in other cases, change it to something that describes what kind of data the query is returning).

Searching for Data

3. Open a new AOT window, expand the **Data Dictionary** node, and then click on the **Tables** node.
4. Drag the `CarTable` and drop it onto the **Data Sources** node of the new query. You can also drag maps or views to the data source of a query.

You have now created the skeleton of the query. Now, we need to change the **Dynamic** property of the **Fields** node. This property is used to define which fields are pulled from the database when the query is executed.

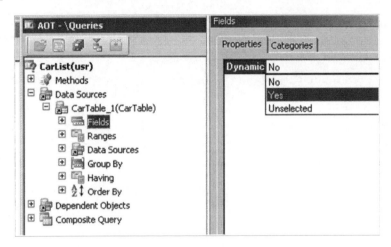

The following options are available under the **Dynamic** property:

- **Unselected**: This is the default option. This means that no fields have been selected and the query is not ready for execution.
- **Yes**: If the **Dynamic** property is set to **Yes**, then AX will effectively pull all the fields from the database at execution time. This covers both fields present on the table now and any new fields that will be added in future.
- **No**: This means that the user must specify the list of fields that should be selected from the database under the **Field** node in the query. If new fields are added to the table, then a developer must remember to add them to the query as well (only if needed by the query). This option is generally better for performance.

Let's take a look at how to add sorting and ranges to the query.

Adding a sort order to the query

To add sorting to the query, just drag the selected field from the **Fields** node under the data source and drop it under the **Order By** node. In our example, we'll use the `Mileage` field. You can then choose to sort it in ascending or descending order by changing the direction property on the `sort` field.

When the query prompt is executed in a report, the user has the ability to change the sort order.

Adding a range to the query

You can also add ranges to the data source by dragging a field from the **Fields** node and dropping it under **Ranges**. A range can be used to ask the user for input to narrow down the result returned by the query or it can be used as a fixed range that the user can never change. This is done by adding a value to the **Value** property of the range.

Values in a range can be used like this:

Range operator	Description	Example
,	This selects records where the range field matches any of the values listed	BMW, VW, Volvo
=	This selects records where the range field is a matching value	=VW
..	This selects records where the range field is between the values specified including the values used	1000..3000
<	This selects records where the range field is less than the value specified	<2000
>	This selects records where the range field is greater than the value specified	>2000
!	This selects records where the range field is not equal to the value specified	!BMW
?	This selects records where the ? symbol can be any character	Merc??es
*	This selects records where the range field matches the characters before or after the asterisk	Merc*

When the **Status** property is set to **Open**, the users can change the range value. If it's set to **Lock**, the users can see the range value before executing the query, but they are not allowed to change it. If the **Status** property is set to **Hidden**, the users won't even be allowed to see the range value.

In our example, we add the `ModelYear` field from the data source **CarTable_1**:

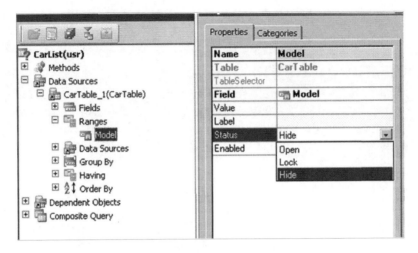

Joining data sources in the query

In order to select data from more than one table, you can join the data sources in your query. Data sources can be joined in a couple of different ways depending on how you would like to link them. This is done by setting the **JoinMode** property to the different values shown in the following table:

JoinMode	Description
InnerJoin	This will return the records where the joined data sources have matching values in the joined fields.
	For example, by using the `CarTable` as the primary data source and using `RentalTable` as the joined data source, the inner join will fetch all records from the `CarTable` where there is a corresponding record in the `RentalTable`. The corresponding records in `RentalTable` will also be fetched.
OuterJoin	This will return all the records from the joined table even if they don't match the joined field.
	For example, compared to the example using the **InnerJoin** property, this will return all records from the `CarTable`, but also records from the `RentalTable` that do not have a match in the `CarTable`.

[146]

JoinMode	Description
ExistsJoin	This is just like the **InnerJoin** property, except the records from the joined data source are not returned. They are only used to filter the primary data source. In our example, it will only return records in the `CarTable` where there is a match in the `RentalTable`. Records from the `RentalTable` will not be fetched.
NoExistsJoin	This is the opposite of the **ExistsJoin** property. It will select records from the primary data source when matching records in the joined data source do not exist. In our example, it will return records from the `CarTable` that do not have any matching records in the `RentalTable` (cars that have never been rented).

Follow these steps to add a new data source and join it to the first one:

1. First, we will create a duplicate of the query we have created so far, since we would like to use the original query in the Reporting Services report in the previous chapter. To duplicate any AOT object, right-click on the object and select **Duplicate**. A duplicate is then created with the prefix **CopyOf**.

2. Now, rename the new query and call it `RentalCarList`.

3. Also, change the range under the **CarTable_1** data source to `ModelYear` instead of `Model`, since this range will be used later in this chapter.

4. Drag another table, map, or view and drop it onto the data source node below the first data source. In our example, we will add the `RentalTable`. So, open a new AOT window and go to **Data Dictionary | Tables | RentalTable**. Drag the **RentalTable** and drop it onto the **Data Sources** node under the **CarTable** data source in the query.

5. Open the properties of the **RentalTable** data source in the query and change the **Relations** property to **Yes**, This will automatically fetch the relationship that is defined on the table. A developer can manually create relationships on the query as well.

6. If you expand the **Relations** node under the **RentalTable** data source, you should now see that the **CarTable** data source is linked to the **RentalTable** data source by the **CarId** and your AOT should look like this:

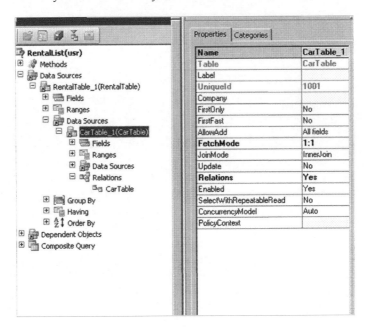

Creating a dynamic query using X++

A query can also be built dynamically using the X++ code. This can be the only way of creating the query if you would like the query to work in one way in some cases and in another way in other cases. An example can be where you would like to join one table if one condition is true and another table if the condition is false. To do this, you need to understand how the Query object model works. Some of the terms associated with the Query object model are explained here:

- `Query`: This contains the definition of the query. It can consist of one data source or several data sources if they are related.
- `QueryRun`: This is a class that is used to execute the given query and loop through the result.
- `QueryBuildDataSource`: This acts as a link to a data source in the query. It can be linked to another `QueryBuildDataSource` object to join linked data sources.

- `QueryBuildRange`: This enables the end user to limit the result by adding a value in the specified query range.
- `QueryBuildFieldList`: This gives a list of all the fields present in a data source—one `QueryBuildFieldList` object for each `QueryBuildDataSource` instance. By default, the **Dynamic** property is set to **true** so that all fields are returned.
- `QueryBuildLink`: This links two data sources in a join. It is usually set on the child data source.

The query definition is set up by creating and linking objects from the Query object model together and the following example shows how this is done in order to create the same query as we did in the previous section of this chapter when we created a query called `RentalCarList` in AOT:

```
static void queryRentalCarList(Args _args)
{
    Query                    query;
    QueryBuildDataSource     queryBuildDataSource1,
queryBuildDataSource2;
    QueryBuildRange          queryBuildRange;
    QueryBuildLink           queryBuildLink;


    // Create a new query object
    query = new Query();
    // Add the first data source to the query
    queryBuildDataSource1 = query.addDataSource(tablenum(CarTable));
    // Add the range to this first data source
    queryBuildRange = queryBuildDataSource1.
addRange(fieldnum(CarTable, ModelYear));
    // Add the second datasource to the first data source
    queryBuildDataSource2 = queryBuildDataSource1.addDataSource(tablen
um(RentalTable));
    // Add the link from the child data source to the parent data
source
    queryBuildLink = queryBuildDataSource2.addLink(fieldnum(CarTable,
CarId),fieldnum(RentalTable, CarId));
}
```

Searching for Data

Using a query

Now we have the query definition, but that doesn't help us much unless we are able to execute the query, right?

The following example uses the previous example and just adds `QueryRun` and loops through the result by using the `next()` method on the `QueryRun` object:

```
static void queryRunRentalCarList(Args _args)
{
    Query                   query;
    QueryBuildDataSource    queryBuildDataSource1,
queryBuildDataSource2;
    QueryBuildRange         queryBuildRange;
    QueryBuildLink          queryBuildLink;
    QueryRun                queryRun;
    CarTable                carTable;
    RentalTable             rentalTable;


    // Create a new query object
    query = new Query();
    // Add the first data source to the query
    queryBuildDataSource1 = query.addDataSource(tablenum(CarTable));
    // Add the range to this first data source
    queryBuildRange = queryBuildDataSource1.
addRange(fieldnum(CarTable, ModelYear));
    // Set the range
    queryBuildRange.value("2008..");
    // Add the second datasource to the first data source
    queryBuildDataSource2 = queryBuildDataSource1.addDataSource(tablen
um(RentalTable));
    // Add the link from the child data source to the parent data
source
    queryBuildLink = queryBuildDataSource2.addLink(fieldnum(CarTable,
CarId),fieldnum(RentalTable, CarId));

    // Create a new QueryRun object based on the query definition
    queryRun = new QueryRun(query);
    // Loop through all the records returned by the query
    while (queryRun.next())
    {
        // Get the table data by using the get() method
        carTable = queryRun.get(tablenum(CarTable));
        rentalTable = queryRun.get(tablenum(RentalTable));
        info (strfmt("CarId %1, RentalId %2", carTable.CarId,
rentalTable.RentalId));
    }
}
```

Chapter 5

The following result is obtained after running the query:

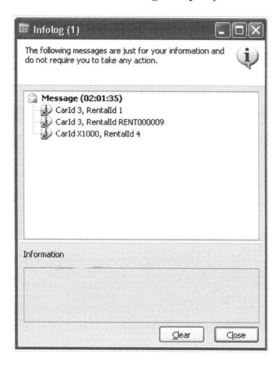

The exact same result will show up if we execute the query that was defined in AOT in the previous section of this chapter.

The code would then look something like this:

```
static void queryRunRentalCarListAOT(Args _args)
{
    Query                   query;
    QueryBuildDataSource    queryBuildDataSource;
    QueryBuildRange         queryBuildRange;
    QueryRun                queryRun;
    CarTable                carTable;
    RentalTable             rentalTable;


    // Create a new query object based on the Query in AOT called RentalCarList
    query = new Query(querystr(RentalCarList));
    // Find the datasource for the CarTable
    queryBuildDataSource = query.dataSourceTable(tablenum(CarTable));
    // Find the range that we added to the query in AOT
    queryBuildRange = queryBuildDataSource.findRange(fieldnum(CarTable, ModelYear));
```

Searching for Data

```
    // Set the value of the range
    queryBuildRange.value("2008..");
    // Create a new QueryRun object based on the query definition
    queryRun = new QueryRun(query);
    // Loop through all the records returned by the query
    while (queryRun.next())
    {
        // Get the table data by using the get() method
        carTable = queryRun.get(tablenum(CarTable));
        rentalTable = queryRun.get(tablenum(RentalTable));
        info (strfmt("CarId %1, RentalId %2", carTable.CarId,
rentalTable.RentalId));
    }
}
```

Views

In AX, views are objects that are used to retrieve data from the database and stored in the memory on the layer in which the view is instantiated. The views are actually stored as database views on the SQL server. This means that there are potentially great performance benefits of using views compared to using an equivalent query. This depends on the complexity of the query but, in general, the performance benefits of using a view compared to a query will increase and the complexity of the query will increase.

Views can be used throughout AX in all places where tables can be used; this includes forms, queries, and reports in the X++ code.

Views in AX can never be used to write data; they are used only to read data from the database. This differs from the SQL implementation that has write back possibilities for views.

Creating a view

We will now create a view that consists of car ID, car brand, car model, customer's name, from date, and to date.

1. First, we locate the **Views** node under the **Data Dictionary** node in AOT.
2. Right-click on the **Views** node and select **New View**. A new view will be created and you can see its properties by right-clicking on it and selecting **Properties**.
3. Change the name of the view to `CarCustRental` and give it a label that describes the contents of the view.

Chapter 5

4. The views can actually use already created queries as a base for the data selection. This is done in the **Properties** tab of the view by choosing the query from the **Query** property. However, in our example, we will create the view from scratch.

5. Under the **Metadata** node under the view, select the **Data Sources** node, right-click on it, and select **New Data Source**.

6. Select the newly created data source and enter `CarTable` in the **Table** property. The name of the data source will automatically change to **CarTable_1** and this is OK.

7. Under the **CarTable** data source, find the **Data Sources** node, right-click on it, and select **New Data Source**. This time, we want to use the `RentalTable`, so change the table property to `RentalTable`. Also, change the **Relations** property to **Yes** in order to get the link between the two tables active in the view.

8. Do the same to add the **CustTable** as a child data source to the **RentalTable**.

9. The next step now is to define the fields that should be made available when this query is executed. Simply drag the fields you need to use in the view from **CarTable_1**, **RentalTable_1**, and **CustTable_1** data sources and drop them onto the **Fields** node.

You should now have a view that looks like this:

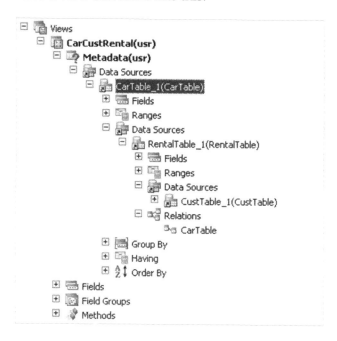

[153]

Searching for Data

After saving the view, you can browse the contents of the view in the same way as you can with a table by using the table browser. Just open the view and the table browser will display the view with its contents.

You can also take a look at the view in the SQL Management Studio by opening the **AX database** node, selecting the **Views** node, and looking for the view you just created. Right-click on the view and select **Design** to open it in Design view. It should then look something like this:

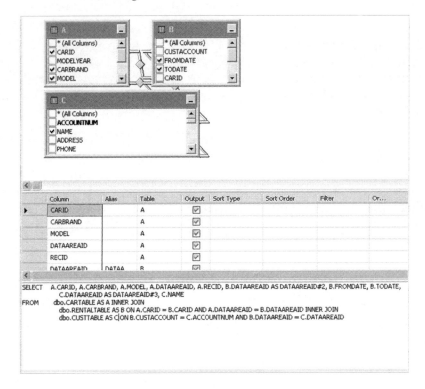

The select statement

One of the really great features of Dynamics AX as a development tool is the possibility to write embedded SQL. This basically means that you can write `select` statements that are controlled by the compiler and get results back directly to table variables.

The following list is taken from the SDK and shows the syntax for the `select` statement and the parameters allowed with the it:

Description	Syntax
SelectStatement	`select` Parameters
Parameters	[[FindOptions] [FieldList `from`]] TableBufferVariable [IndexClause] [Options] [WhereClause] [JoinClause]
FindOptions	`crossCompany` | `reverse` | `firstFast` | [`firstOnly` | `firstOnly10` | `firstOnly100` | `firstOnly1000`] | `forUpdate` | `noFetch` | [`forcePlaceholders` | `forceLiterals`] | `forceselectorder` | `forceNestedLoop` | `repeatableRead`
FieldList	Field { , Field} | *
Field	Aggregate (FieldIdentifier) | FieldIdentifier
Aggregate	`sum` | `avg` | `minof` | `maxof` | `count`
Options	[`order by`, `group by`, FieldIdentifier [`asc` | `desc`] { , FieldIdentifier [`asc` | `desc`]}] | [IndexClause]
IndexClause	`index` IndexName | `index hint` IndexName
WhereClause	`where` Expression
JoinClause	[`exists` | `notexists` | `outer`] `join` Parameters

Check out the SDK for a more in-depth explanation of all the different keywords.

In the following examples, we will have a look at how to create different select statements depending on what data we would like to have available for the rest of the code.

To give you a better understanding of how the different select statements work and what data is returned, we will use the data from the following subsections.

CarTable

The following list shows the test data for the `CarTable`:

CarId	ModelYear	CarBrand	Model	Mileage
1	2007	BMW	320	2299
2	2007	Mercedes	C220	2883
3	2008	Toyota	Corolla	4032
4	2006	Volkswagen	Golf	49902
5	2002	Jeep	Grand Cherokee	65662
6	2003	BMW	Z3	11120
7	2000	Volkswagen	Golf	76322

RentalTable

The following list shows the test data for the `RentalTable`:

RentalId	CustAccount	FromDate	ToDate	CarId
1	1101	24.03.2009	25.03.2009	1
2	1103	23.03.2009	25.03.2009	3
3	1103	02.05.2009	11.05.2009	1
4	1102	10.05.2009	17.05.2009	5
5	1104	10.12.2009	20.12.2009	6

CustTable

The following list shows the test data for the `CustTable`:

AccountNum	Name	CustGroup	Blocked
1101	Forest Wholesales	10	No
1102	Sunset Wholesales	20	No
1103	Cave Wholesales	10	No
1104	Desert Wholesales	30	Yes

How to write a simple select statement

A `select` statement can be written specifically to return only one record or to return many records. If we expect the `select` statement to return multiple records and we would like to loop through these records, we simply embed the `select` statement within a `while` loop.

The following examples will demonstrate how to write simple `select` statements that return different data from the same table.

The first example will select all columns from all records in the `CarTable`:

```
static void selectAllRecordsStatic(Args _args)
{
    CarTable        carTable;
    int             records;

    info("------------------START------------------");
    while select carTable
    {
        info("--------------NEW RECORD--------------");
        info (strfmt("CarId:     %1", carTable.CarId));
        info (strfmt("CarBrand:  %1", carTable.CarBrand));
        info (strfmt("Model:     %1", carTable.Model));
        info (strfmt("ModelYear: %1", carTable.ModelYear));
        info (strfmt("Mileage:   %1", carTable.Mileage));
        records++;
    }
    info("------------------END------------------");
    info(strfmt("%1 records was selected", records));
}
```

Searching for Data

Executing this job will result in the following output to the infolog. Note that only the first records are shown in the following infolog window. When executing it yourself, you can scroll down to see the other records and the **END** line:

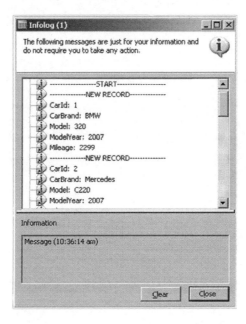

The next example actually does pretty much the same as the first example, but some code has been added to be able to dynamically write the fields in the table. On the other hand, it will also print all the system fields for each record, but it can be a nice exercise for you to understand how you can use the Dict classes (Dict classes are system classes that enable developers to query AOT element metadata at runtime) to create dynamic functionality as follows:

```
static void selectAllRecordsDynamically(Args _args)
{
    CarTable        carTable;
    DictField       dictField;
    DictTable       dictTable;
    int             field;
    int             fieldId;
    int             records;
    str             header, line;
```

```
    // Create a new object of type DictTable based on the carTable
    dictTable = new DictTable(tablenum(carTable));

    // Loop through the fields on the table.
    // For each field, store the field-label in the header variable.
    for (field=1; field <= dictTable.fieldCnt(); field++)
    {
        fieldId = dictTable.fieldCnt2Id(field);
        dictField = new DictField(tablenum(carTable), fieldId);
        header += strfmt("%1, ",  dictField.label());
    }
    info(strupr(header)); // strupr changes the string to UPPERCASE


    // Loop through all the records in the carTable
    while select carTable
    {
        line = "";
        // For each record in the carTable, loop through all the
fields
        // and store the value of the field for this record in the
line variable.
        for (field=1; field <= dictTable.fieldCnt(); field++)
        {
            fieldId = dictTable.fieldCnt2Id(field);
            dictField = new DictField(carTable.TableId, fieldId);
            // Instead of referencing to the fieldname, I reference to
the fieldId
            // the get the fields value.
            line += strfmt("%1, ",  carTable.(fieldId));
        }
        info(line);
        records++;
    }
    info(strfmt("%1 records were selected", records));
}
```

Searching for Data

Executing this job will result in the following output in the infolog:

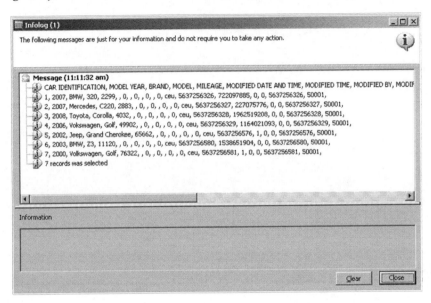

The next example will select all columns from the record in CarTable where the CarId equals 1. This means that we will only select one (the first) record and so we do not need the while loop:

```
static void selectOneRecord(Args _args)
{
    CarTable        carTable;

    select firstonly carTable
        where carTable.CarId == "1";

    info (strfmt("Car Brand: %1", carTable.CarBrand));
    info (strfmt("Car Model: %1", carTable.Model));
    info (strfmt("Model Year: %1", carTable.ModelYear));
    info (strfmt("Mileage: %1", carTable.Mileage));
}
```

Executing this job will result in the following output in the infolog:

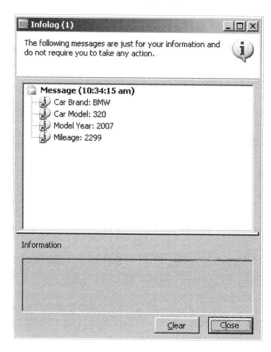

The next example will select only the CarBrand and Model columns from all records in the CarTable where the ModelYear value is higher than 2005:

```
static void selectWhereStatement(Args _args)
{
    CarTable         carTable;

    info(strupr("CarBrand, Model"));
    while select CarBrand, Model from carTable
        where carTable.ModelYear > 2005
    {
        info (strfmt("%1, %2  ", carTable.CarBrand, carTable.Model));
    }
}
```

Executing this job will result in the following output to the infolog:

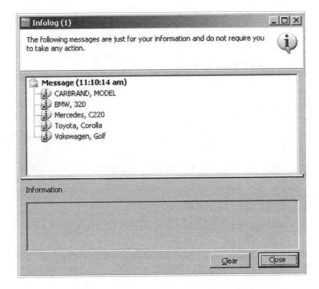

How to use sorting in the select statements

By default, a `while select` statement that returns multiple rows will sort the result ascending by the primary index on the table. You can see this in the first two examples in the previous section.

If you would like to have a statement return the rows in a different order, you have to use the `order by` parameter in the `select` statement and specify which fields you would like to sort the result by. If you have an index that corresponds with the sorting, you can use the name of the index to order by as well, but then you will have to use the `index` statement instead of `order by`. The following example will return all the records in the `CarTable` sorted in a descending order of mileage:

```
static void selectRecordsSortedDesc(Args _args)
{
    CarTable         carTable;
    int              records;

    info("-----------------START-------------------");
    while select carTable
        order by Mileage desc
    {
        info("--------------NEW RECORD--------------");
        info (strfmt("CarId:    %1", carTable.CarId));
```

```
            info (strfmt("CarBrand:   %1", carTable.CarBrand));
            info (strfmt("Model:   %1", carTable.Model));
            info (strfmt("ModelYear:   %1", carTable.ModelYear));
            info (strfmt("Mileage:   %1", carTable.Mileage));
            records++;
        }
        info("------------------END------------------");
        info(strfmt("%1 records was selected", records));
    }
```

Executing this job will result in the following output in the infolog:

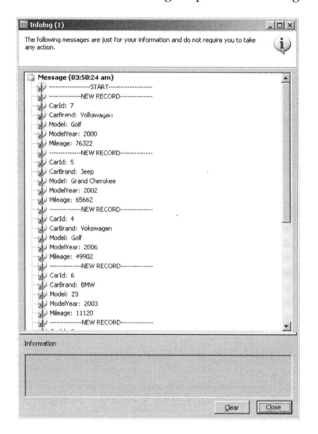

How to use joins in a select statement

If you would like to retrieve data from several tables or at least use ranges from different tables in the `select` statement, you should use one of the join parameters listed in the following sections.

Searching for Data

The inner join

The `inner` join is the most common join as it joins two tables that are linked together typically by a one-to-many relationship.

The first table used in the `select` statement, should be the "many" part of the relationship, so in our example, we can say that a record from the `CarTable` can exist many times in the `RentalTable` making the `RentalTable` being used first.

As you might notice, the sorting in a joined select is done first with the innermost table; in this case, the `CarTable`. When no sorting has been specified, AX uses the primary index set on the table. In this case, it uses the `CardIdx` index on the `CarTable`:

```
static void selectInnerJoin(Args _args)
{
    CarTable        carTable;
    RentalTable     rentalTable;

    while select rentalTable
        join carTable // same as writing inner join
            where carTable.CarId == rentalTable.CarId
    {
        info(strfmt("RentalId %1 is a %2 %3", rentalTable.RentalId,
carTable.CarBrand, carTable.Model));
    }
}
```

Executing this job will result in the following output in the infolog:

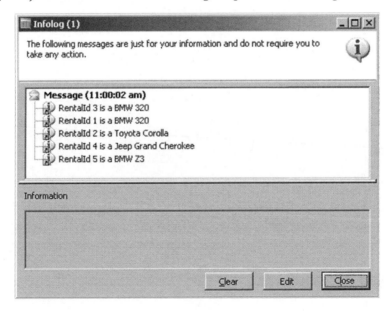

[164]

The outer join

An `outer` join is used to join two tables but to also include the records that do not have a corresponding match in the joined table. In the following example, you will see that all records in the `CarTable` are selected even though some of the cars have never been rented:

```
static void selectOuterJoin(Args _args)
{
    CarTable         carTable;
    RentalTable      rentalTable;


    while select carTable
        outer join rentalTable
            where rentalTable.CarId == carTable.CarId
    {
        if (!rentalTable.RecId)
            info(strfmt("No rentals for the car with carId %1",
carTable.CarId));
        else
            info(strfmt("RentalId %1 is a %2 %3", rentalTable.
RentalId, carTable.CarBrand, carTable.Model));
    }
}
```

Executing this job will result in the following output in the infolog:

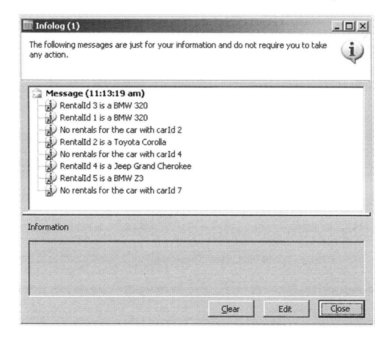

The exists join

The `exists` join does pretty much the same as the `inner` join except for one important thing; it does not fetch the records from the joined table. This means that the `rentalTable` variable cannot be used within the `while` loop in the following example as it will never have any data:

```
static void selectExistsJoin(Args _args)
{
    CarTable        carTable;
    RentalTable     rentalTable;


    while select carTable
        exists join rentalTable
            where rentalTable.CarId == carTable.CarId
    {
        info(strfmt("CarId %1 has a matching record in rentalTable",
CarTable.CarId));
    }
}
```

Executing this job will result in the following output in the infolog:

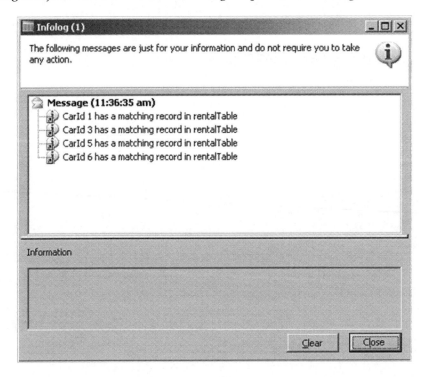

The notexists join

Obviously, the `notexists` join is the opposite of the `exists` join in terms of how it works. This means that it will return all records from the main table where there does not exist a record in the joined table as described by the `where` clause. This means that the following example will produce the opposite result from the previous example:

```
static void selectNotExistsJoin(Args _args)
{
    CarTable        carTable;
    RentalTable     rentalTable;


    while select carTable
        notexists join rentalTable
            where rentalTable.CarId == carTable.CarId
    {
        info(strfmt("CarId %1 does not has a matching record in rentalTable", CarTable.CarId));
    }
}
```

Executing this job will result in the following output in the infolog:

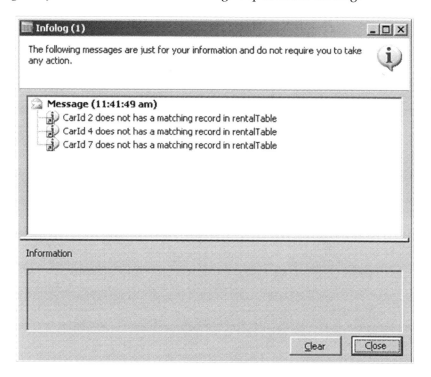

How to write aggregate select statements

In a lot of cases, you would like to write `select` statements that return aggregate data like the sum or average of a field in a set of data. You can also use the count aggregate option to count the number of records in a table matching a `where` statement if any. The `minof` and `maxof` options can be used in the same way to find the minimum or maximum value of a field in a record set that corresponds to the `where` statement.

The following examples show how the different aggregate options can be used.

sum

The `sum` aggregate option is used as follows:

```
static void selectSumMileage(Args _args)
{
    CarTable    carTable;

    select sum(Mileage) from carTable;

    info(strfmt("The total mileage of all cars is %1", carTable.Mileage));
}
```

Executing this job will result in the following output in the infolog:

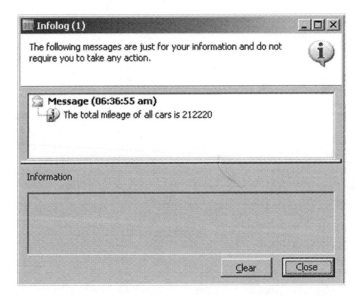

Chapter 5

avg

The `avg` aggregate option is used as follows:

```
static void selectAvgModelYear(Args _args)
{
    CarTable    carTable;

    select avg(ModelYear) from carTable;

    info(strfmt("The average ModelYear is %1", carTable.ModelYear));
}
```

Executing this job will result in the following output in the infolog:

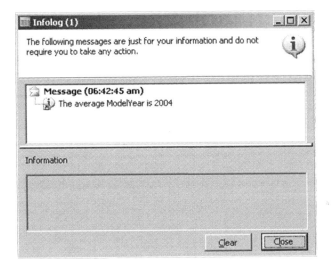

count

The `count` aggregate option is used as follows:

```
static void selectCountRentals(Args _args)
{
    RentalTable    rentalTable;

    select count(recId) from rentalTable;

    info(strfmt("There are %1 rentals registered in the system", rentalTable.RecId));
}
```

[169]

Executing this job will result in the following output in the infolog:

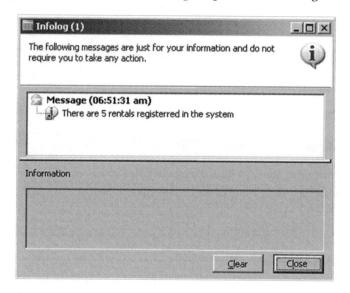

minof and maxof

The `minof` and `maxof` aggregate options are used as follows:

```
static void selectMinofMileage(Args _args)
{
    CarTable    minCarTable, maxCarTable;

    select minof(Mileage) from minCarTable;
    select maxof(Mileage) from maxCarTable;

    info(strfmt("The car with the lowest mileage has a mileage of %2", minCarTable.CarId, minCarTable.Mileage));
    info(strfmt("The car with the highest mileage has a mileage of %2", maxCarTable.CarId, maxCarTable.Mileage));
}
```

Executing this job will result in the following output in the infolog:

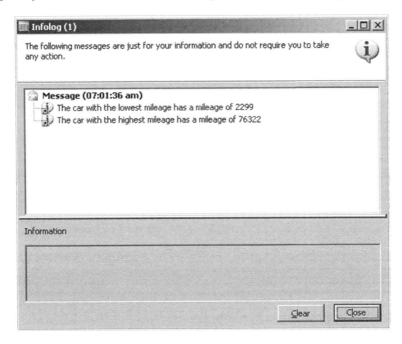

Group by

In many cases, aggregate options are used together with the group by parameter in order to list the aggregate for each subpart of a table.

In the next example, we will find the number of rentals for each customer who has rented cars. I will also demonstrate how to use the next command together with the select statement instead of the while select statement to loop through the records in the result. You will frequently see the while select statement being used in standard AX, but in case you see the next command, at least now you know it does the same as a while select statement.

```
static void selectCountRentalsPerCustomer(Args _args)
{
    RentalTable    rentalTable;

    // Normal while select to loop data
    info ("Using while select:");
```

```
    // The result of the count operation is put
    // into the recId field of the tableBuffer
    // since it is an integerfield.
    while select count(recId) from rentalTable
        group by rentalTable.CustAccount
    {
        info(strfmt("    Customer %1 has rented cars %2 times",
rentalTable.CustAccount, rentalTable.RecId));
    }

    // Looping the rentalTable cusrsor using the next command
    info ("Using next command:");
    select count(recId) from rentalTable
        group by rentalTable.CustAccount;

    while (rentalTable.RecId)
    {
        info(strfmt("    Customer %1 has rented cars %2 times",
rentalTable.CustAccount, rentalTable.RecId));
        next rentalTable;
    }
}
```

Executing this job will result in the following output in the infolog:

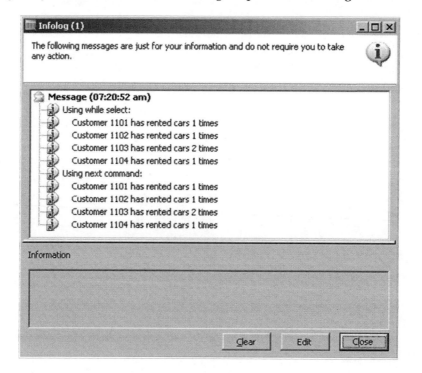

Optimizing data retrieval

There can be several different steps you as a developer should take in order to optimize the process of fetching data from the database to the application, and I will try to cover the most important things for you to have in mind here.

Using the correct data retrieval method

One important issue, not only for optimization but also for usability, is to select the correct data retrieval method based on what you would like to achieve.

Use queries when you want the users to be able to change the range of data to be retrieved and when the selection criteria are simple enough for the query to handle.

If the selection criteria are complex and there is no need for the users to be able to change the selection criteria, you should opt for a `select` statement.

If you would like to be able to use the query definition at multiple places, you should create a query in AOT instead of writing it in X++ every time you need to use it. It can also be easier to get a visual overview of a query created in AOT compared to a query written in X++.

Also, if the selection criteria are complex, there is no need to update or delete the data selected. If you would like to be able to use the same selection in many places in the application, you should consider creating a view in AOT instead of writing the `select` statement every time.

Field selects

The first and perhaps the most important thing to do in order to optimize the data retrieval is actually very simple: you should only fetch the data that you need. This means that you should eliminate any `select` statements that you don't really need and you should also fetch only the fields that the program really needs.

In order to do this, you should never use the `select` statement like this unless you actually need all fields in the record(s) selected:

```
select carTable; // Is the same as select * from carTable
```

You should rather select only the fields needed from the table with the following command:

```
select CarBrand, Model from carTable;
```

This will reduce the amount of data that has to be transferred from the database and to the application layer and thus reduce the time needed to wait for the data to be transferred.

Indexing

Another thing you need to consider is the use of indexes and perhaps even adding the missing indexes. This part could actually cover a book all by itself, but I'll try to explain the most important things you need to know about the use of indexes in AX.

As we already covered in *Chapter 3, Storing Data*, all tables should have a unique index that represents the primary key of the tables.

If a lot of data selection is done to the table using constraints other than the primary key, consider creating an index for those constraints as well. However, creating too many indexes on a table to optimize the speed when searching for data may slow down the operations of inserting, updating, and deleting data from the table as all of the indexes must be updated as well.

Using views to optimize data retrieval

When using views, the data retrieved is limited to the fields in the **Fields** node of the view. This means that the field select can easily be narrowed down when joining several tables. Also, joining several tables will execute faster because the `select` statement is already compiled and exists in the database layer when the view is executed, as opposed to queries that have to compile the `select` statement at runtime.

Other ways to improve data retrieval

There are many different ways of optimizing the retrieval of data from the database, of which the most obvious are discussed in the preceding sections. There are also other ways of optimization that haven't been discussed here.

The **CacheLoopup** property on the tables in AX specifies which type of caching is used for the table. If the wrong type of cache is used, it can give a significant decrease in performance when the table is accessed.

Find options such as `firstonly`, `forcePlaceholders`, and `forceLiterals` can also give a performance boost in certain occasions. Please refer to the SDK for more information regarding caching and find operations.

Summary

In this chapter, you learned how to write different kind of `select` statements in order to retrieve data from the database and how to create queries and views.

We also went through the reasons for choosing which of the data retrieval mechanisms to use in different scenarios. We also discussed how to optimize the data retrieval so that each transfer of data from the database to the application only contains the data necessary for the further operations in the application and how to make sure that the correct index is used to find the data.

In the next chapter, we will look at how to manipulate data by inserting, updating, and deleting records.

6
Manipulating Data

Throughout Dynamics AX, you can find data manipulation in code with the `insert()`, `update()`, and `delete()` methods, for example, when posting an invoice. When this is done, the system has to create records in journals and update data in different tables based on the data that already exist in an order and in other base data tables.

In this chapter, we will look at the following topics:

- The validation methods used to validate the data to be inserted/updated/deleted
- The `insert()` method used to insert data
- The `update()` method used to update existing data
- The `delete()` method used to delete records
- The `insert_recordset` operator used to send a request to the database to insert a chunk of data
- The `update_recordset` operator used to send a request to the database to update a chunk of records
- The `delete_from` operator used to send a request to the database to delete a chunk of records
- Direct handling for direct data manipulation without running any code within the update, insert, or delete methods
- Unit of work as a new framework in AX 2012 that allows for bulk/mass data create/update operations

The validation methods

Before manipulating the data, it's a good idea to make sure that the data you are inserting, updating, or deleting doesn't break any of the rules you have set for the table you are manipulating.

These rules are typically to check that all mandatory fields have data in the buffer that you are trying to insert or update, or to check that the record you are about to delete doesn't have any related records in the tables set up with a restricted delete action.

A validation method should always return a Boolean value. This value will be `true` if the validation is OK and `false` if it's not OK.

If you don't use the validation methods, you will be allowed to have records with mandatory fields empty when inserting or updating records from X++. You will also be allowed to delete records that have restricted delete actions against other tables. This means that you are likely to get unreferenced data if you don't use validation methods.

There are three data validation methods used in tables and data sources in AX forms and they all have default functionality defined in the system class `Common` available when they call `super()`:

- `validateWrite`: This method validates records to be inserted or updated and checks for mandatory fields. This method's data is automatically triggered when a user writes or updates data in an AX form (before the record is committed to the database). A developer must explicitly call this method when creating/updating records via code.

- `validateDelete`: This method validates records to be deleted and checks for delete actions. This method's data is automatically triggered when a user tries to delete the record in an AX form (before the record is physically deleted from the database). A developer must explicitly call this method when deleting records via code.

- `validateField`: This method checks whether the value of the given field is a legal value. This method's data is automatically triggered when a user writes or updates data on a field in an AX form (before the field is committed to the database). A developer must explicitly call this method when creating/updating records via code.

Validation rules (set using table/form metadata) are automatically triggered when the user creates, updates, or deletes a record using a form. If, however, the same actions are performed using the X++ code, the developer needs to write the code to validate the action. Another type of validation methods called `aosValidate` methods are used to ensure that the user performing the action has the proper access rights according to the user group setup.

Record-based manipulation

The record-based manipulation is used to manipulate one record at a time. The typical usage of record-based manipulation is when you need to manipulate only one record or if you have to manipulate many records and you are unable to use the set-based operators or would like to commit each record at a time.

In the following sections, we will look closer at the insert, update, and delete operations.

Insert

Perhaps the most common method to manipulate tables in AX is to insert them using the `insert()` method. It is used to insert the data currently held in a table variable (an object) to a new record in the database (that is, the data is physically committed to the database). The `insert()` method in X++ is a table instance method and so it is performed on a table variable, which is also referred to as a table buffer.

This means that the `insert()` method will only be able to insert one record in the database at a time.

If you need to insert multiple records, you will have to create a loop that calls the `insert()` method multiple times. In turn, this will generate more traffic between the AOS and the database than what perhaps is necessary. An alternative option could be to use the `insert_recordset` operator (explained later in this chapter).

When inserting multiple records using the `insert()` method, it is important that you clear the table buffer each time the loop iterates. This is done by using the table instance method `clear()` at the beginning of the loop. There is an example on how to insert many records to a table by using a loop in *Chapter 7, Integrating Data*.

Manipulating Data

All tables in AX also have a method called `initValue` that can be used to initialize default values for some of the fields (see the `InventTable` for an example of how `initValue` is implemented). Tables also often have `initFrom` methods that are used to initialize the records if a related record is already known. An example of this is the `initFromSalesTable` method in the `SalesLine` table. The `initFrom` method has to be created manually, while the `initValue` method is inherited from the system table `Common`.

> The `InitValue` method is automatically called when the user creates a record through an AX form.

The following example shows how to insert one record into the `CarTable` with fixed values:

```
static void InsertMethod(Args _args)
{
    CarTable            carTable;

    // Initialize the table variable
    carTable.initValue();

    // Write some values to the table variable
    carTable.CarId = "100";
    carTable.CarBrand = "Audi";
    carTable.Model = "A4";
    carTable.ModelYear = 2012;
    carTable.Mileage = 0;

    // Check if all values are legal and if so, insert the values of
the table variable into a record in the table
    if (carTable.validateWrite())
        carTable.insert();
}
```

Update

In many cases, you will need to update data in an existing record. In our case, it could be to update the mileage in the `CarTable` each time a car is delivered after being rented.

The `update()` method is used in order to update the selected record with the values of the active table variable.

Chapter 6

When updating data, it is essential to have a locking system that locks the records about to be updated so that no one else can update the same data at the same time. To do this in AX, we use the `ttsbegin` keyword giving a hint to AX that a rollback segment should be created in the database when the next `select` statement or the `update()`, `insert()` or `delete()` methods are executed. Only then will we write the data to the rollback segment of the database instead of the table itself whenever the `update()` method is called. Then when we use the `ttscommit` keyword, the contents of the rollback segment will be written to the actual table in the database. If an error occurs while we are updating a chunk of data, we can use the `ttsabort` keyword to roll back the database transaction. This means that with the records we have done updates on so far, nothing is ever written to the actual table in the database.

Another slightly better way of rolling back the transaction is to throw an error message as the throw statement will call `ttsabort` implicitly.

> It is important that the number of `ttscommit` statements executed matches the number of `ttsbegin` statements executed. If they do not match, AX will throw a message saying that an unbalanced X++ **TTSBEGIN/TTSCOMMIT** has been detected. You will then have to close AX and open it again to reset the Transaction (tts) level and to roll back the transactions done within the rollback segment.

Another keyword that we have to use in order to update records in AX is the `forupdate` keyword. This keyword is used to tell a select statement that the records fetched from the database are going to be updated and lock these records so that no one else can update these records until the `ttscommit` or `ttsabort` is executed.

> The term rollback segment is used only in the Oracle databases. MS SQL writes to the logfile(s) and copies the transaction to the datafile(s) when the transaction is committed. As a general term, it can also be called the transaction scope.

This means that a single record update would look something like this:

```
static void UpdateMethodSingle(Args _args)
{
    CarTable            carTable;

    // Start the database transaction
    ttsbegin;

    // Find the record to be updated and flag the record with the forupdate flag
```

[181]

Manipulating Data

```
        select forupdate carTable
            where carTable.CarId == "1";

        // Change a value in the table variable
        carTable.Mileage = 23999;
        // Copy the values of the table variable to the actual record
        carTable.update();

        // End the database transaction
        ttscommit;
    }
```

In some cases though, you will need to update many records in a table at once. In such cases, you should write a `while select` statement but then another issue arises. If you are updating a huge amount of data, the rollback segment will also increase accordingly and then it becomes slower and slower to update. To cope with this, you could perhaps commit a smaller chunk of data like in the following example, where chunks of 300 records are committed at a time. This option cannot be used though if you want to make sure that if one of the records fails, none of the records are updated.

```
    static void UpdateMethodMultiple(Args _args)
    {
        CarTable            carTable;
        int                 records;

        // Start the database transaction
        ttsbegin;

        // Find the records to be updated and flag the record with the forupdate flag
        while select forupdate carTable
        {
            // For each 300 records updated, commit the chunk and start a new rollback segment
            if (records mod 300 == 0)
            {
                ttscommit;
                ttsbegin;
            }
            // Change a value in the table variable
            carTable.Mileage = 23999;
            // Copy the values of the table variable to the actual record
            carTable.update();
            // Count how many records have been updated
```

```
            records++;
    }
    // End the database transaction
    ttscommit;

    info(strfmt("%1 records was updated.", records));

}
```

Delete

When deleting records in a table, it is important to also have in mind the effect the delete actions on that table will have for records in other tables.

If a restricted delete action exists and the linked table has records related to the record you are trying to delete, you should not be able to delete the record. This is handled automatically in the user interface (in forms), but when deleting records from X++, you have to add the `validateDelete()` method first and perform the `delete()` *only* if the `validateDelete()` method returns `true`.

However, if a cascade delete action exists and the linked table has records related to the record you are trying to delete, all of the related records will also be deleted when using the `delete()` method in X++.

Another important thing to remember when deleting a record is to always create a rollback segment using the `ttsbegin` keyword before selecting the record(s) to be deleted and using the `ttscommit` keyword after the `delete()` method.

The following example shows how to use the delete method to delete a single record from this table (and all records related to this record where a cascade delete action exists):

```
static void DeleteMethod(Args _args)
{
    CarTable            carTable;

    // Start the database transaction
    ttsbegin;
    // Find the record to be deleted and flag the record with the
forupdate flag
    select forupdate carTable
        where carTable.CarId == "1";

    // Check if this record can be deleted
    if (carTable.validateDelete())
```

```
        // Delete the selected record
        carTable.delete();

    // End the database transaction
    ttscommit;
}
```

Set-based data manipulation

As you will see in this section, you can also manipulate a set of data by sending only one command to the database. This way of manipulating data improves performance a lot when trying to manipulate large sets of records. There are, however, a couple of things to consider before using set-based data manipulation.

All of the operators discussed in the following sections will be converted back to their record-based counterparts' runtime if any of the following is true:

- A record-based method such as `insert()`, `update()`, `delete()`, or `aosValidate()` has been overridden
- An AX database logging is set up to log when records based operations occur or if the standard AX Alerts are set up to alert when inserts, updates, or deletes occur
- The cache lookup property on the table is set to entire cache

The insert_recordset operator

A very efficient way of inserting a chunk of data compared to using the `insert()` method is to use the `insert_recordset` operator. The `insert_recordset` operator can be used in two different ways, either to copy data from one or more tables to another or simply to add a chunk of data into a table in one database operation.

The first example will show how to insert a chunk of data into a table in one database operation. To do this, we simply use two different table variables for the same table and set one of them to act as a temporary table. This means that its content is not stored in the database, but simply held in memory on the tier where the variable was instantiated. The code is as follows:

```
static void Insert_RecordsetInsert(Args _args)
{
    CarTable    carTable;
    CarTable    carTableTmp;
```

```
    /*
    Set the carTableTmp variable to be a temporary table.
    This means that its contents are only store in memory
    not in the database.
    */
    carTableTmp.setTmp();
    // Insert 3 records into the temporary table.
    carTableTmp.CarId = "200";
    carTableTmp.CarBrand = "MG";
    carTableTmp.insert();
    carTableTmp.CarId = "300";
    carTableTmp.CarBrand = "SAAB";
    carTableTmp.insert();
    carTableTmp.CarId = "400";
    carTableTmp.CarBrand = "Ferrari";
    carTableTmp.insert();

    /*
    Copy the contents from the fields carId and carBrand
    in the temporary table to the corresponding fields in
    the table variable called carTable and insert the chunk
    in one database operation.
    */
    Insert_Recordset carTable
        (carId, carBrand)
        select carId, carBrand from carTableTmp;
}
```

The other and perhaps the more common way of using the `insert_recordset` operator is to copy values from one or more tables into new records in another table. A very simple example on how to do this can be to create a record in the `InventColor` table for all records in the `InventTable`. The code is as follows:

```
static void Insert_RecordsetCopy(Args _args)
{
    InventColor     inventColor;
    InventTable     inventTable;
    InventColorId   defaultColor = "B";
    Name            defaultColorName = "Blue";


    insert_recordset inventColor (ItemId, InventColorId, Name)
        select itemId, defaultColor, defaultColorName from
inventTable;
}
```

Manipulating Data

The field list inside the parentheses points to fields in the `InventColor` table. The fields in the selected or joined tables are used to fill values into the fields in the field list.

The update_recordset operator

The `update_recordset` operator can be used to update a chunk of records in a table in one database operation. As with the `insert_recordset` operator, the `update_recordset` operator is very efficient because it only needs to call an update in the database once.

The syntax for the `update_recordset` operator can be seen in the following example:

```
static void Update_RecordsetExmple(Args _args)
{
    CarTable        carTable;

    info("BEFORE UPDATE");
    while select carTable
        where carTable.ModelYear == 2007
    {
        info(strfmt("CarId %1 has run %2 miles", carTable.CarId, carTable.Mileage));
    }

    update_recordset carTable
        setting Mileage = carTable.Mileage + 1000
        where carTable.ModelYear == 2007;


    info("AFTER UPDATE");
    while select carTable
        where carTable.ModelYear == 2007
    {
        info(strfmt("CarId %1 has now run %2 miles", carTable.CarId, carTable.Mileage));
    }
}
```

When this job is executed, it will print some messages to the info log, as shown in the following screenshot:

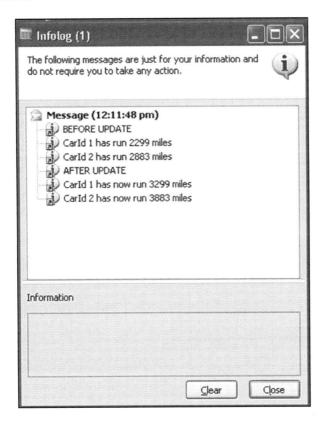

Notice that no error was thrown even though the job didn't use the selectforupdate, ttsbegin, and ttscommit statements in this example. The selectforupdate statement is implicit when using the update_recordset, ttsbegin, and ttscommit are not necessary when all the updates are done in one database operation. However, if you were to write several update_recordset statements in a row or perform other checks that should make the update fail, you could use ttsbegin and ttscommit and force an abort by using ttsabort if the checks fail.

 Throwing an info, warning, or error inside a rollback segment (between ttsbegin and ttscommit) will automatically result in a ttsabort statement.

Manipulating Data

Consider modifying the previous example so that it gets a rollback segment and a check that makes sure to break the update operation:

```
static void Update_RecordsetExmpleTts(Args _args)
{
    CarTable        carTable;
    // Change the check to false to make the
    // transaction go through
    boolean         check = true;

    info("BEFORE UPDATE");
    while select carTable
        where carTable.ModelYear == 2007
    {
        info(strfmt("CarId %1 has run %2 miles", carTable.CarId, carTable.Mileage));
    }
    ttsbegin;   // Added ttsbegin
    update_recordset carTable
        setting Mileage = carTable.Mileage + 1000
        where carTable.ModelYear == 2007;

    if (check)
        throw info("This is a test");

    ttscommit; // Added ttscommit

    info("AFTER UPDATE");
    while select carTable
        where carTable.ModelYear == 2007
    {
        info(strfmt("CarId %1 has now run %2 miles", carTable.CarId, carTable.Mileage));
    }
}
```

The update will now never be committed in the database, so the result will look like this every time you run the job:

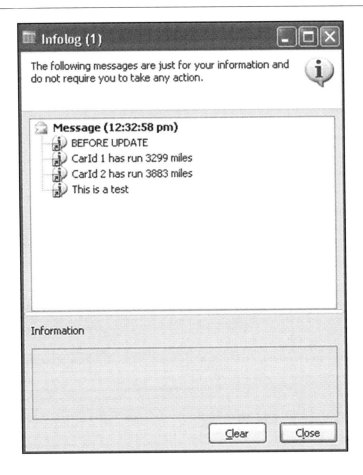

The delete_from operator

As with the `insert_recordset` and `update_recordset` operators, there is also an option to delete a chunk of records. This operator is called `delete_from` and is used as the following example shows:

```
static void Delete_FromExample(Args _args)
{
    CarTable        carTable;


    delete_from carTable
        where carTable.Mileage == 0;

}
```

Manipulating Data

Unit of work

Though set-based operations work great when mass updating or deleting records, we get into a bit of a problem when mass inserting records into multiple tables that have a parent/child type relation, for example, transaction headers and transaction lines.

As an ID (key) is needed from the transaction header before transaction lines can be created, developers are forced to make multiple calls to the database within a large transaction block.

In Dynamics AX 2012, this problem was addressed by the UnitOfWork class.

UnitOfWork is a system class and is used to comment a number of records in a single transaction. The class is aware of the relationship between tables and can automatically fill in the related value fields. For example, transaction header and transaction line records can be created with a single instruction.

Consider the following example. For testing purposes, let's create two tables called UOWHeader and UOWLines and then add a couple of fields to both the tables (be creative).

Now let's add a relation between the two tables. Note the properties of the relation carefully in the following screenshot:

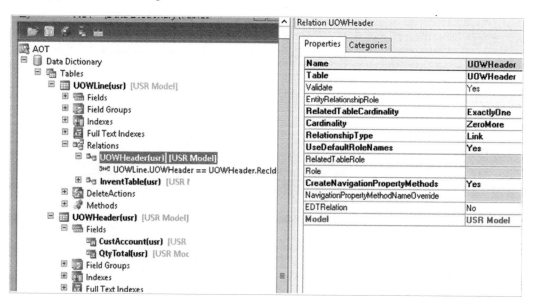

The **CreateNavigationPropertyMethods** property is important here; if this is set to **Yes**, then Dynamics AX will automatically create navigation methods for the related table. This method allows us to link two table buffer (parent and child) instances.

The value set in the **RelatedTableRole** property is used to define the name of the navigation method.

If the **UseDefaultRoleNames** property is set to **Yes** (and the **RelatedTableRole** property is blank), then the table names are effectively used as the navigation methods.

In addition, the **NavigationPropertyMethodNameOverride** property can be used to specify a navigation method name. This property is typically used if the `relatedTableRole` is already a method or if the table name is too long.

It's important to note that the navigation methods are neither displayed in the **Methods** node, nor are they visible under the table buffer methods displayed by IntelliSense. They are similar to `Map` methods in the sense that the developer can type them in and the compiler we know, despite the fact that the method name is not available in the list of methods.

Now, let's create a class called `UOWClass` and change the **RunOn** property of this class to **Server**. The reason we are doing this is because the `UnitOfWork` class can only be executed in the server tier. This is an important point to bear in mind when developing scripts (data migration or data updates) that use unit of work.

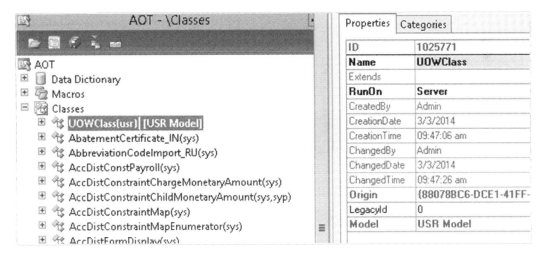

Manipulating Data

To keep things simple, let's write a static method as follows that populates the line table with 10 lines. The key point to note in the following code is that the join between line and header is not being specified within the code (as a field value). Instead, we are use navigation methods to set the link and then `UnitofWork` sets the value. The code is as follows:

```
static void UOWMethod()
{
    UOWHeader               uowHeader;
    UOWLine                 uowLine;

    UnitofWork              unitofWork;

    int                     i;
    Qty                     totalQty;

    //Demo data
    CustAccount             custAccount = "US-012";
    ItemId                  itemid      = "D0001";

    // RandomGenerate will be used to set random qty on lines section.
    RandomGenerate          randomGenerate;

    unitofWork              = new UnitofWork(); // Initialize  Unit of Work

    randomGenerate          = RandomGenerate::construct(); // Initialize random number generator

    //Now lets start setting the table buffers
    uowHeader.CustAccount   = custAccount;

    // This section of the code will create 10 lines for the same item with random qtys
    for(i=1;i<=10;i++)
    {
        uowLine = null;

        uowLine.ItemId      = itemid;

        uowLine.Qty         = randomGenerate.randomInt(1,30); // random number between 1 and 30

        uowLine.UOWHeader(UOWHeader); //link line to header using navigation method.
```

```
            unitofWork.insertonSaveChanges(uowLine); // set the line
buffer for insertion.

        //track total qty
        totalQty            += uowLine.Qty;

    }

    uowHeader.QtyTotal      = totalQty;

    unitofWork.insertonSaveChanges(uowHeader); //ready the header
buffer for insertion.

    unitofWork.saveChanges(); // commit changes to database.

}
```

Next, we will write some code to call the static methods. We can either do this as a job or as a call to the `main` method in the class, as shown in the following code:

```
static void main(Args _args)
{
    UOWClass::UOWMethod();
}
```

If you view the data within the tables using the table browser, you will notice that the `recId` field from the header table was correctly set on all the lines.

Direct handling

In many tables in AX, the `insert`, `update`, and `delete` methods have been overridden to include checks or other form of logic. As you can see in the overridden `insert` method here, you can put code before or after the `super()` call if you need something to happen before or after the record has been inserted into the record buffer:

```
public void insert()
{
    // Put code to happen before inserting
    // the record here
    super(); // The INSERT INTO statement in SQL is executed
    // Put code to happen after the record
    // has been inserted here
}
```

Manipulating Data

In some cases though, you will need to be able to insert, update, or delete a record in the table without running the code inside the method. You could then override the method as shown in the preceding code, but you would then always be stuck with the code in the overridden method.

> If insert and/or delete methods are overridden, then set-based DB methods, such as update_recordset() or delete_recordset(), will be downgraded so that the update or delete operation is performed record by record. This will obviously have a negative impact on performance.

You can then use the doInsert, doUpdate, or doDelete methods that exist with all tables in AX. These methods can never be overridden and can guarantee that the only thing they will do is to insert, update, or delete the record on which you execute the transaction. This means that calling the doInsert method will do the same as super() inside the insert method.

The following figure shows a very simplified example of the difference between using insert() and doInsert(). The difference is the same in the case of using update() and doUpdate() as well delete() and doDelete().

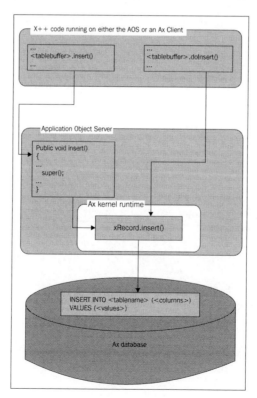

Summary

In this chapter, we discussed how to manipulate data using X++. We also saw how to write code that inserts, updates, and deletes records without breaking the relationship that the record has with data in other tables.

The `ttsbegin`, `ttscommit`, and `ttsabort` operators and the `selectforupdate` keyword were also introduced to show you how to create and handle a transaction scope.

After reading about `insert_recordset`, `update_recordset`, and `delete_from`, you also learned how to manipulate many records within one database transaction, which is a lot more efficient than using the `insert`, `update`, or `delete` methods.

In addition, we also went through the difference between the `insert`, `update`, and `delete` methods and the `doInsert`, `doUpdate`, and `doDelete` methods.

In the next chapter, we will use the knowledge gained in this chapter and look at how we can use it to integrate data with other systems. We do this by reading and writing text files and XML files in addition to other databases using an ODBC connection. We will also create a class library that can be used for specialized data import and export operations to and from AX.

7
Integrating Data

As you learned in the previous chapter, manipulating a huge chunk of data is more easily done by running a periodic job rather than user data entry. So the data that is being inserted or updated must come from somewhere, right? Let's say you have a semicolon-separated file, or maybe even an XML file, that contains data that you would like to read into AX. Or perhaps you need to generate such a file from AX so that it can be read by another system?

In this chapter, you will learn how to:

- Read/write data from/to a character-separated file
- Read/write data from/to a binary file
- Read/write data from/to an XML file
- Read/write data from/to a database using ODBC
- Use **DictTable** and **DictField** to create generic code for data manipulation
- Create a simple module to export and import data to/from AX

What is the need to create import/export routines in code when I can use the standard data import and export functionality in AX, you might ask. Well, you will notice after a while that the standard data import/export functionality in AX is fairly limited. It treats each table as its own entity while you might have the need to include data from several tables.

This chapter focuses on how to generate the different file formats and not on the transport of the data. We will only generate files that are stored on the disk. When integrating data between two systems, you will have to take the data transport into account as well. If the system that integrates with AX exists in the same domain, storing the files in a shared folder might be sufficient. If the system exists in a different domain, perhaps at a customer or vendor site, you will have to establish a transport link between these two systems. This can be done using FTP, web services, and message queuing, to mention a few.

Integrating Data

While setting up such a transport, you should also consider creating a subsystem that logs data that is being communicated over the transport in order to pick up data that causes errors or unwanted situations.

One way of doing this can be to use the **EventWriter** that is shown in *Chapter 10, Working with .NET and AX*.

The **Application Integration Framework (AIF)** can be used as a middle layer between AX and the transport links mentioned earlier. The AIF is most commonly used in business-to-business (B2B) integration scenarios where there is a need to exchange electronic business documents.

The AIF is not covered in detail in this book, but you can read more about it in the SDK here at `http://msdn.microsoft.com/en-us/library/bb496535(lightweight).aspx`.

Text files

The most common way of integrating data is by reading/writing some sort of text files where the records are separated with a new line and the fields are separated by a certain character. This is typically achieved using the `TextIo` or `CommaIo` class.

As you can see in the following figure, these classes belong to a class hierarchy where the `Io` class is the main class.

> Remember to place the code that will read or write data at the correct tier. If it runs on the server, the `C:/` drive used by the code will be the `C:/` drive of the AOS server. Also remember to consider access rights to the folder that you are reading or writing to.

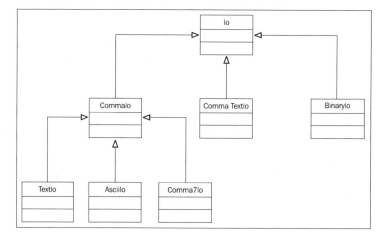

The data in AX are stored using Unicode fields in the SQL database. When these data are exported from AX, you need to make sure that the files generated will also be in Unicode. To achieve this, always use the `TextIo` or `CommaTextIo` class.

The `AsciiIo` and `CommaIo` classes should only be used if there is an absolute demand for files using the ASCII encoding.

The difference between the `TextIo` and the `CommaTextIo` is that by using the `CommaTextIo` class, the files will by default set the field delimiter to comma and the record delimiter to carriage return plus the line feed. It will also wrap all of the string fields between the quotation marks (" and "); the numbers will not be wrapped.

Writing data to a text file

Let's look at how we can write data from AX to a text file in a very easy way using a job.

First, we will put all the code in the method into a try/catch statement to make sure we can pick up any errors that are thrown.

We also need to set a filename for the file. We will use this filename when creating a new `Io` object, but before we do so, we have to ask the system for permission to write the file to the file path specified. This is achieved by using the `FileIoPermission` class that extends the `CodeAccessPermission` class. The second parameter in `new()` specifies whether we want to read, write, or append a file. When using the `TextIo` class as shown in the example, we also have the option of setting a third parameter in `new()` that specifies the code page that we would like to use in the file. This is necessary when writing language-specific characters. You can find a list of these code pages at http://msdn.microsoft.com/en-us/goglobal/bb964653.aspx.

The following table shows how to use the three different options. The macros used are taken from the #File macro library.

Operation	Code	Macro	Description
Read	R	`#io_read`	Read data from a file.
Write	W	`#io_write`	Write data to a file. Overwrite any existing data.
Append	A	`#io_append`	Write data to a file. Start writing at the end of the file if it already exists.
Translate	T	`#io_translate`	<not in use>
Binary	B	`#io_binary`	<not in use>

Integrating Data

If the specified filepath doesn't exist, or if we do not have permission to write to this folder, a new object will not be created. We should therefore check to see if a new object of the `TextIo` was created and throw an exception if the variable is null.

In order to write fields from a table to a file, we use a container and put all the field data into the container first. Then we simply write the container to the file. It is important to remember to empty the container each time it is looped through the records by using the `connull()` method.

The last thing we do is revert the code access permission by calling the static method `revertAssert()` which is defined in the `CodeAccessPermission` class.

Here is an example:

```
static server void WriteTextFile(Args _args)
{
  TextIo              file;
  // Using the @ before the filename
  // enables us to use single path
  // delimiters. If you don't use it
  // you will have to write the path like this:
  // "c:\\temp\\cars.txt"
  FileName            filename = @"c:\temp\cars.txt";
  CarTable            carTable;
  container           con;
  FileIoPermission    permission;
  #File

  try
  {
    // Create the permission class
    permission = new FileIoPermission(filename, #io_write);
    // Add a request for permission before new TextIo()
    permission.assert();
    // Create the TextIo object
    file = new TextIo(filename, #io_write);
    if (!file)
    throw Exception::Error;
    // Specify the delimiters
    file.outRecordDelimiter(#delimiterCRLF);
    file.outFieldDelimiter(";");

    // Loop through the data source
    while select carTable
    {
```

```
            // Empty the container
            con = connull();
            // Set the data into the container
            con = conins(con, 1, carTable.CarId);
            con = conins(con, 2, carTable.CarBrand);
            con = conins(con, 3, carTable.Mileage);
            con = conins(con, 4, carTable.Model);
            con = conins(con, 5, carTable.ModelYear);
            // Write the container to the file
            file.writeExp(con);
        }
    }
    catch(Exception::Error)
    {
        error("You do not have access to write the file to the
        selected folder");
    }
    // Revert the access privileges
    CodeAccessPermission::revertAssert();
}
```

This is how the exported file looks:

```
1;BMW;2299;320;2007
4;Volksvagen;49902;Golf;2006
5;Jeep;65662;Grand Cherokee;2002
6;BMW;11120;Z3;2003
7;Volksvage;76322;Golf;2000
X1001;Alfa Romeo;29982;166;2005
3;Toyota;4032;Corolla;2008
XX1;BMW;2299;320;2007
2;Mercedes;3883;C220;2007
X1000;Mazda;0;Miata;2009
```

You can now play around by changing the class used from TextIo to CommaIo or TextIo to CommaTextIo and see the difference in the result, as stated earlier in this chapter.

In the preceding example, we used a container to out the data into before writing the content of the container to the file. You can also write the data directly to the file by using the write() method instead of the writeExp() method. The while loop would then look as follows:

```
while select carTable
{
    // Write the data to the file
```

Integrating Data

```
        file.write(carTable.CarId,
          carTable.CarBrand,
          carTable.Mileage,
          carTable.Model,
          carTable.ModelYear);
    }
```

Reading from a file

Reading from a file is very similar to writing to the file, but you now have to change the direction of the data by changing the filemode to `#io_read` instead of `#io_write`. The methods that set the delimiters also have to change from `outDelimiters` to `inDelimiters`.

The `while` loop will now loop through the file content instead of the AX table. In my example, we simply print the information from the file to the Infolog. You can, however, play around and find out how to insert and update the data in the `carTable`.

```
    static void ReadTextFile(Args _args)
    {
      TextIo             file;
      FileName           filename = @"c:\temp\cars.txt";
      CarTable           carTable;
      container          con;
      FileIoPermission   permission;
      #File

      try
      {
        // Create the permission class
        permission = new FileIoPermission(filename, #io_read);
        // Ask for permission to write the file
        permission.assert();
        // Create the TextIo object
        file = new TextIo(filename, #io_read);
        if (!file)
        throw Exception::Error;
        // Note that we now use inDelimiters
        // instead of outDelimiters as in the
        // previous example
        file.inRecordDelimiter(#delimiterCRLF);
        file.inFieldDelimiter(";");
```

```
    // Write the header info
    info("CarId - CarBrand - Mileage - Model - ModelYear");
    // Read the first record from the file
    con = file.read();
    // Loop as long as the file status is ok
    while (file.status() == IO_Status::Ok)
    {
      // Write the content to the infolog
      info(strfmt("%1 - %2 - %3 - %4 - %5",
      conpeek(con,1),
      conpeek(con,2),
      conpeek(con,3),
      conpeek(con,4),
      conpeek(con,5)));
      // Read the next record from the file
      con = file.read();
    }
  }
  catch(Exception::Error)
  {
    error("You do not have access to write the file to the
    selected folder");
  }
  // Revert the access privileges
  CodeAccessPermission::revertAssert();
}
```

> If you would like to read/write a tab delimited file, change `outFieldDelimiter`/`inFieldDelimiter` to \t instead of ; in the preceding example.

Binary files

Binary files can actually be written and read the same way as text files. The binary files are, of course, not readable in a text editor, but they can easily be read back into AX again.

The only change you have to make to the previous two examples is to use the `BinaryIo` class instead of the `TextIo` class.

The use of binary files to export data from AX is rare, as the data will only be readable from AX. You can use it if you don't want the data exported to be readable outside AX.

Integrating Data

XML files

AX has its own data integration module called Application Integration Framework (AIF) that uses XML documents as a data layer when transporting data. This book does not cover the AIF as it could probably fill a book on its own. It does, however, cover the same generic base classes that the AIF is based upon, so it is a good idea to read this part even if you will be using the AIF.

The use of XML files to transport data between systems is increasing rapidly. As you read in the beginning of this chapter, the transport channels used to carry the files are not covered in this chapter. You can, however, learn more on how to use web services as transport for XML files in *Chapter 11, Web Services*. In this chapter, we simply store and read the XML files to/from the disk as we did with the text file that we created earlier in this chapter.

Let's now have a look at how we can create an XML document and have it written and read to/from the disk.

I have created a macro library for the example that follows, which stores the tag names, so that I don't have to hardcode the text into the code. The name of the macro library is `CarsXmlTags` and contains the following two tags:

```
#define.CarRootNode("Cars")
#define.CarRecords("CarRecords")
```

Creating an XML file and writing to it

The following example shows how to create and write data to an XML file by using the `XmlDocument`, `XmlElement`, and `XmlWriter` classes. It loops through all of the records in the `CarTable` and finds all the fields in the table automatically, by using the `DictTable` and `DictField` classes.

```
static void WriteXml(Args _args)
{
    XmlDocument  xmlDoc;
    XmlElement   xmlRoot;
    XmlElement   xmlField;
    XmlElement   xmlRecord;
    XMLWriter    xmlWriter;
    CarTable     carTable;
    DictTable    dTable = new DictTable(tablenum(CarTable));
    DictField    dField;
    int          i, fieldId;
    str          value;
```

```
    #CarsXmlTags

// Create a new object of the XmlDocument class
xmlDoc = XmlDocument::newBlank();
// Create the root node
xmlRoot = xmlDoc.createElement(#CarRootNode);

// Loop through all the records in the carTable
while select carTable
{
  // Create a XmlElement (record) to hold the
  // contents of the current record.
  xmlRecord = xmlDoc.createElement(#CarRecords);
  // Loop through all the fields in the record
  for (i=1; i<=dTable.fieldCnt(); i++)
  {
    // Get the fieldId from the field count
    fieldId = dTable.fieldCnt2Id(i);
    // Find the DictField object that matches
    // the fieldId
    dField = dTable.fieldObject(fieldId);
    // Skip system fields
    if (dField.isSystem())
    continue;
    // Create a new XmlElement (field) and
    // have the name equal to the name of the
    // dictField
    xmlField = xmlDoc.createElement(dField.name());

    // Convert values to string. I have just added
    // a couple of conversion as an example.
    // Use tableName.(fieldId) instead of fieldname
    // to get the content of the field.
    switch (dField.baseType())
    {
      case Types::Int64 :
      value = int642str(carTable.(fieldId));
      break;
      case Types::Integer :
      value = int2str(carTable.(fieldId));
      break;
      default :
      value = carTable.(fieldId);
      break;
```

```
        }
        // Set the innerText of the XmlElement (field)
        // to the value from the table
        xmlField.innerText(value);
        // Append the field as a child node to the record
        xmlRecord.appendChild(xmlField);
    }
    // Add the record as a child node to the root
    xmlRoot.appendChild(xmlRecord);
}
// Add the root to the XmlDocument
xmlDoc.appendChild(xmlRoot);
// Create a new object of the XmlWriter class
// in order to be able to write the xml to a file
xmlWriter = XMLWriter::newFile(@"c:\temp\cars.xml");
// Write the content of the XmlDocument to the
// file as specified by the XmlWriter
xmlDoc.writeTo(xmlWriter);
}
```

The file that is created looks as follows (only the first part of the file is shown):

```xml
<?xml version="1.0" encoding="utf-8" ?>
- <Cars>
    - <CarRecords>
        <CarId>1</CarId>
        <ModelYear>2007</ModelYear>
        <CarBrand>BMW</CarBrand>
        <Model>320</Model>
        <Mileage>2299</Mileage>
      </CarRecords>
    - <CarRecords>
        <CarId>4</CarId>
        <ModelYear>2006</ModelYear>
        <CarBrand>Volksvagen</CarBrand>
        <Model>Golf</Model>
        <Mileage>49902</Mileage>
      </CarRecords>
    - <CarRecords>
        <CarId>5</CarId>
        <ModelYear>2002</ModelYear>
        <CarBrand>Jeep</CarBrand>
        <Model>Grand Cherokee</Model>
        <Mileage>65662</Mileage>
      </CarRecords>
    - <CarRecords>
        <CarId>6</CarId>
        <ModelYear>2003</ModelYear>
        <CarBrand>BMW</CarBrand>
        <Model>Z3</Model>
        <Mileage>11120</Mileage>
      </CarRecords>
```

As you can see, this file is based on a standard XML format only with tags and values. You can, however, use tag attributes as well. To put the values from the table into tag attributes instead of their own tags, simply change the following lines of code in the preceding example:

```
// Set the innerText of the XmlElement (field)
// to the value from the table
xmlField.innerText(value);
// Append the field as a child node to the record
xmlRecord.appendChild(xmlField);
```

Substitute these with the following lines:

```
// Add the attribute to the record
xmlRecord.setAttribute(dField.name(), value);
```

The file that is created now looks as follows:

```xml
<?xml version="1.0" encoding="utf-8" ?>
- <Cars>
    <CarRecords CarId="1" ModelYear="2007" CarBrand="BMW" Model="320" Mileage="2299" />
    <CarRecords CarId="4" ModelYear="2006" CarBrand="Volksvagen" Model="Golf" Mileage="49902" />
    <CarRecords CarId="5" ModelYear="2002" CarBrand="Jeep" Model="Grand Cherokee" Mileage="65662" />
    <CarRecords CarId="6" ModelYear="2003" CarBrand="BMW" Model="Z3" Mileage="11120" />
    <CarRecords CarId="7" ModelYear="2000" CarBrand="Volksvage" Model="Golf" Mileage="76322" />
    <CarRecords CarId="X1001" ModelYear="2005" CarBrand="Alfa Romeo" Model="166" Mileage="29982" />
    <CarRecords CarId="3" ModelYear="2008" CarBrand="Toyota" Model="Corolla" Mileage="4032" />
    <CarRecords CarId="XX1" ModelYear="2007" CarBrand="BMW" Model="320" Mileage="2299" />
    <CarRecords CarId="2" ModelYear="2007" CarBrand="Mercedes" Model="C220" Mileage="3883" />
    <CarRecords CarId="X1000" ModelYear="2009" CarBrand="Mazda" Model="Miata" Mileage="0" />
  </Cars>
```

Reading an XML from a file

The following example will enable you to read a file that is in the same format as the previous example.

```
static void ReadXml(Args _args)
{
  XmlDocument  xmlDoc;
  XmlElement   xmlRoot;
  XmlElement   xmlField;
  XmlElement   xmlRecord;
  XmlNodeList  xmlRecordList;
  XmlNodeList  xmlFieldList;
  CarTable     carTable;
```

```
    DictTable   dTable = new DictTable(tablenum(CarTable));
    int         i, j, fieldId;
    #CarsXmlTags

    // Create an XmlDocument object to hold the
    // contents of the xml-file
    xmlDoc = new XmlDocument();
    // Load the content of the xml-file
    // into the XmlDocument object
    xmlDoc.load(@"c:\temp\cars.xml");
    // Get the root node
    xmlRoot = xmlDoc.getNamedElement(#CarRootNode);
    // Get all child nodes (records)
    xmlRecordList = xmlRoot.childNodes();
    // Loop through the list of records
    for (i=0; i<xmlRecordList.length(); i++)
    {
      carTable.clear();
      // Get the current record from the
      // record list
      xmlRecord = xmlRecordList.item(i);
      // Get all child nodes (fields)
      xmlFieldList = xmlRecord.childNodes();
      // Loop through the list of fields
      for (j=0; j<xmlFieldList.length(); j++)
      {
        // Get the current field from the
        // field list
        xmlField = xmlFieldList.item(j);
        // Set the matching field in the carTable
        // to be equal to the inner text
        // (the text between the tag and end tag).
        carTable.(dTable.fieldName2Id(xmlField.name())) =
        xmlField.innerText();
      }
      // Insert the record into the carTable
      carTable.insert();
    }
}
```

Open Database Connectivity

Sometimes you need direct access to another database, either to read data from the tables, or in some cases, to write data to the tables. You can do that in AX by using an **ODBC** connection to the other database.

In most cases though, I would recommend having AX integrated with the application layer of the other system rather than the data layer, but I know that sometimes that is not an option.

Reading data from the database:

The following example shows how to set up a connection to a database using ODBC, how to create a SQL statement, how to execute the statement, and how to retrieve and loop through the result.

The database used in these examples is the AX database itself. Remember to consider access permissions. The user executing the job should have read access to the database. If the connection is created on the AOS, the user setup as the execution account of the AOS should have proper access to the database that you are trying to read from.

Reading from a database using ODBC

Let's learn how to create a connection to another database by using the ODBC API with an example. In our example, the steps used to create a connection and read data from the external database using ODBC are as follows:

1. Create an object of the `LoginProperty` class to hold the login information for the external database.
2. Connect to the database by creating an object of the `OdbcConnection` class.
3. Define the SQL statement to be executed.
4. Ensure that the SQL statement is safe by using the `SqlStatementExecutionPermission` class.
5. Create an object for the `Statement` class and execute the SQL statement.
6. Loop through the result of the statement execution.

Integrating Data

The code will be as follows:

```
static void ReadOdbc(Args _args)
{
  OdbcConnection                    connection;
  LoginProperty                     loginProp;
  Statement                         statement;
  ResultSet                         result;
  str                               sqlStmt;
  SqlStatementExecutePermission     permission;

  // Create an object of the LoginProperty class
  loginProp = new LoginProperty();
  // Set the servername and database to the
  // LoginProperty object
  loginProp.setServer("AX-SRV-01"); //specify server name
  loginProp.setDatabase("AX593"); // specify DB name

  // Check to see if the executing user has access
  try
  {
    // Create a new connection based on the information
    // set in the LoginProperty object
    connection = new OdbcConnection(loginProp);
  }
  catch
  {
    error ("You do not have access to the database
    specified");
    return;
  }
  // Set the select statement to the string variable
  sqlStmt = 'SELECT Dataareaid, AccountNum, Name from dbo.
CustTable';
  // Check if it's ok to use sql statement
  permission = new SqlStatementExecutePermission(sqlStmt);
  permission.assert();
  // Create and prepare a new Statement object
  // from the connection
  statement = connection.createStatement();
  // Execute the query and retrieve the resultset
  result = statement.executeQuery(sqlStmt);

  // Loop through the records in the resultset and print
  // the information to the infolog
```

```
    while (result.next())
    {
       info (strfmt("(%1)    %2:    %3", result.getString(1), result.
  getString(2), result.getString(3)));
    }
    // Revert the permission assert
    CodeAccessPermission::revertAssert();
  }
```

Writing to a database using ODBC

The next example shows how to update data in a database using an ODBC connection in AX. The same method can be used to insert or delete data. It can even be used to execute a stored procedure in the database. The steps needed are pretty much the same, except that there is no result set to loop after executing the update statement.

```
  static void WriteOdbc(Args _args)
  {
    OdbcConnection                     connection;
    LoginProperty                      loginProp;
    Statement                          statement;
    str                                sqlStmt;
    SqlStatementExecutePermission      permission;

    // Create an object of the LoginProperty class
    loginProp = new LoginProperty();
    // Set the servername and database to the
    // LoginProperty object (consider creating a
    // fixed odbc in windows and reference it here
    // by using setDBS() instead of setServer/setDatabase
    loginProp.setServer("AX-SRV-01"); // specify server name
    loginProp.setDatabase("AX593"); // specify DB name

    // Check to see if the executing user has access
    try
    {
      // Create a new connection based on the information
      // set in the LoginProperty object
      connection = new OdbcConnection(loginProp);
    }
    catch
    {
      error ("You do not have access to the database specified");
```

```
        return;
    }
    // Set the select statement to the string variable
    sqlStmt = strfmt("UPDATE dbo.CustTable SET Name='test' WHERE
    AccountNum='%1' AND Dataareaid='%2'", "1101", "ceu");
    // Check if it's ok to use sql statement
    permission = new SqlStatementExecutePermission(sqlStmt);
    permission.assert();
    // Create and prepare a new Statement object
    // from the connection
    statement = connection.createStatement();
    // Execute the query and retrieve the resultset
    statement.executeUpdate(sqlStmt);

    // Revert the permission assert
    CodeAccessPermission::revertAssert();
}
```

The import/export activity

Importing and exporting data is most likely something that you have to do more than once. It can be nice to have your own module for testing purposes.

I know that the standard import/export tool in AX also lets you do many of these things, but you are a programmer, right? So you might prefer to write the code yourself.

Anyway, I just wanted to get you started with a simple example that shows how to build a simple dialog where the user can select what to import/export, the filenames, and so on.

Here is the class model diagram for the example:

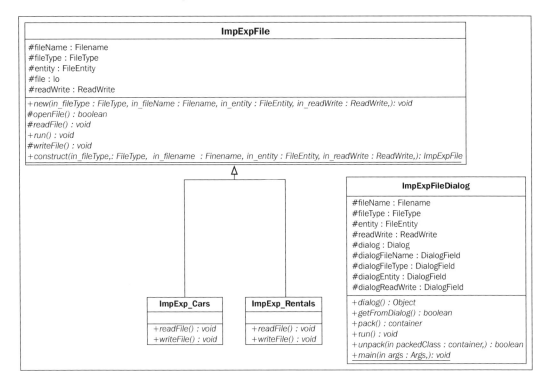

The ImpExpFileDialog class

This is the dialog class that is common for all the different import/export entities. You do not need to change this class when adding a new entity class. Change this class only if you would like the dialog to look different or want to add additional fields to the dialog. The methods in this class (and the rest of the classes in this example) are explained by header comments.

Integrating Data

The classDeclaration method

This class provides the starting point for the `ImpExpFile` classes by presenting a dialog for the user, creating an object of the `ImpExpFile` class hierarchy, and then passing the control to the created object. The following code shows you how to implement it:

```
class ImpExpFileDialog extends RunBase
{
  // Global variables
  FileName            fileName;
  FileType            fileType;
  FileEntity          entity;
  ReadWrite           readWrite;
  Dialog              dialog;
  // Dialog fields
  DialogField         dialogFileName;
  DialogField         dialogFileType;
  DialogField         dialogEntity;
  DialogField         dialogReadWrite;

  #define.CurrentVersion(1)
  // Macro that contains the global variables
  // to be kept until the next time the user
  // executes this class.
  #localmacro.CurrentList
    fileName,
    fileType,
    entity,
    readWrite
  #endmacro
}
```

The dialog method

The `dialog` method defines the dialog that is presented to the user when the prompt method is executed. The following code shows us how the `dialog` method is implemented:

```
public Object dialog()
{
  // Create a new object of the DialogRunbase class
  dialog = new DialogRunbase("Import data from file", this);
```

```
    // Add the fields to the dialog and
    // set the initial value to be equal to
    // the value selected last time.
    dialogReadWrite = dialog.addFieldValue(typeid(ReadWrite),
    readWrite);
    dialogFileName = dialog.addFieldValue(typeid(FileName),
    fileName);
    dialogFileType = dialog.addFieldValue(typeid(FileType),
    fileType);
    dialogEntity = dialog.addFieldValue(typeid(FileEntity),
    entity);

    return dialog;
}
```

The getFromDialog method

This method, originated from the `RunBase` class, is initiated when the user presses OK in the dialog, and it is used to store the user-selected values. The following code shows us how the `getFromDialog` method is implemented:

```
public boolean getFromDialog()
{
    fileName      = dialogFileName.value();
    fileType      = dialogFileType.value();
    entity        = dialogEntity.value();
    readWrite     = dialogReadWrite.value();

    return super();
}
```

The pack method

The pack method is a standard method inherited from the `RunBase` class. It is used to save the values that the user selects and store them until the next time the user executes the class. The following code shows us how the `pack` method is implemented:

```
public container pack()
{
    return [#CurrentVersion,#CurrentList];
}
```

Integrating Data

The run method

The standard methods from the `RunBase` class are typically used to start the main execution flow of the class. The following code shows us how the run method is implemented:

```
public void run()
{
  // Create a new object of the ImpExpFile class-hierarchy
  // based on the values selected in the dialog.
  ImpExpFile    impExpFile = ImpExpFile::construct(fileType,
  fileName, entity, readWrite);

  // Start the main flow of the ImpExpFile object
  impExpFile.run();
}
```

The unpack method

It is the standard method inherited from the `RunBase` class and is used to fetch the values that the user selected the last time he executed the class. The following example shows us how the unpack method is implemented:

```
*/
public boolean unpack(container packedClass)
{
  Version version = RunBase::getVersion(packedClass);

  switch (version)
  {
    case #CurrentVersion:
    [version, #CurrentList] = packedClass;
    break;
    default:
    return false;
  }

  return true;
}
```

The main method

This is the class entry point, executed when a menu item that points to it is started, or if it is opened directly from the **Application Object Tree (AOT)**. The following code shows us the `main` method:

```
static void main(Args args)
{
  // Create an object of the ImportFile class
  ImpExpFileDialog    importFileDialog = new ImpExpFileDialog();
  // Prompt the user with the fields
  // specified in the dialog() method
  if (importFileDialog.prompt())
  // If the user hits the Ok-button
  // execute the run() method
  importFileDialog.run();
}
```

The ImpExpFile class

This is the main class in this class hierarchy. Any code generic to the entity classes that extend this class are set here. The class is abstract, which means that you can never create an object of this class, only its subclasses can be created (the entity classes). The following are the methods within this class:

The classDeclaration method

It is the main class for the `ImpExpFile` class hierarchy. The class is abstract to ensure that an object cannot be created based on it (only subclasses of this class can have objects created). The following code shows us the `classDeclaration` method:

```
abstract class ImpExpFile
{
  // Use the file macro to set IO flags
  #File
  // Global variables
  FileName           fileName;
  FileType           fileType;
  FileEntity         entity;
  IO                 file;
  ReadWrite          readWrite;
}
```

The new method

It is the constructor that is used to set default values for some of the global variables. The following code shows us the `new` method:

```
void new(FileType _fileType, FileName _fileName, FileEntity
_entity, ReadWrite _readWrite)
{
  fileType = _fileType;
  fileName = _fileName;
   entity = _entity;
  readWrite = _readWrite;
}
```

The openFile method

This method is used to open the selected file either to read from or to write to. The following code shows us the `openFile` method:

```
protected boolean openFile()
{
  boolean ret = true;
  str      rw;
  if (readWrite == ReadWrite::Read)
  rw = #io_read;
  else
  rw = #io_write;
  switch (fileType)
  {
    case FileType::Binary :
    file = new BinaryIo(filename, rw);
    break;
    case FileType::Comma :
    file = new CommaIO(filename, rw);
    break;
    default :
    ret = false;
    break;
  }
  return ret;
}
```

The readFile method

This method is used to initialize the file that is to be read. The following code shows us the `readFile` method:

```
protected void readFile()
{
  if(!this.openFile())
  throw error("Unable to open the selected file");

  file.inFieldDelimiter(';');
  file.inRecordDelimiter('\r\n');
}
```

The run method

This is the main execution flow of the `ImpExpFile`. It decides whether to read to or write from the file and catch any exceptions that might occur. The following code shows us the `run` method in it:

```
void run()
{
  try
  {
    // Use this function to make sure that
    // the mouse-pointer changes to a timeglass.
    startLengthyOperation();
    if (readWrite == ReadWrite::read)
    this.readFile();
    else
    this.writeFile();
  }
  catch (Exception::Deadlock)
  {
    retry;
  }
  catch (Exception::Error)
  {
    error(strfmt("An error occured while trying to read the file
    %1 into the %2 entity", filename, enum2str(entity)));
  }

  // Mous-pointer can switch back
  // to normal again.
  endLengthyOperation();
}
```

The writeFile method

This method is used to initialize the file that is to be written to. The following code shows us the `writeFile` method in it:

```
protected void writeFile()
{
  if(!this.openFile())
  throw error("Unable to open the selected file");
  file.outFieldDelimiter(';');
  file.outRecordDelimiter('\r\n');
}
```

The construct method

Create an object for one of the subclasses based on the user input in the dialog. The following code shows us the `construct` method:

```
static ImpExpFile construct(FileType _fileType, FileName _filename,
FileEntity _entity, ReadWrite _readWrite)
{
  ImpExpFile          impExpFile;
  switch(_entity)
  {
    case FileEntity::Cars :
    impExpFile = new ImpExp_Cars(_fileType, _filename, _entity,
    _readWrite);
    break;
    case FileEntity::Rentalts :
    impExpFile = new ImpExp_Rentals(_fileType, _filename, _entity,
    _readWrite);
    break;
  }
  return impExpFile;
}
```

The ImpExp_Cars class

This is one of the entity classes that I have created to demonstrate how you can use this example framework. It allows for the export and import of data from and to the `CarTable` respectively. Note that it only supports the insertion of new records into the `CarTable`, not updating. You can, of course, add that part yourself if you have read the previous chapter. The following are the methods within this class.

The classDeclaration method

It's an empty class declaration as there are no global variables in this class, and it is as follows:

```
class ImpExp_Cars extends ImpExpFile
{
}
```

The readFile method

This example shows a hardcoded way of reading the file that is to be used to insert new records into the `CarTable`. Each line in the file is read into a container. Each field is fetched from the container using the `conpeek()` function:

```
void readFile()
{
  CarTable        carTable;
  container       con;
  super();

  con = file.read();

  if (conlen(con) != 5)
  throw error("The file has an illegal format");
  // Read the file as long as the file is ok.
  // The status changes when the cursor hits
  // the end of the file.
  while (file.status() == IO_Status::Ok)
  {
    carTable.clear();
    carTable.CarId = conpeek(con, 1);
    carTable.CarBrand = conpeek(con, 2);
    carTable.Model = conpeek(con, 3);
    carTable.ModelYear = conpeek(con, 4);
    carTable.Mileage = conpeek(con, 5);

    if (carTable.validateWrite())
    carTable.insert();
    con = file.read();
  }
}
```

Integrating Data

The writeFile method

It is used to write information from the `carTable` to the file, and it is implemented as shown in the following code:

```
void writeFile()
{
  CarTable        carTable;
  container       con;

  super();

  while select carTable
  {
    con = conins(con, 1,
    carTable.CarId,
    carTable.CarBrand,
    carTable.Model,
    carTable.ModelYear,
    carTable.Mileage);
    file.writeExp(con);
  }
}
```

The ImpExp_Rentals class

This entity class is written to export and import all fields from the rental table. It can also be rewritten so that it is generic and it works with all tables; but for now I just want to show you how to use the `DictTable` and `DictField` classes while exporting and importing. The following are the methods within this class.

The classDeclaration method

It is an empty class declaration as there are no global variables in this class, and is as follows:

```
class ImpExp_Rentals extends ImpExpFile
{
}
```

The readFile method

This method uses the `DictTable` and `DictField` classes to find all the fields in the `RentalTable` and insert the data from the file to the matching fields in the `RentalTable`. The following code shows us the `readFile` method in it:

```
void readFile()
{
   RentalTable      rentalTable;
   container        con;
   DictTable        dTable = new DictTable(tablenum(RentalTable));
   DictField        dField;
   int              i, fields, field;

   super();

   con = file.read();

   while (file.status() == IO_Status::Ok)
   {
     for (i=1; i <= conlen(con); i++)
     {
       field = dTable.fieldCnt2Id(i);
       dField = dTable.fieldObject(field);
       switch (dField.baseType())
       {
         case Types::Guid :
         rentalTable.(field) = str2guid(conpeek(con, i));
         break;
         case Types::Int64 :
         rentalTable.(field) = str2Int64(conpeek(con, i));
         break;
         case Types::Date :
         rentalTable.(field) = str2Date(conpeek(con, i),321);
         break;
         default :
         rentalTable.(field) = conpeek(con, i);
         break;
       }
     }
     if (rentalTable.validateWrite())
     rentalTable.insert();
     con = file.read();
   }
}
```

The writeFile method

This method uses the `DictTable` and `DictField` class to loop through all the fields in RentalTable and write their content to the file. The following code shows us the `writeFile` method:

```
void writeFile()
{
  RentalTable      rentalTable;
  container        con;
  int              fields, i, fieldId;
  DictTable        dt = new DictTable(tablenum(RentalTable));

  super();

  while select rentalTable
  {
    con = connull();
    fields = dt.fieldCnt();
    for (i=1; i<=fields; i++)
    {
      fieldId = dt.fieldCnt2Id(i);
      con = conins(con, i, rentalTable.(fieldId));
    }
    file.write(con);
  }
}
```

Summary

In this chapter, you have learned how to write data from AX to text files, XML files, and binary files, and also how to write the data back into AX again. You have also learned how to read the data and how to manipulate it in a database using ODBC.

We have also gone through the basics of how to use the `DictTable` and `DictField` elements in order to generate dynamic routines for data manipulation.

You have also seen how to create a simple class hierarchy that can be used for data import or data export in different formats.

In the next chapter, we will look at how to modify standard AX modules such as Inventory, Ledger, Accounts Receivable, and Accounts Payable.

For each of the modules, we will start by having a look at the entity schema and the main class hierarchies before looking at how to perform some of the most common tasks using the X++ programming language.

8
Integrating with Standard AX

If you have come this far, you are most likely ready to figure out how to change or add functionality in standard AX. This chapter takes you through some of the challenges you will face when trying to modify how some of the standard modules in AX behave.

We will look at some typical problems that you might have faced when integrating to standard AX in the main modules of Dynamics AX:

- Inventory
- Ledger
- Accounts Receivable and Accounts Payable

You will also get to know the important tables within each module, how they are related to each other, and take a look at some of the classes that control the behavior of the module.

One of the main procedural concepts of AX is the way journals and posting of journals work. A journal is like a draft and does not have any related financial transactions until it is posted. Whenever a posting occurs, AX will generate transactions related to the parts of the journal that is being posted. The type of transactions depends on what kind of posting takes place.

The inventory module

The inventory module in AX contains the storage and setup of items and explains how they are stored in the physical inventory. It is also heavily integrated to most of the other modules; the production module has to know which items to produce and which items the production consists of. To create a sales order in the **Accounts Receivable** module, you need to know which items to sell and so on.

Integrating with Standard AX

The InventTable entity schema

The main entity of the inventory, as you have figured out probably, is the **Product Information Management** module. There are two main concepts that you need to understand—the concept of product and item.

A product can be considered to be a definition (dare I call it a template) of an item. The product table is a shared table (which means it is not company specific) and it holds basic details about the product. A product is then *released* into a company where it becomes an item (also referred to as Released product). The following two diagrams published by Microsoft illustrate the product data structure and key relations:

 Not all fields have been captured in these diagrams.

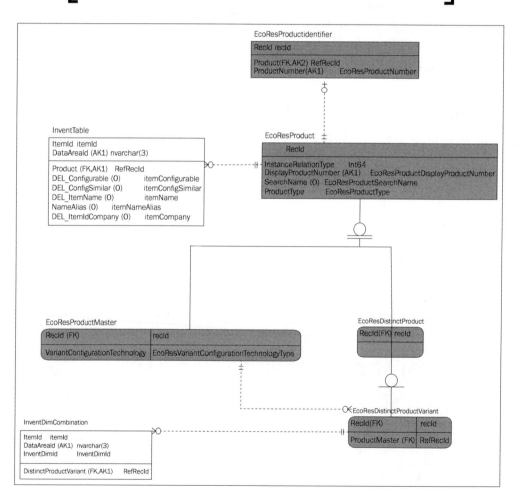

The following table gives a brief description of each of the tables shown in the preceding `InventTable` entity schema:

Table name	Description
`EcoResProduct`	This is a base table for the inherited tables that follow next.
`EcoResProductMaster`	This table holds information on products that can have variants (color, size, and so on.). Within the application, these products are referred to as product masters.
`EcoResDistinctProduct`	A distinct product is effectively a product that does not have variants (it is not associated with inventory dimensions color, size, and so on).
`InventTable`	This table contains information about the released items.
`InventItemGroup`	This table contains information about item groups.
`InventDimGroup`	This table contains information about a dimension group.
`InventTableModule`	This table contains information about purchase, sales and inventory specific settings for items.
`InventModelGroup`	This table contains information about inventory model groups.
`InventItemSalesSetup`	This table contains default settings for items, such as site and warehouse. The values are related to sales settings.
`InventItemPurchSetup`	This table contains default settings for items, such as site and warehouse. The values are related to purchase settings.
`InventItemInventSetup`	This table contains default settings for items, such as site and warehouse. The values are related to inventory settings.
`InventItemLocation`	This table contains information about items and related warehouse, and counting settings. The settings can be made specific based on the items configuration and vary from warehouse to warehouse.
`InventDim`	This table contains values for inventory dimensions.

> The table description in the list below each entity schema in this chapter is taken from the Dynamics AX SDK, also known as the Developer Help.

Integrating with Standard AX

As you can see, this diagram is very simplified as I have left out most of the fields in the tables to make the preceding diagram more readable. The purpose of the diagram is to give you an idea of the relations between these tables.

The diagram shows that items have tables linked to them that describe their behavior in purchase, inventory and sales, and how the items should be treated with regards to financial posting and inventory posting.

The InventTrans entity schema

The `InventTransaction` schema is another important in the inventory module. Again, this is very simplified with only the main entities and the fields that make up the primary and foreign keys, as shown in the diagram from a Microsoft whitepaper

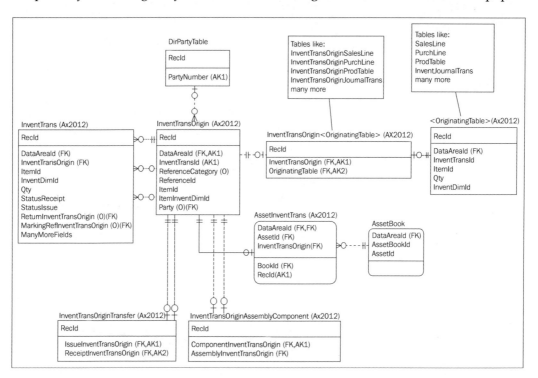

The following table gives a brief description of each of the tables shown in the preceding `InventTrans entity` schema:

Table name	Description
`InventTransOrigin`	This was a new table added in AX 2012 and is effectively used to join `InventTrans` table to the origination (sales line, purchase lines, inventory adjustment, and so on) transaction line via the `InventTransOrigin` tables.
`InventTransOrigin` tables	There are multiple tables such as `InventTransOrigin Salesline` and `InventTransOriginPurchLine`, and they are fundamentally used to link the transaction origin document to an inventory transaction record.
`InventTrans`	This table contains information about inventory transactions. When order lines, such as sales order lines or purchase order lines are created, they generate related records in this table. These records represent the flow of material that goes in and out of the inventory.
`InventTable`	This table contains information about inventory items.
`InventSum`	This table contains information about the present and expected on-hand stock of items. Expected on-hand stock is calculated by looking at the present on-hand values and adding whatever is on order (has been purchased but not arrived yet).
`InventDim`	This table contains values of inventory dimensions.
`VendTable`	This table contains information on vendors for Accounts Payable.
`CustTable`	This table contains the list of customers for Accounts Receivable and customer relationship management.

Understanding main class hierarchies

In addition to the entity schemas, it is important to know a little about the main class hierarchies within the `Inventory` module. We use the classes that the main class hierarchies consist of to validate, prepare, create, and change transactions.

The InventMovement classes

The `InventMovement` classes are used to validate and prepare data that will be used to generate inventory transactions. The super class in the hierarchy is the abstract class called `InventMovement`. All of the other classes in the hierarchy are prefixed `InventMov_`.

Integrating with Standard AX

For example, `InventMov_Sales` is used to validate and prepare inventory with sales line transactions, or `InventMov_Transfer`, which is used when dealing with inventory transfer journals.

The following figure is taken from the type hierarchy browser of the `InventMovement` class and shows the whole class hierarchy under `InventMovement`:

Chapter 8

The InventUpdate classes

The `InventUpdate` classes are used to insert and update inventory transactions. Whenever a transaction should be posted, the `updateNow()` method in the correct `InventUpdate` subclass will execute. The super class in the hierarchy is the `InventUpdate` class and the other classes in the hierarchy are prefixed `InventUpd_`.

For example, `InventUpd_Estimated` is used whenever an item line is entered in the system that will most likely generate a physical transaction in future. This can be, for example, a sales order line that has the on order sales status. When a line like this is entered or generated in AX, the `InventUpd_Estimated` class is triggered so that the inventory transactions will reflect that the item is on order.

The following figure shows the type hierarchy browser of the `InventUpdate` class and its subclasses:

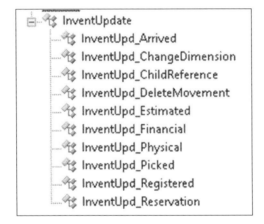

The InventAdj classes

Whenever an adjustment to an inventory transaction takes place, the `InventAdj` classes are used. The adjustments typically occur when you are closing the inventory.

The following figure shows the application hierarchy tree of the `InventAdj` class and its subclasses:

The InventSum classes

The `InventSum` classes are used to find the on-hand information about a certain item at a certain date. The `InventOnHand` class is used to find the current on-hand information. The `InventSum` classes are not structured in a hierarchy as the previously mentioned classes.

Now that you have seen how some of the main tables in the inventory module are related to each other, we will discuss how to write code that integrates with the inventory module.

Working with inventory dimensions

One thing that you will have to learn sooner rather than later is how the inventory dimensions work. Basically, the `InventDim` table holds information about all the different dimensions that are related to an item. These dimensions can be divided into three types: item, storage, and tracking dimensions. By default, AX comes with the following dimensions:

- **Four item dimension:** The dimensions are Color, Size, Style, and Configuration
- **Six storage dimension:** The dimensions are Site, Warehouse, Location, Pallet, Inventory status, and License plate
- **Five tracking dimension:** The dimensions are Batch, Serial, Owner, Inventory Profile, and GTD number

> The number of dimensions visible within the application will vary based on the configuration keys enabled.

Finding an inventory dimension

When combinations of these dimensions are needed in a journal or a transaction, we always check to see whether the combination already exists. If it does, we link to that record in the `InventDim` table. If it doesn't exist, a new record is created in the `InventDim` table with the different dimensions filled out. Then, we can link to the new record. This is done by using a method called `findOrCreate` from the `InventDim` table. You can see how to use it in the following code:

```
static void findingDimension(Args _args)
{
    InventDim           inventDim;

    // Set the values that you need for
```

```
    // the journal or transaction
    inventDim.InventLocationId = "01";
    inventDim.InventColorId = "02";
    // Use findOrCreate and use the inventDim
    // variable that you have set values into
    inventDim = InventDim::findOrCreate(inventDim);
    // Use the inventDimId to link to the
    // InventDim record that was either
    // found or created
    info(inventDim.inventDimId);
}
```

Finding the current on-hand information

Another thing you should know is how to find how many items are available within a certain `InventDim` scope. You can do this by converting the `InventDim` fields into an `InventDim` variable and then specifying which dimension fields or combination of dimension fields you would like to get on-hand information on. In the following example, we search for the on-hand information for an item in a specific color:

```
static void findingOnHandInfo(Args _args)
{
    ItemId              itemId;
    InventDim           inventDimCriteria;
    InventDimParm       inventDimParm;
    InventOnhand        inventOnhand;

    // Specify the item to get onhand info on
    itemId = "1001";

    // initilise inventOnHand
    inventOnhand = InventOnhand::newItemId(itemId);

    // Specify the dimensions you want
    // to filter the onhand info on
    inventDimCriteria.InventColorId = "02";
    // Set the parameter flags active
    // according to which of the dimensions
    // in inventDimCriteria that are set
    inventDimParm.initFromInventDim(inventDimCriteria);

    // Specify the inventDim,
    // inventDimParm and itemId
    inventOnhand.parmInventDim(inventDimCriteria);
```

Integrating with Standard AX

```
        inventOnhand.parmInventDimParm(inventDimParm);
        inventOnhand.parmItemId(itemId);

        // Retrieve the onhand info
        info(strfmt("Available Physical: %1",inventOnhand.availPhysical()));
        info(strfmt("On order: %1",inventOnhand.onOrder()));
    }
```

You could easily narrow the information down to a specific warehouse by setting a warehouse (`InventLocationId`) to the `inventDimCriteria` method, as we have done for the `InventColorId` value.

Finding on-hand information by a specific date

The following example will let you find the on-hand quantity information of a specific item with a specific color (inventory dimension) at a specific date. The code is as follows:

```
    static void findingOnHandByDate(Args _args)
    {
        ItemId              itemId;
        InventDim           inventDimCriteria;
        InventDimParm       inventDimParm;
        InventSumDateDim    inventSumDateDim;

        // Specify the item to get onhand info on
        itemId = "1001";
        // Specify the dimensions you want
        // to filter the onhand info on
        inventDimCriteria.InventColorId = "02";
        // Set the parameter flags active
        // accoring to which of the dimensions
        // in inventDimCriteria that are set
        inventDimParm.initFromInventDim(inventDimCriteria);

        // Specify the transaction date, inventDimCriteria,
        // inventDimParm and itemId to receive a new object
        // of InventSumDateDim
        inventSumDateDim =
        InventSumDateDim::newParameters(mkdate(01,01,2014),
        itemId, inventDimCriteria, inventDimParm);
        // Retrieve the on hand info using the methods
        // of InventSumDateDim
```

```
    info(strfmt("PostedQty: %1",inventSumDateDim.postedQty()));
    info(strfmt("DeductedQty: %1",inventSumDateDim.deductedQty()));
    info(strfmt("ReceivedQty: %1",inventSumDateDim.receivedQty()));
}
```

Entering and posting an inventory journal from code

One of the things you will need to know when dealing with the inventory module is how to automate journal entry and posting. This example will show you one way of doing this. This method is typically used when performing data migration. The code is as follows:

```
static void enterPostInventJournal(Args _args)
{
    InventJournalName       inventJournalName;
    InventJournalTable      inventJournalTable;
    InventJournalTrans      inventJournalTrans;

    InventJournalTableData  inventJournalTableData;
    InventJournalTransData  inventJournalTransData;

    InventTable             inventTable;
    InventDim               inventDim;

    select firstonly inventTable; // find item

    // find a movement journal name
    select firstOnly inventJournalName
    where inventJournalName.JournalType ==
    InventJournalType::Movement;

    // Initialize the values in the inventJournalTable
    // from the inventJournalName and insert the record
    inventJournalTable.clear();
    inventJournalTable.initValue();
    inventJournalTable.initFromInventJournalName
    (inventJournalName);
    inventJournalTable.insert();

    inventJournalTableData =
    JournalTableData::newTable(inventJournalTable);
```

Integrating with Standard AX

```
    // Insert to records into the inventJournalTrans table
    inventJournalTrans.clear();
    inventJournalTrans.initFromInventJournalTable
    (inventJournalTable);
    inventJournalTrans.TransDate = systemdateget();
    inventJournalTrans.initFromInventTable(inventTable);
    inventJournalTrans.Qty = 3;

    // Find the default dimension
    inventDim.initFromInventTable
    (inventJournalTrans.inventMovement().inventTable(),
    InventItemOrderSetupType::Invent,inventDim);
    // Set additional mandatory dimensions - based on item
    selected
    //inventDim.InventColorId    = "02";
    //inventDim.InventSizeId     = "50";
    //inventDim.configId         = "HD";
    // See if the inventDim with the selected values
    // allready exist in the InventDim table. If not, it's
    // created automatically

    inventDim = InventDim::findOrCreate(inventDim);
    inventJournalTrans.InventDimId  = inventDim.inventDimId;

    inventJournalTransData =
    inventJournalTableData.journalStatic()
    .newJournalTransData(inventJournalTrans,
    inventJournalTableData);
    inventJournalTransData.create();

    // Use the InventJournalCheckPost class to
    // post the journal
    if (InventJournalCheckPost::newPostJournal
    (inventJournalTable).validate())
    InventJournalCheckPost::newPostJournal
    (inventJournalTable).run();
}
```

The Ledger module

The Ledger module (also known as general ledger) is where all financial transaction in AX is controlled and stored. All of the other modules are connected to the Ledger module in some way as it is the *money central* of AX.

Chapter 8

The main entity of the Ledger module is the Ledger table that consists of the chart of accounts. In addition, there are transaction tables and other tables related to the Ledger table and, hopefully, you will understand how some of these tables relate to each other by taking a look at the following entity schema from Microsoft:

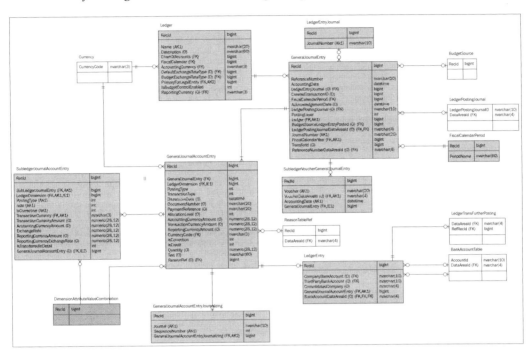

The following table gives a brief description of each of the tables shown in the Ledger entity schema in the preceding diagram:

Table name	Description
Ledger	This table contains the definitions of the general ledger accounts.
GeneralJournalAccountEntry	This table contains information about the general ledger entry.
GeneralJournalEntry	This table contains transaction metadata such as posting layer, transaction date, and so on.
SubledgerVoucherGeneralJournalEntry	This table links the subledger voucher to the general ledger entry.
LedgerEntry	This table contains general ledger bank transaction information.

[237]

Posting ledger transactions

There are two ways of posting ledger transactions:

- **Ledger Journal**: Enter data into a journal and post the journal using the `LedgerJournalCheckPost` class.
- **Ledger Voucher**: Create a list of vouchers (`LedgerVoucherObject`) and post them using the `LedgerVoucher` class.

Entering and posting a LedgerJournal class

The easiest way to post a ledger transaction is using the `LedgerJournal` class. This is similar to the example in the previous section of this chapter, where you learned how to fill the inventory journal with data and then post the journal from code. The code is as follows:

In the following example, we will post a ledger transaction by filling `LedgerJournalTable` and `LedgerJournalTrans` with data and post the journal using the `LedgerJournalCheckPost` class:

```
static void enterPostLedgerJournal(Args _args)
{
    LedgerJournalName        ledgerJournalName;
    LedgerJournalTable       ledgerJournalTable;
    LedgerJournalTrans       ledgerJournalTrans;

    LedgerJournalCheckPost   ledgerJournalCheckPost;
    container                ledgerDimensions, offsetDimensions;
    Voucher                  voucher;

    // Set ledger account information
    ledgerDimensions = ["22322","Chicago"];
    offsetDimensions = ["22321","London"];

    // You MUST have tts around the code or else
    // the numberSeq will generate an error while
    // trying to find the next available voucher
    ttsbegin;

    // Specify which ledger journal to use
    ledgerJournalName = LedgerJournalName::find("GenJrn");
    // Initialize the values in the ledgerJournalTable
    // from the ledgerJournalName and insert the record
```

```
ledgerJournalTable.initFromLedgerJournalName
(ledgerJournalName.JournalName);
ledgerJournalTable.insert();
// Find the next available voucher number.
voucher = new JournalVoucherNum
(JournalTableData::newTable(ledgerJournalTable)).getNew(false);

ledgerJournalTrans.voucher = voucher;
ledgerJournalTrans.initValue();

// Set the fields necessary in the ledgerJournalTrans
ledgerJournalTrans.JournalNum       =
ledgerJournalTable.JournalNum;
ledgerJournalTrans.currencyCode     = 'USD';
ledgerJournalTrans.ExchRate         =
Currency::exchRate(ledgerJournalTrans.currencyCode);
ledgerJournalTrans.LedgerDimension  =
AxdDimensionUtil::getLedgerAccountId(ledgerDimensions);
ledgerJournalTrans.AccountType      =
ledgerJournalACType::Ledger;
ledgerJournalTrans.AmountCurDebit   = 1220.00;
ledgerJournalTrans.TransDate        = systemdateget();
ledgerJournalTrans.Txt              = 'Transfer to UK';
ledgerJournalTrans.OffsetDefaultDimension =
AxdDimensionUtil::getLedgerAccountId(offsetDimensions);
// Insert to records into the ledgerJournalTrans table
ledgerJournalTrans.insert();

// Use the LedgerJournalCheckPost class to
// post the journal
ledgerJournalCheckPost =
LedgerJournalCheckPost::construct(LedgerJournalType::Daily);
// Set the JournalId, tableId of the journalTable
// and specify to post the journal (not only check it).
ledgerJournalCheckPost.parmJournalNum
(ledgerJournalTable.JournalNum);
ledgerJournalCheckPost.parmPost(NoYes::Yes);
ledgerJournalCheckPost.run();

ttscommit;
}
```

Integrating with Standard AX

 You can also have AX check and validate the content of the journal before posting it. This can be a good idea, especially when the data originates from a different solution—for instance, when migrating data from the previous system and into AX.

Entering and posting a LedgerVoucher class

Using the `LedgerVoucher` classes to post ledger transactions means that you first create vouchers and then post them. This is more controlled and similar to the traditional way of dealing with posting of ledger transactions.

The method is based on having a `LedgerVoucher` object where you can add multiple vouchers (`LedgerVoucherObject`). For each voucher, you typically have two transactions (`LedgerVoucherTransObject`), one for debit and one for credit. You can of course have more transactions in a voucher, but they have to be compatible. This means that if you add the amount of all of the credit transactions and all of the debit transactions, the result has to be 0.

When all transactions have been added to a voucher and all vouchers have been added to the `LedgerVoucher` object, you can simply call the `ledgerVoucher.end()` method in order to validate and post the voucher. The code is as follows:

```
static void createAndPostLedgerVoucher(Args _args)
{
    AxLedgerJournalTable      ledgerJournalTable;
    AxLedgerJournalTrans      ledgerJournalTrans;

    container   ledgerDimensions, offsetDimensions;

    // Set ledger account information
    ledgerDimensions = ["22322","Chicago"];
    offsetDimensions = ["22321","London"];

    ledgerJournalTable         = new AxLedgerJournalTable();
    ledgerJournalTrans         = new AxLedgerJournalTrans();

    ledgerJournalTable.parmJournalName("Gen");
    ledgerJournalTable.save();
```

```
    ledgerJournalTrans.parmAccountType(LedgerJournalACType::Ledger);
    ledgerJournalTrans.parmJournalNum
(ledgerJournalTable.ledgerJournalTable().JournalNum);

    ledgerJournalTrans.parmLedgerDimension
    (AxdDimensionUtil::getLedgerAccountId(ledgerDimensions));
    ledgerJournalTrans.parmAmountCurDebit(500);

    ledgerJournalTrans.parmOffsetLedgerDimension
    (AxdDimensionUtil::getLedgerAccountId(offsetDimensions));

    ledgerJournalTrans.end();
}
```

Understanding the Accounts Receivable / Accounts Payable modules

The **Account Receivable (AR)** and **Accounts Payable (AP)** modules in AX are very similar to one another. On one hand, you have customers and sales orders and on the other hand, you have vendors and purchase orders. The examples in this chapter are only from the AR module, but switching the example to AP should not be a problem for you at this point.

As you will see from the entity schema in the next section, the similarities between the tables on the different sides are taken to a common level using a table map in the in **Application Object Tree (AOT)**. This enables you, as a developer, to write one class that can easily handle both AR and AP at the same time, as you can reference the table map instead of having two classes—one class to reference the AP tables and another class to reference the AR tables.

Integrating with Standard AX

Entity schema – base data and orders

The entity schema shows how the base data in the AR and AP modules relate to one another. It also shows that the fields that are common in the AR and AP modules are put into maps to enable one piece of code to refer to the map and have it work for both the AR and the AP modules.

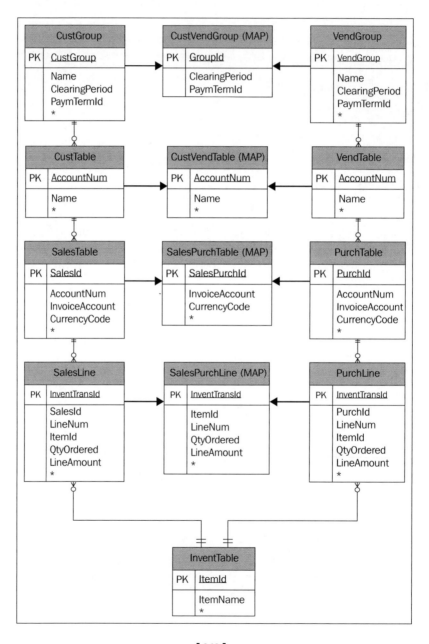

Again, this schema is very simplified as there are many more fields and other entities that also relate to the tables in the schema.

The following table gives a brief description of each of the tables shown in the preceding entity schema:

Table name	Description
CustGroup	This table contains a list of groups into which customers can be added. All customers must specify a CustGroup value with which they are associated. The group contains information such as default payment terms and settlement periods, and it is also used for reporting.
VendGroup	This table contains definitions of vendor groups.
CustTable	This table contains the list of customers for AR and customer relationship management.
VendTable	This table contains vendors for AP.
SalesTable	This table contains all sales order headers regardless of whether they have been posted or not.
PurchTable	This table contains all purchase order headers regardless of whether they have been posted or not.
SalesLine	This table contains all sales order lines regardless of whether they have been posted or not.
PurchLine	This table contains all purchase order lines regardless of whether they have been posted or not.

Integrating with Standard AX

Entity schema – transactions

The transactions entity schema shows how the customer and vendor transactions link to settlement tables and the ledger transactions, and how all of these tables relate to the ledger dimensions. The following shows a transaction entity schema:

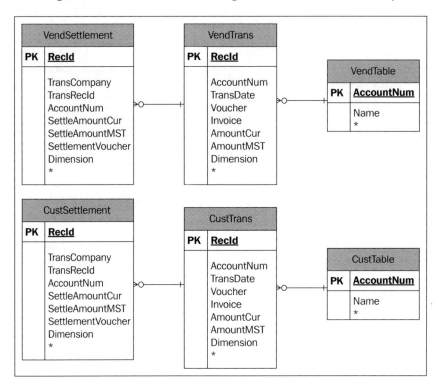

The following table gives a brief description of each of the tables shown in the preceding transactions entity schema:

Table name	Description
CustTrans	This table contains posted transaction information for the customer.
VendTrans	This table contains posted transaction information for the vendor.
CustSettlement	This table contains information relating to the settlement or reverse settlement of two transactions. They are used to link a transaction with the transaction it was settled against.
VendSettlement	This table contains information relating to the settlement or reverse settlement of two transactions. They are used to link a transaction with the transaction it was settled against.

The trade agreements

The trade agreements module in AX is where prices and discounts are handled. An item can, for example, have a default sales price / discount that is valid for all customers. This information is then stored in the `InventTableModule` table (see the `InventTable` entity schema under the *The inventory module* section of this chapter).

At other times, however, you may like to give either a certain customer, a group of customers, or perhaps all customers special prices/discounts on an item, a group of items, or all items. This is achieved by setting up trade agreements in the `PriceDiscTable` table.

A price cannot be set up for a group of items or all items only for a specific item. Discounts can, however, be set up on all items, a group of items, or on a specific item.

The trade agreements can also be combined so that, for example, multiple discounts are used to give the customer the correct price. This is done by checking the `Find Next` flag in the trade agreements form. Explaining all the details of the trade agreements in AX is not in the scope of this book, but I suggest that you play around in AX to set up several different price agreements and try them out in a sales order to see the different effects they give.

Finding the price of an item for a specific customer

Finding the correct price for an item can be pretty messy if you start to write code that searches the `PriceDisc` table for the price and, luckily, you don't have to because this has already been taken care of in standard AX. The question is how to use the code that is present in standard AX to get the correct prices when you write your code. The code is as follows:

```
static void findPrice(Args _args)
{
    PriceDisc            priceDisc;
    InventDim            inventDim;
    Price                price;
    CustTable            custTable;
    InventTable          inventTable;
    InventTableModule    sales;
```

```
        // Specify the inventDim that we would like
        // to get the price for
        inventDim.configId = "HD";
        inventDim.InventSizeId = "50";
        inventDim.InventColorId = "01";
        inventDim = InventDim::findDim(inventDim);

        // Specify the item and customer
        inventTable = InventTable::find("1003");
        custTable = CustTable::find("1101");
        sales = inventTable.inventTableModuleSales();

        // Create a new object of the PriceDisc
        // class with the specifications of parameters
        priceDisc = new PriceDisc(ModuleInventPurchSales::Sales,
        inventTable.ItemId,
        inventDim,
        sales.UnitId,
        systemdateget(),
        1, // Quantity
        custTable.AccountNum);

        // Find the price from PriceDiscTable if one exist
        // for the specification
        if (priceDisc.findPrice(custTable.PriceGroup))
        price = priceDisc.price();

        // If no record in PriceDiscTable matches, then
        // get the default item price
        else if (priceDisc.findItemPrice())
        price = priceDisc.price();

            info(strfmt("Price: %1", priceDisc.price()));
    }
```

Posting and printing sales/purchase updates

One of the most commonly used classes in AX are the `form letter service` classes—theses classes define how to post different status updates against sales orders and purchase orders.

The following figure shows the class hierarchy of `FormLetterServiceController` with all its subclasses:

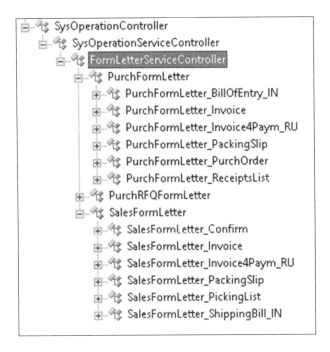

As you can see, there are four main operations on both the sales side and the purchase side that are fairly similar:

Sales	Purchase
Confirmation	Purchase order confirmation
Picking list	Receipt list
Packing slip	Packing slip
Invoice	Invoice

In addition, the class hierarchy contains classes for updating **Request For Quotes (RFQ)**.

Since the process of posting orders can include several orders in one update and also only posts parts of an order, AX uses the `Parm` tables that are filled with data before the actual posting. For example, on the sales side, the `SalesParmUpdate` table contains information regarding the update taking place and can be linked to several records in the `SalesParmTable` table, which again contains information regarding the sales orders being updated. The `SalesParmLine` table is linked to the `SalesParmTable` table and contains information regarding the lines being updated.

Integrating with Standard AX

The normal flow when a posting is being performed is that the `Parm` tables are populated with data and then the update itself is being performed.

Updating a single sales order is, however, a lot easier, as shown in the following example. It will then update only that order and update all the lines in the order. The code is as follows:

```
static void postSalesInvoice(Args _args)
{
  // Define a classvariable according to the
  // type of posting being performed
  SalesFormLetter_Invoice    invoice;
  SalesTable                 salesTable;

  // Select the salesTable to update
  salesTable = SalesTable::find("SO-101297");

  // Create a new object of the SalesFormLetter_Invoice
  // by using the construct-method in SalesFormLetter
  invoice = SalesFormLetter::construct(DocumentStatus::Invoice);
  // Post the invoice
  invoice.update(salesTable,
  SystemDateGet(),
  SalesUpdate::All,
  AccountOrder::None,
  false,
  true); // Set to true to print the invoice
}
```

The voucher settlement

When a payment is made or received toward an invoice, either on the vendor side or on the customer side, the transactions have to settle against each other in order to close the transaction. Obviously, the standard functionality in AX lets the users take care of this in a very neat way using the payment journal form where they can enter the payment into AX and mark the invoices to settle the payment against, as shown in the following screenshot:

Chapter 8

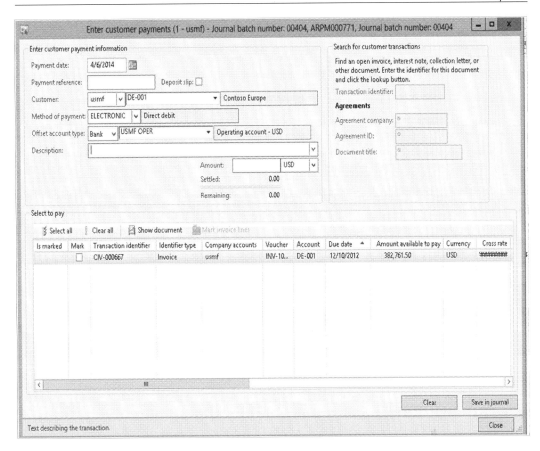

However, you might find yourself creating an integration that should take care of this automatically and then it would be nice to know how to do this using AX, right?

Ok, so let's assume that a payment has been registered by the customer account shown in the form shown previosly (3001), but the settlement hasn't been done yet and it is our task to write the code that takes care of it:

The following code should then do the trick:

```
static void settlePayment(Args _args)
{
    CustTable custTable;
    CustTrans invCustTrans, payCustTrans;
    SpecTransManager   manager;
    CustVendTransData    custVendTransData;
```

```
    custTable = CustTable::find("3001");
    // Find the oldest invoice that hasn't been settled yet
    // for this customer
    select firstonly invCustTrans
    order by TransDate asc
    where invCustTrans.AccountNum == custTable.AccountNum &&
    invCustTrans.TransType == LedgerTransType::Sales &&
    !invCustTrans.LastSettleDate;

    // Find the oldest payment that hasn't been settled yet
    // for this customer
    select firstonly payCustTrans
    order by TransDate asc
    where payCustTrans.AccountNum == custTable.AccountNum &&
    payCustTrans.TransType == LedgerTransType::Payment &&
    !payCustTrans.LastSettleDate;
       ttsbegin;

    // Create an object of the CustVendTransData class
    // with the invoice transaction as parameter and mark
    // it for settlement
    custVendTransData = CustVendTransData::construct(invCustTrans);
    custVendTransData.markForSettlement(CustTable);

    // Create an object of the CustVendTransData class
    // with the payment transaction as parameter and mark
    // it for settlement
    custVendTransData = CustVendTransData::construct(payCustTrans);
    custVendTransData.markForSettlement(CustTable);
    ttscommit;

    // Settle all transactions marked for settlement for this customer
    if(CustTrans::settleTransact(custTable, null, true,
SettleDatePrinc::DaysDate, systemdateget()))
    info("Transactions settled");
}
```

Summary

In this chapter, you have seen how to trigger the standard functionality in AX, which is normally done manually using a code. Being able to automate processes and extend the standard functionality will most likely be something that you will do over and over again if you work with customer development.

You should now know how the main tables and the transactional tables in the inventory, Ledger, AR, and AP modules are related to each other.

In the *The inventory module* section, you learned how to find an inventory dimension, how to find the current inventory stock for an item, how to find the inventory stock for an item by a specific date, and how to enter and post an inventory journal.

In the *The Ledger module* section, you learned how to use financial dimensions in code and how to enter and post a ledger journal.

In the AR/AP section, you learned how to find an item price from the trade agreements for a specific customer, how to post a sales order invoice, and how to settle a payment against an invoice.

In the next chapter, you will learn how to create and set up a new module in AX by creating number sequences, parameter tables, and configuring the security framework.

Creating a New Module

At some point, you might get a new idea of creating a fantastic module in AX that solves some of the difficulties your customers might be having; there are a couple of things that we need to bear in mind, and we will cover the following points in this chapter:

- Number sequences
- Parameter tables
- The security framework

As you have learned in *Chapter 4, Data User Interaction*, a module in AX should have its own area page that contains menu items grouped by the following subgroups that are added to the menu element for the module:

- **Places**
- **Common forms**
- **Journals**
- **Reports**
- **Inquiry**
- **Periodic**
- **Setup**

The **Places** and **Common forms** groups are added automatically based on the content of the menu, but the other groups have to be added manually.

Creating a New Module

After implementing the examples in this chapter, you should have an area page for the `Car Rental` module that looks like this:

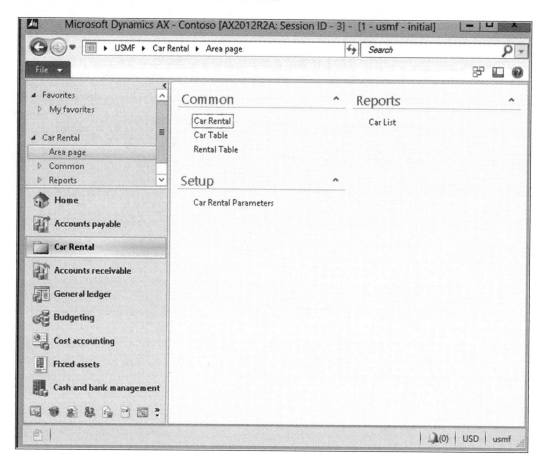

Setting up a number sequence reference

Number sequences are used to automatically create values for specific fields when a new record is created. They are typically used by identifier fields and can have prefix, infix, postfix, and number formatting options, and a specification of how to increment an identifier field.

The number sequences that already exist in AX can be adjusted and set up using the **Number Sequence** form that can be found in the main menu by navigating to **Organization Administration | Common | Number sequences | Number sequences**. New number sequences can also be created in this form, but in order to set up a new number sequence, you will need to perform the following steps:

1. Create a new enum value (CarRental) in the base enum NumberSeqModule.
2. Create a new extended data type (RentalId for example).
3. Create a new class named NumberSeqModuleCarRental that extends NumberSeqApplicationModule module.
4. Create a number sequence reference page in the **Car Rental Parameter** form. RentalId value will then be used as the unique identifier in the RentalTable table.

The following example will demonstrate how to add a new module to the number sequences framework as well as add a new number sequence reference. If you only need to add a new number sequence reference to an existing module, some of the steps are obsolete.

1. The first thing to do in order to add a new module to the number sequence framework is to add a new element to the base enum called NumberSeqModule.

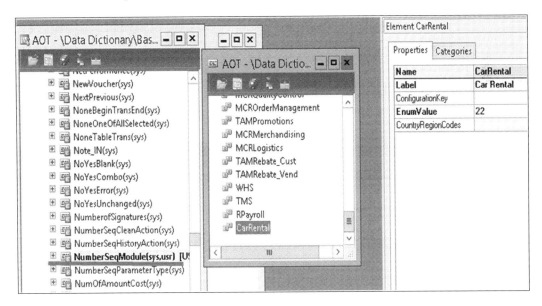

Creating a New Module

2. We will add a new element named `CarRental`. We will also create a new configuration key named `CarRental`. This configuration key will enable us to turn the module on and off in an AX installation. This is done by right-clicking on **Configuration Keys** under the **Data Dictionary** node in AOT and selecting a new configuration key. Then simply name the configuration key as `CarRental` and change the label to `Car rental`.

3. When the configuration key has been created, we will modify the `ConfigurationKey` parameter to `CarRental` on the following elements. The following image shows the `ConfigurationKey` parameter changed on the extended data type `RentalId`:

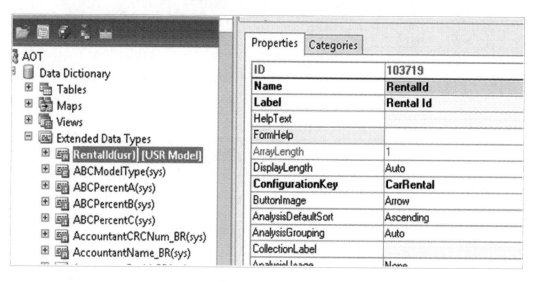

4. Now, add a new class that extends the `NumberSeqApplicationModule` class. Our new class will be called `NumberSeqModuleCarRental` and will look like this:

```
public class NumberSeqModuleCarRental extends
NumberSeqApplicationModule
{
}
public static client server NumberSeqModule numberSeqModule()
{
    return NumberSeqModule::CarRental;
}
protected void loadModule()
{
    NumberSeqDatatype datatype =
    NumberSeqDatatype::construct();
    /* Rental Id */
```

[256]

```
        datatype.parmDatatypeId(extendedtypenum(RentalId));
        datatype.parmReferenceHelp("Unique key for RentalId");
        datatype.parmWizardIsContinuous(false);
        datatype.parmWizardIsManual(NoYes::No);
        datatype.parmWizardIsChangeDownAllowed(NoYes::No);
        datatype.parmWizardIsChangeUpAllowed(NoYes::No);
        datatype.parmWizardHighest(999999);
        datatype.addParameterType(NumberSeqParameterType::
        DataArea, true, false);
        this.create(datatype);
    }
```

5. In order to set up the number sequence reference, we have to add a parameter that will link the number sequence reference to a number sequence created in the number sequence table. We will go through the steps needed to do this in the next section of this chapter.

The parameter table

Most modules need a parameter table that can only consist of one record. The values in the table specify general options for the module. They typically consist of the number sequences needed for the module and default values that are used throughout the module.

In the following example, we will create a parameter table for the `Car Rental` module. The following are the steps:

1. First off, we will create a table in the same way that we did in *Chapter 3*, *Storing Data*, name the table `CarRentalParameters`, and set the label of the table to be `Car rental parameters`.

2. We then add a field to the parameter table that will work as the key for the parameter table, ensuring that at maximum only one record can exist in the table. In order to do this, we open an additional AOT window and browse to the extended data type named `ParametersKey`. Then, we drag-and-drop it onto the **Fields** node of our newly created parameter table and change the name of the field in the table to `Key`. We also change some of the properties of the `Key` field in the parameter table as follows:
    - **AllowEditOnChange**: `No`
    - **AllowEdit**: `No`
    - **Visible**: `No`

3. We also create an index that consists of this field only, call the `KeyIdx` index and set the parameter `Allow Duplicates` to `No`.

4. Then, we add a field that will be used to hold the default file location to import and export data in the module. This field is used in the example at the end of this section. We name this field `DefaultFilepath` and make it extend the extended data type `Filename`.

5. Then, we change some of the parameters of the `CarRentalParameter` table as follows:
    - **TableContents**: `Base + default data`
    - **MaxAccessNode**: `Edit`
    - **CacheLookup**: `Found`
    - **TableGroup**: `Parameter`
    - **PrimaryIndex**: `KeyIdx`
    - **ClusterIndex**: `KeyIdx`
    - **ModifyDateTime**: `Yes`
    - **ModifyBy**: `Yes`

6. We will also create a `find` method for the table, which will look something like this:

```
client server static CarRentalParameters find(boolean _forupdate = false)
{
    CarRentalParameters parameter;

    // Try/catch added because of issues that
    // might occur during upgrade
    try
    {
        if (_forupdate)
            parameter.selectForUpdate(_forupdate);

        // Find the one and only record in
        // the table if any
        select firstonly parameter
            index KeyIdx
            where parameter.Key == 0;

        // If the record doesn't exist and
        // the table buffer used has not been
        // set as temporary, then create the record.
        if (!parameter && !parameter.isTmp())
            Company::createParameter(parameter);
```

```
        }
        catch (Exception::DuplicateKeyException,parameter)
        {
            retry;
        }
        return parameter;
    }
```

The CarRentalParameter table should now look like this in AOT:

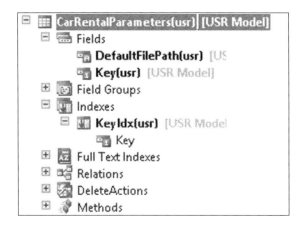

We can now use the parameter table in the ImpExpFileDialog class that we created in *Chapter 7, Integrating Data*. We will modify the dialog method and add the code between the NEW comments, as shown in the following code:

```
public Object dialog()
{
    // Create a new object of the DialogRunbase class
    dialog = new DialogRunbase("Import data from file", this);

    // +++ NEW +++
    // Find the default filepath if it has been set
    // in the parameter table if the fileName variable
    // is empty (no value fetched while unpacking).
    if (!fileName)
    fileName = CarRentalParameters::find().DefaultFilepath;
    // --- NEW ---

    // Add the fields to the dialog and
    // set the initial value to be equal to
    // the value selected last time.
```

Creating a New Module

```
    dialogReadWrite = dialog.addFieldValue(typeid(ReadWrite),
    readWrite);
    dialogFileName = dialog.addFieldValue(typeid(FileName),
    fileName);
    dialogFileType = dialog.addFieldValue(typeid(FileType),
    fileType);
    dialogEntity = dialog.addFieldValue(typeid(FileEntity),
    entity);

    return dialog;
}
```

As we haven't created a form for the parameter table yet, we will have to use the table browser to change the parameter in order to test the import/export classes. Remember to delete the usage data after implementing the changes done in the preceding code. If you don't, you will get the previous selected file location and filename instead of the file location from the parameter table.

Also, add the following methods to the parameter table. This method will be used to get the number sequence reference:

```
Public server static NumberSequenceReference numRefRentalId ()
{
  // scope definition
  NumberSeqScopeFactory::CreateDataAreaScope(selectableDataArea
   _dataArea = curext());

  return NumberSeqReference::findReference(extendedtypenum
    (RentalId));
}
```

Setting up the number sequence

In the first section of this chapter, you learned how to set up a number sequence reference by adding a new class. Now, you have to create a number sequence and to link it to the number sequence reference.

The first thing that we need to do is initialize the number sequence by calling the `LoadAll` method on the class `NumberSequenceModuleSetup`. Create a job that can call the `LoadAll` function.

Next, go to the **Number sequence** form and set up the number sequence by navigating to **Organization administration | Common | Number sequences | Number sequences**.

Chapter 9

It is also common to be able to do this from the page in the last tab in the parameter form for the module where it is relevant to set up the number sequence. The following screenshot shows a **Number Sequence** form:

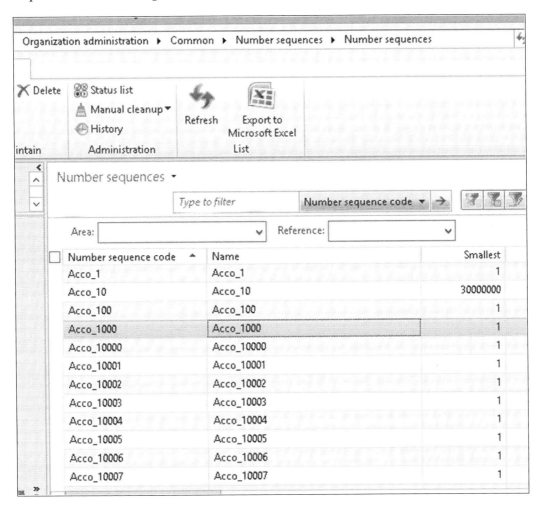

Using the number sequence

There are a few steps you have to perform in order to use the number sequence as well, and I will try to demonstrate how to use the number sequence for the `RentalId` value in the `RentalTable` form. The steps are as follows:

1. First of all, we add a global variable in the `RentalTable` form to hold an object of the `NumberSeqFormHandler` class:

   ```
   public class FormRun extends ObjectRun
   {
       NumberSeqFormHandler    numberSeqFormHandler;
   }
   ```

2. Then, add a global method that creates and holds the reference to the `numberSeqFormHandler` object:

   ```
   NumberSeqFormHandler numberSeqFormHandler()
   {
       if (!numberSeqFormHandler)
       {
           // Create a new object of the NumberSeqFormHandler
           // class by using the static method newForm
           numberSeqFormHandler = NumberSeqFormHandler::newForm(
           CarRentalParameters::numRefRentalId().NumberSequenceId,
           element, RentalTable_DS, fieldnum(RentalTable,
           RentalId));
       }
       return numberSeqFormHandler;
   }
   ```

3. You also need to override the following methods in the `RentalTable` data source, as shown in the following code:

   ```
   public void create(boolean _append = false)
   {
       element.numberSeqFormHandler()
       .formMethodDataSourceCreatePre();
       super(_append);
       element.numberSeqFormHandler()
       .formMethodDataSourceCreate();
   }

   public void delete()
   {
       element.numberSeqFormHandler()
       .formMethodDataSourceDelete();
   ```

```
      super();
    }

    public void write()
    {
      super();
      element.numberSeqFormHandler()
      .formMethodDataSourceWrite();
    }
```

4. Opening the `RentalTable` form now and creating a new record should create a new value for the `RentalId`.

The security framework

The security framework in AX is used to ensure that the user experience is tailored to each user's needs by filtering out functionality that is irrelevant to the users.

To do this, AX uses three main areas of the security framework:

- License codes
- Configuration keys
- Role and permissions

License codes

License codes give access to different modules in AX. In the customer's environment, the customer will have a customized set of license codes activated in AX, depending on which modules they have bought.

Value added resellers and independent software vendors get their own set of license codes that normally include most of the standard modules within AX.

You can look at the existing license codes in AOT by going to **Data Dictionary | License keys**; however, to add a new license code into AX, the VAR/ISV layer has to sign an agreement with Microsoft to make the module available for all other partners and customers to purchase.

Creating a New Module

The set of license codes for an installation is called the license letter and can be viewed in the **License Information (1)** form located at **Main menu | System Administration | Setup | Licensing | License Information**.

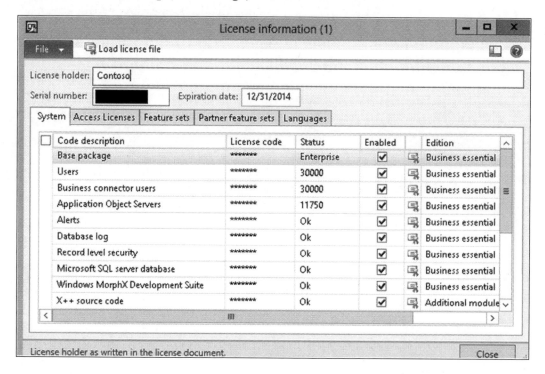

The form will tell you if the current solution has valid licenses for the different modules and a number of users, AOS, Dimensions, details of license holder, serial number, and expiry date.

Configuration keys

In addition to the license codes, AX has a built-in feature to turn on and off parts of a module. This is done from the configuration form found at **Main Menu | System Administration | Setup | Licensing | License Configuration**.

Chapter 9

You can see in the following figure that the configuration key `Car rental` we created earlier in this chapter is shown in the alphabetically sorted list of configuration keys:

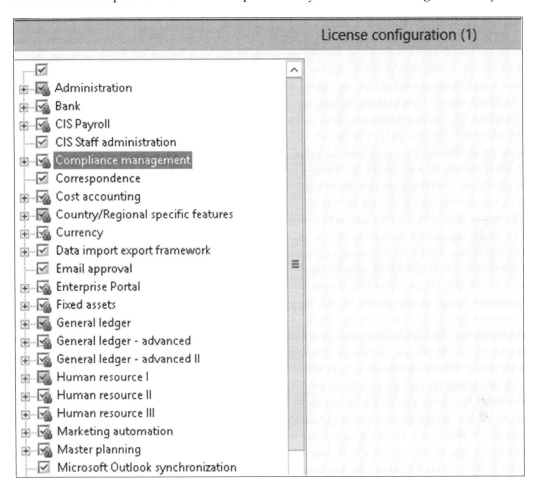

If we turn off a configuration key, the tables using the configuration key will be dropped from the database and all the AOT elements that use the configuration keys will be disabled.

Configuration keys can also be linked to a license code. This means that the set of configuration keys available in the preceding configuration form will be limited to those that have an active license code. If the configuration key is not linked to a license code, it will always be available in the preceding form.

Creating a New Module

Configuration keys can also be linked to other configuration keys so that you can create a hierarchy of configuration keys, as shown in the following screenshot:

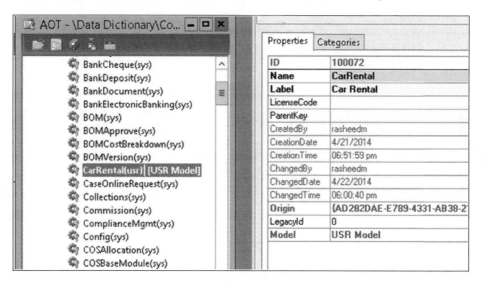

The security hierarchy

The security framework in Dynamics AX 2012 enables us to give certain permissions to certain users in AX, depending on which security roles have been associated with the user account.

It's important to understand the Dynamics AX security hierarchy before starting any security modification. The Dynamics AX 2012 security model is hierarchical and each element in the hierarchy represents a different level of access detail, as shown in the following diagram from MSDN:

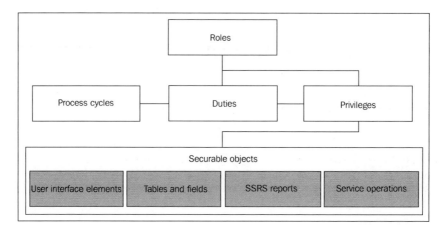

The key points to note here are:

- Permissions represent access to individual securable objects, such as menu items and tables
- Privileges are composed of permissions and represent access to tasks such as posting journals and processing checks
- Duties are composed of privileges and represent parts of a business process, such as maintaining ledger transactions, and both duties and privileges can be assigned to roles

Developers can define new roles or edit existing ones from AOT under the new **Security** node, as shown in the following screenshot:

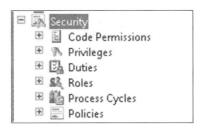

Code permission

Code permission is a group of permissions that are associated with a menu item or a service operation. The degree of access is controlled by the particular permissions that are defined under the node.

Privileges

Privileges define the group of elements that a user has permission to access. A privilege specifies the level of access that is required to perform a job or function. Although privileges can be assigned directly to roles, it is recommended that privileges are assigned to duties (and duties are then assigned to roles).

Duties

Duties are a group of privileges. In terms of organization modeling, they represent a set of privileges (access rights) required to perform an end-to-end business operation.

Policies

Policies define the data that a user is allowed to access. For example, a user might need to have access to the sales table, but the data needs to be restricted to a certain division or business unit.

Roles

Roles are analogous to user groups in active directory—they are effectively a grouping of duties. A user must be assigned to at least one role.

Process cycles

Process cycles are effectively a set of duties that are required to perform a business process. You can think of process cycles as mini roles, as both roles and process cycles are collection of duties. Process cycles are used for organization/security modeling only and cannot be directly associated with a role in AOT.

Open AOT and browse to **Security**. Then, right click on the **Privileges** node and select **New**. We will create two new privileges in our example:

Name	Label
CarRentalView	Car rental clerk
CarRentalMaintain	Car rental administrator

Now, drag and drop the new tables and forms we created and grant read-only access to the **View Privilege** tab and delete access for the **Maintain Privilege**.

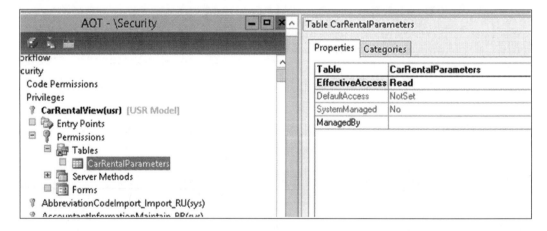

The effective access options are described in the following table:

Name	Description
No access	The user has no access to the features
View access	The user can view the features, but can't update, create, or delete data
Edit access	The user is allowed to view and change the features

Name	Description
Create access	The user is allowed to view and use the features and can also add new records
Correct	Where a data has date effective properties, the user will be allowed to add new date effective records
Delete	The user can view, edit, and even delete records in the specific table

Next, create new duties and roles with the same names as the privileges created earlier and link the appropriate privileges.

The newly defined roles should now be visible in the **Role definition** form located at **System Administration | Setup | Security | Security Roles**. The following screenshot shows the **Security Roles** window:

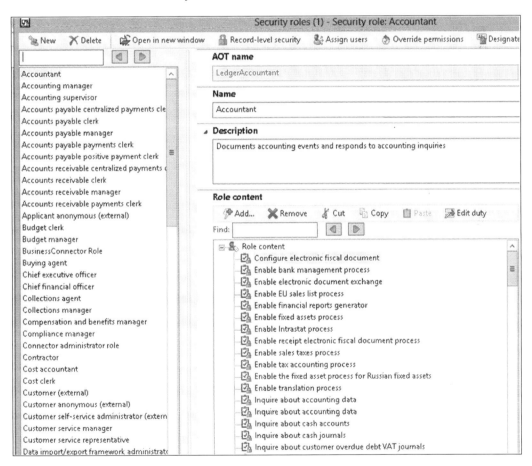

Summary

In this chapter, you learned how to create a parameter table that is used to hold default values and other settings for your module. You also learned how to create a number sequence to be used with an identifier field and how to take advantage of the security framework within AX in order to lock down the module.

This should enable you to create a module in AX that follows the standard principals used by the rest of the modules in AX.

In the next chapter, you will learn how to use .NET assemblies in X++ and look at some of the possibilities the common language runtime give us in AX.

We will also make some simple .NET programs that use the .NET Business Connector to execute functionality in AX and get results.

10
Working with .NET and AX

After going through this chapter, you should be able to use .NET classes as reference classes in AX using Common Language Runtime. This chapter will also guide you through the process of creating a .NET class in Visual Studio and using it in AX. You will also learn how to use the AX logic from external applications by using .NET Business Connector.

 All the examples in this chapter that are written in Visual Studio are in C# programming language.

It's also important to understand that .NET is one of the many ways by which external applications can invoke the AX functionality. Perhaps the best and most recommended approach is to use web services that are deployed using the **Application Integration Framework (AIF)**.

In this chapter, we will cover the following topics:

- Common Language Runtime
- .NET Business Connector

Common Language Runtime

So you have done some development before looking into X++, right? Maybe you're a .NET expert? If so, you must have heard of Common Language Runtime before. **Common Language Runtime (CLR)** is a component of .NET that enables objects written in different languages to communicate with each other. CLR can be used in AX to consume functionality from .NET classes and libraries, including the ones you have created in .NET. Technically, you cannot use AX objects in .NET by using CLR. However, to facilitate interoperability, Dynamics AX provides the managed code with managed classes (called proxies) that represent X++ artifacts.

Working with .NET and AX

One very nice feature in AX when dealing with integration between AX and .NET is the way AX can implicitly convert common data types. For the data types listed in the following table, you do not need to convert the data manually. For all other data types, you will have to convert them manually.

.NET CLR	X++
System.String	Str
System.Int32	Int
System.Int64	int64
System.Single	Real
System.Double	
System.Boolean	Boolean
System.DateTime	Date
System.Guid	Guid

> The enums are stored as integers in SQL and are treated as integers when they are implicitly converted between .NET and AX.

We prove this by executing the following example that shows the conversion between `System.String` and `str`:

```
static void ImplicitDataConversion(Args _args)
{
   System.String netString;
   str xppString;

   // Converting from System.String to str
   netString = "Hello Ax!";
   xppString = netString;
   info(xppString);

   // Converting from str to System.String
   xppString = "Hello .NET!";
   netString = xppString;
   info(netString);
}
```

This can be done for any of the other data types in the preceding table.

> Although X++ is case insensitive, when dealing with CLR, it is not. This means that writing System.string in the preceding example will result in a compile error, while writing Str instead of str will not result in any error.

The result will look like this:

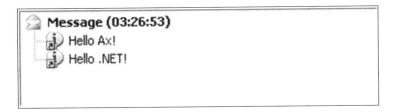

Adding a reference to a .NET class in AX

To be able to use .NET classes in AX, you have to make sure that the .NET assembly that you would like to use in AX exists under the **References** node in AOT. If you can't find the .NET assembly there, you have to add it by adding a reference to the .dll file that contains the assembly in the AOT under **References**.

Assembly existing in the Global Assembly Cache

Here are the steps to add a reference that exists in the Global Assembly Cache:

1. If the .dll file has been added to the Global Assembly Cache, you can right-click on the **Reference** node in AOT and select **Add Reference**.
2. In the form that opens (see the following screenshot), you should be able to find the desired .dll file. Add it by clicking on the **Select** button.

3. When you have selected the desired reference, click on the **OK** button. The assembly has now been added to AOT and can be used when writing X++ code.

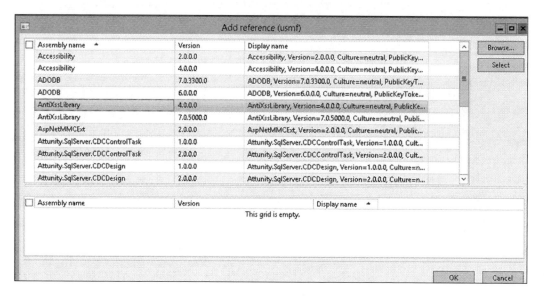

Assembly not in Global Assembly Cache

If the file does not exist in the Global Assembly Cache, you have to perform the following steps:

1. Click on the **Browse** button in the **Add Reference** form shown earlier and find the .dll file.
2. Then click on **Open**. If the .dll file is a valid assembly, it will be added to AOT under **References**.

Another option is to add the .dll file to the Global Assembly Cache first and select it as described in the *Assembly existing in the Global Assembly Cache* section.

Using a .NET class in X++

After adding a reference to the .NET assembly you want to use in AX, you can start writing the X++ code that will use the assembly.

When referencing classes in the assembly, you will need to write the whole namespace and class name. In my example, I am using an assembly that has been added to AOT in the sys layer. The example shows a nice feature that enables AX to send info messages to the **Windows Event Log**.

This can be particularly nice when you use the Windows Event Log to monitor AX batch jobs.

First, we create a new static method called `writeLogEntry` to the global class:

```
static void writeLogEntry(Exception e, str caller, int line, str text)
{
  // Use the standard .NET class EventLog from
  // the System.Diagnostics assembly
  System.Diagnostics.EventLog        eventLog;
  // Also use a .NET enumeration from the
  // System.Diagnostics assembly
  System.Diagnostics.EventLogEntryType    entryType;
  System.Exception    clrException;
  str stack;
  Batch batch;
  str batchInfo;

  try
  {
    // Create a new object of the EventLog class
    eventLog = new System.Diagnostics.EventLog();
    eventLog.set_Source("Dynamics Ax");
    // Set the enumeration value based on the Exception
    // type in Ax
    switch (e)
    {
      case Exception::Info :
      entryType =
      System.Diagnostics.EventLogEntryType::Information;
      break;
      case Exception::Warning :
      entryType = System.Diagnostics.EventLogEntryType::Warning;
      break;
      case Exception::Error :
      entryType = System.Diagnostics.EventLogEntryType::Error;
      break;
    }
    // If the current user is running a batch job
    // we can assume that the info message came
    // from the batch job and add additional information
    // to the event log
    while select batch
    where batch.Status == BatchStatus::Executing &&
    batch.ExecutedBy == curuserid()
```

```
    {
      batchInfo += batch.GroupId + ': '+
      classid2name(batch.ClassNumber) + '\n';
    }

    if (batchInfo)
    eventLog.WriteEntry(strfmt("Batch info from Ax: %1 \n\nThe
    message originated from :%2 \nat line %3 \n\nMessage: %4",
    batchInfo, caller, line, text), entryType);
    else
    eventLog.WriteEntry(strfmt("Info from Ax: \n\nThe message
    originated from :%1 \nat line %2 \n\nMessage: %3", caller,
    line, text), entryType);
  }
  catch(Exception::CLRError)
  {
    // If not able to write the info to the eventlog
    // print an error in the print window instead.
    print "EventWriter: Unable to write entry to the windows
    eventlog";
  }
}
```

Then, we add a line of code at the end of the add method in the Info class so that the end of the method will look like the following code:

```
        writeLogEntry(_exception, conpeek(packedAction,2) ,
conpeek(packedAction,3), _txt);

        this.addSysInfoAction(_helpUrl, actionClassId, packedAction);
    }

    return super(_exception, (buildprefix?getprefix():'')+_txt);
}
```

To test the feature, simply create a new job that can print something to infolog:

```
static void TestEventLog(Args _args)
{
  info("This is a test");
}
```

Chapter 10

You will now see an `infolog` message in AX and if you open the Windows Event Viewer, you should see this message in the list:

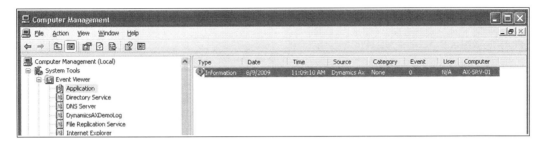

Double clicking on the event will bring up information about the origin of the information and the message that was printed to the `infolog` in AX.

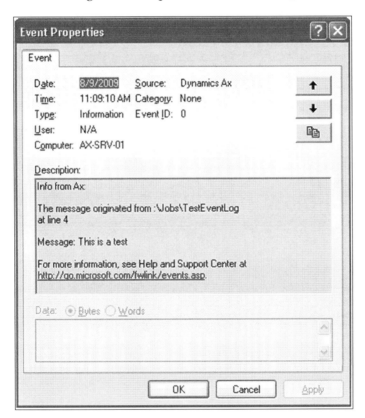

This example can be extended easily so that you can select to switch the feature on and off for different users and to select the level of messages to be sent to `EventLog`.

.NET Business Connector

If you have external applications that need to integrate directly to the AX logic, you can easily achieve this by using .NET Business Connector. A typical scenario can be that you would like your .NET application to execute some code in AX and have the result sent back to the .NET application.

In standard AX, .NET Business Connector is also used by the Enterprise Portal through **Web Parts** in Microsoft SharePoint so that they can expose the AX data and logic directly to the web. We will see how this is achieved in *Chapter 12*, *Enterprise Portal*. It is also used by the standard Application Integration Framework.

.NET Business Connector enables Visual Studio to create proxies (managed classes) that are generated behind the scene to represent the Microsoft Dynamics AX tables, enumerations, and classes. Proxies are also created at build time, hence they are in sync with the methods/fields available in AX (AOT).

Another big difference in the .NET Business Connector in AX 2012 as compared to the previous releases is its ability to maintain sessions. In the previous version of .NET Business Connector, the system invoked a new session before executing a process. In this release of the session, the system maintains sessions, thereby allowing developers to use .NET as a natural extension of the AX programming model.

Using .NET Business Connector in .NET classes

In the next sections of this chapter, we will look at some examples that show how we can use the methods in .NET Business Connector to call AX methods, insert data into AX tables, and read data from AX tables.

In the next example, we will do a simple transfer of some text from AX to our .NET application.

Creating a static method in AX in the global class

This means that you have to open AOT in AX and find the global class in AOT. Add the following method to a new class called `MyClass`:

```
static str AxHelloWorld()
{
  return "HelloWorld!";
}
```

Creating a new project in Visual Studio and adding it to AOT

In the following example, we will create a new console application project in Visual Studio and add the project to AOT. If you already have a project where you would like to use .NET Business Connector, you can skip this step.

1. Open Visual Studio and create a new project (as shown in the following screenshot). Once you press **OK**, you will have a new C# file called `Program.cs`.

2. Right-click on the **Project** node, select **Add** `<ProjectName>` **to AOT**, and then save and close Visual Studio.

3. Now, the .NET project is actually stored in AOT. To check, open AX and launch the development workspace under the **.NET Project**. You should be able to see the project.

4. The project is now fully stored in the AX and is part of the layer and model that is set as the default option for the developer. This implies that the .NET project can be moved from development to a test environment as a part of the normal code migration method (in previous versions, .NET references had to be moved separately from X++ artifacts).

5. The developer can now actually start editing the .NET project from AX. In AOT, right-click on the project and select **Edit**; this will launch Visual Studio.

Application Explorer

In Visual Studio, you should now be able to view the application explorer. If you cannot see it, then select **Application Explorer** (shown in the following screenshot) from the **View** menu.

Chapter 10

Application Explorer is effectively a representation of AX elements present in AOT.

Now, the developer can simply drag the required elements from **Application Explorer** and drop them into the project. This will allow the developer to use AX elements as though they were built in C#. When the developer adds the element, the system is effectively creating a proxy in the background.

You now need to drag-and-drop the class that was created earlier. Note that the developer does not have to worry about creating a (creating a connection) connection with AX; all that has been covered in the proxy.

In the project, we open the `Program.cs` file again and enter the following code:

```
using System;
namespace GetAxInfo1
{
  class Program
  {
    /// <summary>
    /// This class connects to Ax throught the
    /// .NET Business Connector and call the static method
    /// AxAXHelloWorld in Ax class.
    /// The result is sent to the console (command prompt).
    /// </summary>
    /// <param name="args"></param>
    static void Main(string[] args)
    {
    try
      {
        Console.WriteLine(MyClass.AxHelloWorld());
      }
      catch (Exception e)
      {
        Console.WriteLine(e.Message);
      }
      Console.ReadKey();
    }
  }
}
```

Working with .NET and AX

Execute the program by pressing *Ctrl + F5*. You should now get the following result in the console (command prompt) that will open:

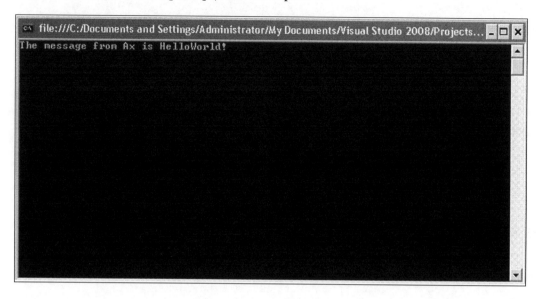

If you are getting a different result, it is possible that you haven't set up .NET Business Connector correctly. If so, please refer to the installation guide to set it up properly. Also, check the Windows Event Viewer to see if there are any error messages that can lead you in the right direction.

Inserting data in an AX table

As mentioned earlier in this chapter, you can use the methods in some of the marshalled classes in .NET Business Connector to manipulate data. However, the best practice is to avoid this and make AX handle all data selection and manipulation and make your .NET application call a method in AX that does the job and return the result to the .NET application again.

First, you should create a new project in Visual Studio in the same way we did earlier in this chapter. I'll call my new project `InsertAxRecord` and then add the project to AOT. Also, this time we will be using a different method to interface with AX.

In the `Program.cs` file (or whatever you call your file), you write the following code:

```
using System;
using Microsoft.Dynamics.BusinessConnectorNet;

namespace InsertAxRecord
{
```

```
class Program
{
  static void Main(string[] args)
  {
    try
    {
      // Create ax object and log on to Ax
      ax = new Axapta();
      ax.Logon(null, null, null, null);

      // Create a new AxaptaRecord object with
      // the name of the table as input parameter
      using (record = ax.CreateAxaptaRecord("CarTable"))
      {
        // Remember to clear the tablebuffer if
        // you are inserting inside a loop
        record.Clear();
        record.InitValue();
        // Set the fields in the table
        record.set_Field("CARID", "XXX1");
        record.set_Field("MODELYEAR", 1998);
        record.set_Field("CARBRAND", "FORD");
        record.set_Field("MODEL", "F1");
        record.set_Field("MILEAGE", 89378);
        // Insert the record
        record.Insert();
      }
      // End the ax session
      ax.Logoff();
    }
    catch (Exception e)
    {
      Console.WriteLine(e.Message);
    }
  }
}
```

Working with .NET and AX

If you open the table browser and look at the contents of CarTable in AX now (find the table in the AOT and press *Ctrl + O* to open the table browser), you should now see that the record has been added, as shown in the following screenshot:

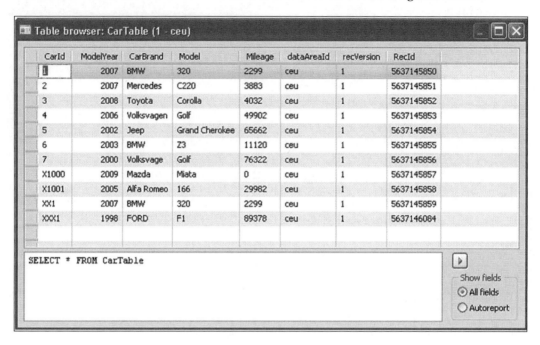

Reading data from an AX table

For our next example, we will observe methods that are the same as the ones used in the previous section *Inserting data in an AX table*, except now we are going to read data from the table instead of writing to the table.

You should start off by creating a new project and then add .NET Business Connector as a reference to the solution.

Then, enter the following code in the Program.cs file (or whatever you have named your program):

```
using System;
using Microsoft.Dynamics.BusinessConnectorNet;
namespace ReadAXRecord
{
  class Program
  {
    static void Main(string[] args)
    {
```

```
        AXapta AX;
        AxaptaRecord record;
        Object carId, carBrand, model, modelYear, mileage;
        try
        {
          // Create Ax object and log on to Ax
          ax = new Axapta();
          ax.Logon(null, null, null, null);

          // Create an AxaptaRecord object from the
          // table that will be used
          using (record = ax.CreateAxaptaRecord("CarTable"))
          {
            // Execute the statement entered as parameter
            record.ExecuteStmt("select * from %1 where %1.CarBrand
            like 'BMW'");

            // Loop through the result of the statement.
            while (record.Found)
            {
              // Set our local variables to be
              // equal to the fields in the table
              // for the current record.
              carId = record.get_Field("CARID");
              carBrand = record.get_Field("CARBRAND");
              model = record.get_Field("MODEL");
              modelYear = record.get_Field("MODELYEAR");
              mileage = record.get_Field("MILEAGE");

              // Write the result to the console
              Console.WriteLine(carId + "\t" + carBrand + "\t" +
model + "\t" + modelYear + "\t" + mileage);

              // Go to the next record in the result set
              record.Next();
            }

            // End the Ax session
            ax.Logoff();

            // Make sure the console stays up
            // until a key is pressed
            Console.ReadKey();
          }
```

```
            }
            catch (Exception e)
            {
                Console.WriteLine(e.Message);
            }
          }
        }
    }
```

Execute the program by pressing *Ctrl + F5* and take a look at the result. It should look something like this:

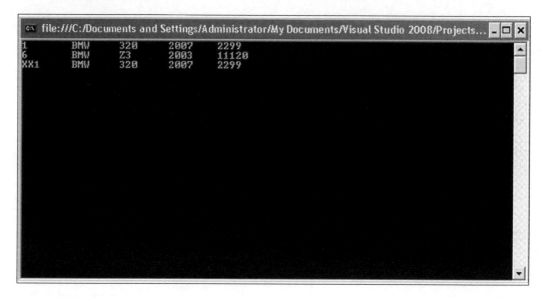

Exception classes

.NET Business Connector also consists of a number of exceptions that AX can raise. These exceptions are controlled by exception classes that will help you determine further actions if an exception occurs. In the examples shown earlier, I have only used the standard .NET exception class. However, if you would like to write solid code, you should consider using the exceptions from .NET Business Connector instead.

The information in the following table is taken from the Dynamics AX SDK and shows all of the exception classes that exist within .NET Business Connector:

Exception	Description
AlreadyLoggedOnException	This exception is thrown when log on to AX fails because the user session is already logged on.
AXBufferNotValidException	This exception is thrown when the AX buffer being referenced is not valid.
AXContainerNotValidException	This exception is thrown when the AX container being references is not valid.
AXObjectNotValidException	This exception is thrown when the AX object being referenced is not valid.
AXRecordNotValidException	This exception is thrown when the AX record being referenced is not valid.
BusinessConnectorException	This exception is thrown when an unexpected error has occurred with the .NET Business Connector.
ConnectionLostException	This exception is thrown when the connection to AOS is lost.
DebuggerStopException	This exception is thrown when the AX debugger has been stopped.
ExecutionErrorException	This exception is thrown when an unexpected system exception has occurred.
FatalErrorLoggedOffException	This exception is thrown when the AX session is closed due to an error.
InitializationFailedException	This exception is thrown when the .NET Business Connector fails to initialize.
InvalidReturnValueException	This exception is thrown when a return value is invalid.
LogonAsGuesNotSupportedException	This exception is thrown when trying to log on as a guest from a non-web (IIS) scenario, for example, directly through .NET Business Connector.
LogonFailedException	This exception is thrown during an AX log on failure.
LogonSystemChangedException	This exception is thrown when log on to AX fails due to log on parameters not matching those currently in use for the .NET Business Connector.

Exception	Description
LogonUserLockedOutException	This exception is thrown when the user attempting a log on is locked out due to exceeding the maximum number of log on attempts.
MethodUnknownException	This exception is thrown when the method being referenced is not known by the system.
NoIISRightsException	This exception is thrown when log on to AX fails because the user has not been granted the proper IIS rights.
NoSecurityKeyException	This exception is thrown when a requested operation fails because the required security key does not exist.
NotLoggedOnException	This exception is thrown then a requested operation cannot be performed because the user is not logged on.
PermissionDeniedException	This exception is thrown when permission is denied to execute an operation.
ServerCommunicationErrorException	This exception is thrown when communication between the client computer and the server fails.
ServerOutOfReachException	This exception is thrown when communication with the server could not be established.
ServerOutOfResourcesException	This exception is thrown when the server terminates the session due to the server not having enough free resources.
ServerUnavailableException	This exception is thrown when the server is unavailable. AX will attempt to connect to other servers listed in the client configuration.
SessionTerminatedException	This exception is thrown when the server terminates the session.
UnknownClassHandleException	This exception is thrown when the class being referenced does not exist.
UnknownRecordException	This exception is thrown when the record being referenced does not exist.

Exception	Description
UnknownTextException	This exception is thrown when an unknown text exception has occurred.
UnknownXPPClassException	This exception is thrown when an unknown X++ exception has occurred.
XppException	This exception is thrown when an X++ exception has occurred.

Summary

Now, you should now be able to use .NET classes in AX and use AX code in .NET classes.

You also learned that in .NET classes in AX, you have to add the reference to the .NET class first and then use the code in the .NET class from X++ code. AX makes this possible by using a bridge to CLR.

You learned that to use the AX functionality in your .NET classes, you have to add the elements to use from the application explorer. Then, you have to use the proxy classes that .NET Business Connector created in your .NET code in order to call class methods, manipulate data, or read data from AX.

In the next chapter, you will learn how to create a web service that exposes AX logic and how to publish it to **Internet Information Services** (**IIS**). We will also discuss how we can make AX consume a web service.

11
Web Services

A **web service** is a way of integrating systems directly over a network. We have learnt to create a file and store it on a disk so that another application can read it; this is all fine, but what if the other application is in a different network somewhere else in the world, without any access to the disk area where the file is stored? We could solve this issue by sending the files using FTP. In some cases though, we would perhaps ask to get data instead of sending data or retrieving the data in certain intervals. As long as the size of the data being transferred is limited, using web services will be a good alternative.

You should know the basics of a web service before reading this chapter and some good starting points are listed here:

- `http://www.w3schools.com/webservices/default.asp`
- `http://www.w3.org/TR/ws-arch/`

We will cover the following topics in this chapter:

- Creating a web service that exposes the AX logic
- Publishing a web service to IIS
- Consuming a web service from AX

> Web services created in this chapter should be used for consumption by external applications that are within the same domain as the AX environment. If the web services are to be consumed by an application that is outside the AX domain, then it is recommended to use **Microsoft Azure** and **AX-Azure connector**. Azure connector is not within the scope of our discussion though.

Exposing AX logic using web services

Before you start learning how to expose AX logic by using a web service, let's see how the AX logic is triggered by the external application.

We would like to enable an external application (it can also be internal) to execute a method in a web service and have that web service start a method in AX. The result is sent back through the same flow as the methods were triggered.

The following conceptual diagram shows that the request is sent from an external application through the Internet to a web service that runs on a Microsoft Internet Information Services web server:

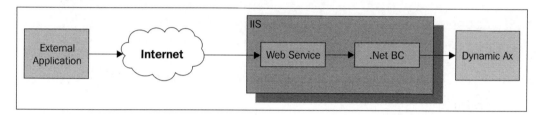

The web service uses .NET Business Connector to create a session in AX and to execute a method in AX. When the result is returned from AX, it is passed back to the calling application the same way the request came.

Creating a web service that exposes the AX logic

In our example, we will create a web service in .NET that will use .NET Business Connector to log on to AX and to execute business logic within AX.

Our web service will contain two methods, one that returns the physical on-hand quantity of one specific item. The other method returns the on-order quantity (what we expect to receive):

1. First, we have to open Visual Studio and create a new project.
2. Select **Web** under **Visual C#** in the **Project types** tree and select **ASP.NET Web Service Application** under **Visual Studio installed templates**. The following screenshot shows the creation of a new project:

Chapter 11

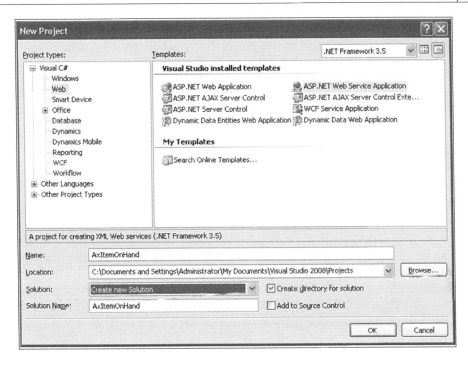

3. Give the project a name and click on **OK**.
4. Then, add a reference to .NET Business Connector. This step was explained in the *Adding a reference to a .NET class in AX* section in *Chapter 10, Working with .NET and AX*.
5. When this is done, we can continue to write our web service.
6. Now, we need to add the reference to .NET Business Connector by adding it to the **using** list.
7. We then add a new private method that will log on to AX and create a new web user session and a private method that we use to log off the web user session from AX.
8. Then, we have to create the two methods that we would like to expose in our web service. We create one method called `AvailableNow` and another one called `AvailableInclOrdered`. They are very similar, except that they call two different methods in the AX class `InventOnHand`.
9. We also create two private methods that are used to log on to AX and log off from AX.

[293]

The preceding steps are implemented in the following code example:

```
using System;
using System.Collections.Generic;
using System.Linq;
using System.Web;
using System.Web.Services;
using Microsoft.Dynamics.BusinessConnectorNet;

namespace AxItemOnHand
{
  /// <summary>
  /// This web service will return OnHand information regarding a
  given item
  /// </summary>

  // Autogenerated code -->
  [WebService(Namespace = "http://tempuri.org/")]
  [WebServiceBinding(ConformsTo = WsiProfiles.BasicProfile1_1)]
  [System.ComponentModel.ToolboxItem(false)]
  // To allow this Web Service to be called from script, using
  ASP.NET AJAX, uncomment the following line.
  // [System.Web.Script.Services.ScriptService]
  // Autogenerated code <--

  public class ItemOnHand : System.Web.Services.WebService
  {
    Axapta   ax;
    string output;

    [WebMethod]
    public string AvailableNow(string itemId)
    {
      AxaptaObject    inventOnHand;
      // Logon to Ax
      this.Logon();
      // Create a new AxaptaObject of the InventOnHand class
      // by executing the static method newItemId
      inventOnHand =
      (AxaptaObject)ax.CallStaticClassMethod("InventOnHand",
      "newItemId", itemId);
      // Call the method availPhysical to get the qty
      // and convert it to a string
      output = inventOnHand.Call("availPhysical").ToString();
      // Release the object to the garbage collection
```

```
        inventOnHand.Dispose();
        // Logoff to release the webuser session in Ax
        this.Logoff();
        // Return the output
        return output;
    }
    [WebMethod]
    public string AvailableInclOrdered(string itemId)
    {
        AxaptaObject inventOnHand;
        this.Logon();
        inventOnHand =
        (AxaptaObject)ax.CallStaticClassMethod("InventOnHand",
        "newItemId", itemId);
        output = inventOnHand.Call("availOrdered").ToString();
        inventOnHand.Dispose();
        this.Logoff();
        return output;
    }
    private void Logon()
    {
        try
        {
            ax = new Ax.Logon("ceu", "", "", "");
        }
        catch(Exception e)
        {
            output = e.Message;
        }
    }
    private void Logoff()
    {
        try
        {
            ax.Logoff();
        }
        catch (Exception e)
        {
            output = e.Message;
        }
    }
}
```

Web Services

The **On-hand** form shown in the following screenshot shows us what we expect to see when we execute our web methods. The `AvailableNow` method will return the available physical value and the `AvailableInclOrdered` method will add the ordered value in total to the available physical.

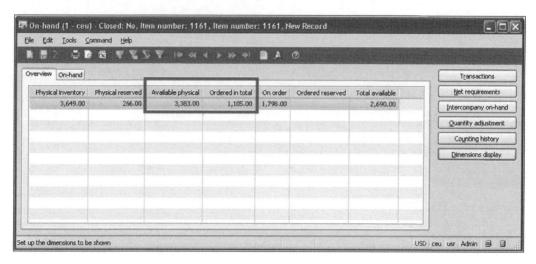

To test the web service, simply press *F5* in Visual Studio and you should get a web page that looks like the following screenshot:

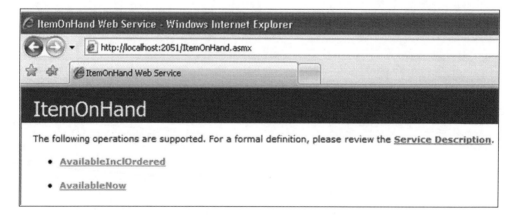

Now, select the `AvailableNow` method and type an item number as shown:

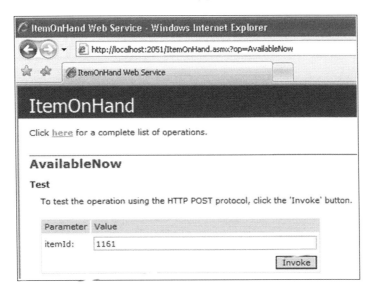

When you click on **Invoke**, you are executing the web method. A new browser window will open, displaying the following result:

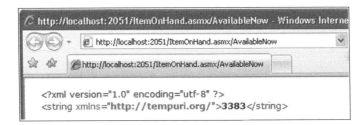

By executing the `AvailableInclOrdered` and using the same `itemId` class, we get the following result:

The result is correct, as *3383 + 1105 = 4488*.

Web Services

Publishing a web service to IIS

Now that our web service is finished, we have to publish it to a web server so that other applications will be able to use it.

As we live in a Microsoft world, the web server we use is IIS, which is short for Internet Information Services. This means that you have to make sure that the server where the web service should be published to has the IIS module installed. The server also needs .NET Business Connector and all its prerequisites installed.

1. To open IIS, press the Windows Start button and go to **Administrative Tools | Internet Information Services (IIS) Manager**.

2. In the tree to the left, expand the `server` node and then click on the **Application Pools** node. Right-click on the **Applications Pools** node and select **Application Pool** under **New**.

3. Enter a name for the **Application pool** that describes the applications that will be used by the pool.

4. Now that the application pool has been created, we have to set the identity of the pool to the user that has been set up as .NET Business Connector Proxy. You can find or set this user in the following form in AX:

Chapter 11

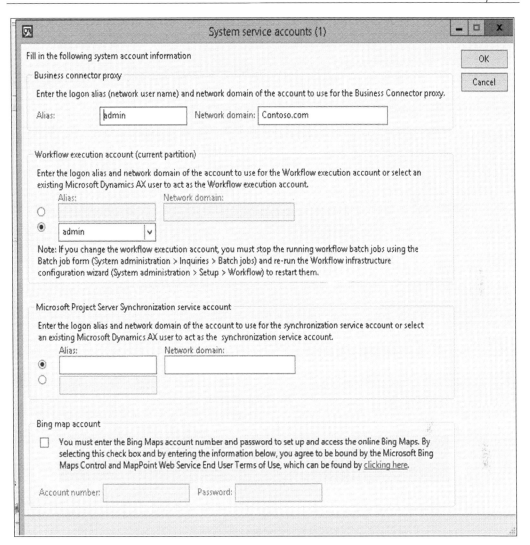

5. To get to the form, you need to go to the main menu and then navigate to **Administration | Setup | Security | System service accounts**. As we can see from the preceding screenshot, the user we have to set up for our application pool is `contoso.com\administrator`.

Web Services

6. Go back to the IIS management tool and right-click on the **Application pool** you just created and select **Properties**. In the form that opens, go to the **Identity** tab page and change to a configurable user and enter the **User name** and **Password** as shown here and click on **OK**:

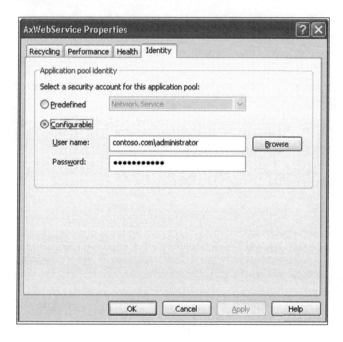

7. After confirming the password in the popup, click on the **OK** button.
8. Then, create a website that uses this **Application pool**. This is done by right-clicking on the **Web Sites** node in the tree in the IIS management tool and selecting **Web Site** under **New**.
9. A wizard comes up and you are prompted for a name of the website and then prompted to enter an IP address, port number, and a host header for the website. In this example, we enter the name and just select port 200, since it's a port that is not in use right now, and then click on **Next**.
10. Now, you will be prompted for the path where the website resides; since we haven't published the web service yet, we create a new folder from Windows Explorer and use this folder in the wizard prompt.

11. Typically, this folder will be under `c:\Inetpub\wwwroot`, so let's create the folder `AXWebService` there.

12. When we now click on **Next**, we have to set the Web Site access permissions. In order to make the web service work, we have to allow scripts (ASP) to run.

13. After the site has been created, you need to set the application pool for the site. This is done by right-clicking on the Web Site and selecting **Properties**. In the window that opens, go to the **Home Directory** tab and select the Application pool.

14. Now that the website is ready, you can go back to the web services project in Visual Studio and select **Build | Publish <your project name>**.

Web Services

15. In the window that opens, you have to specify the website that you have created. This can be done either by entering the URL if you know where it is, or you can press the button with the three dots, as shown in the following screenshot:

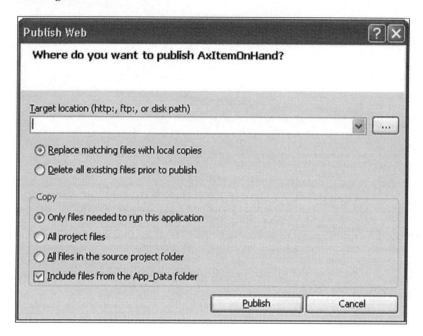

16. A new window will then come up where you can select the folder or website where you want to publish the web service. Select **Local IIS** in the left part of the window if your web server is on the same computer as the Visual Studio installation. Then, select the Web Site in the right part of the window and click on the **Open** button. The following screenshot shows how to open a website:

Chapter 11

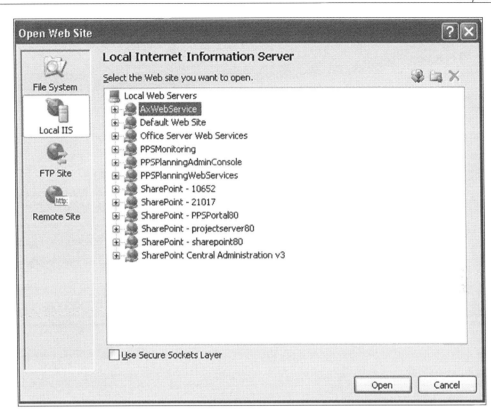

17. Now, you will see that the **Target Location** is filled out in the previous form and you can click on the **Publish** button.

When the status field in Visual Studio (lower-left corner) shows the publish activity has succeeded, you can test that the web service is found at the address by typing the full URL in a web browser and pressing the *Enter* key.

In this example, the full URL is `http://localhost:200/ItemOnHand.asmx` and it will present the following web page:

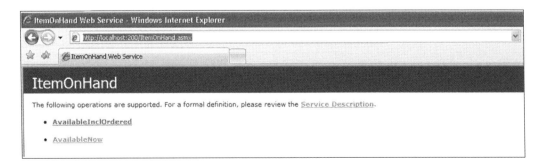

Accessing logic in an external web service

Now that we have seen how we can make other applications trigger the AX logic by exposing the AX logic to web services, we will turn the other way around and see how we can make AX use web services that can expose logic from external applications.

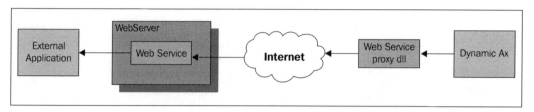

In the preceding diagram, we see that AX uses a web service proxy that is created specifically for the web service that it is about to call. The web service proxy lets AX know everything it needs to know in order to call the web service through the Internet. The web service, in turn, will return a result from the external application and pass it back to AX.

A lot of the examples on the web will show you how you can ask a web service to convert from one currency to another, checking if an email address is valid and some others that most likely is less useful to your AX customers.

Sometimes, however, you will find that your AX customers have several other applications that AX should integrate with to get additional information. Maybe they could even integrate with their vendors to get updated product information automatically from their vendors' applications. If these applications can have web services that trigger actions within these applications, you can consume these web services in AX so that AX can ask for data or trigger some event in the other application.

To show how to achieve this, we will continue to use the example shown earlier. Our web service will then return a result from AX, but it could have been a result returned from any other application that supports web services as well.

Creating a service reference

The first thing we need to do is add a service reference to our web service. We perform this action in Visual Studio, and then add the new project to the AOT. The steps are as follows:

1. To do this, simply open the Visual Studio and create new C# class library project. Call the project `WS.ItemOnHand`.

Chapter 11

2. Under **Solution Explorer**, right-click on the project and select **Add Service Reference**.
3. Type in the **WSDL** and change namespace to **OnHand.**
4. Right-click on the project and select **Add to AOT**.
5. Make changes in the project properties so both **Deploy to client** & **Deploy to Server** options are set to **Yes**.

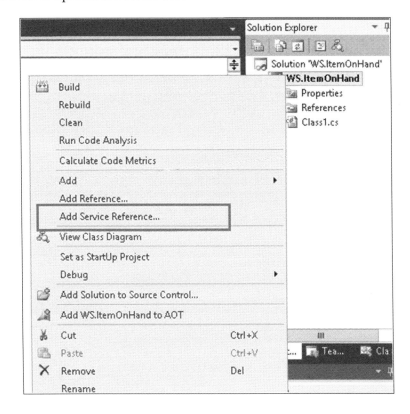

The WDSL URL is the location where the service description of the web service resides.

The .NET code namespace is the namespace that the proxy class will have. The proxy .dll file will also be put in a directory corresponding with .NET namespace.

The reference name is the name of the reference to the proxy that we will use in AX. It will typically be the same as .NET code namespace to have the same naming in the proxy class and in AX.

The service description is just a simple description of the service so that other people will easily recognize what this service is used for in AX.

Web Services

After filling out the required information in the box, click on **OK**. After a little while, you should see an infolog with information regarding the creation of the proxy class. There should be no errors or warnings in the infolog.

Creating a class that consumes the web service

We can now create a class that uses the web service:

1. Create a new class and call it `OnHand`. Add a new method that looks like this:

   ```
   public static server str getOnHand(str itemId)
   {
     // Reference the class in the WS.ItemOnHand namespace
     // Remember that the namespace and its classes are case
     sensitive
     WS.ItemOnHand.OnHand.ItemOnHandSoapClient soapClient;
     str ret;

     try
     {
        // Make sure that we get permission to use the clr
   interop
        new InteropPermission(InteropKind::ClrInterop).assert();

        // Create a new object of the ItemOnHandSoapClient
        class
        // The endpoint configuration must be equal to the
        // wsdl:portType name value in the WSDL file
        soapClient = new
        WS.ItemOnHand.ItemOnHandSoapClient('ItemOnHandSoap');
        // Execute one of the method in the web service
        ret = soapClient.AvailableNow(itemId);
        // Revert the clr interop access when we are done
        // using it.
        CodeAccessPermission::revertAssert();
     }
     catch (Exception::CLRError)
     {
        throw error(AifUtil::getClrErrorMessage());
     }
     return ret;
   }
   ```

Chapter 11

 A method that executes an object that requires `ClrInteropPermission` must be executed on the server by a static method.

2. We also will create a `main` method as a starting point of our class:

```
static void main(Args args)
{
    str itemId;

    itemId = "1161";
    info (strfmt("On-hand for item %1: %2", itemId,
    OnHand::getOnHand(itemId)));
}
```

If we execute the previous class now, we get the same result as we did when we were testing the web service directly from the web browser earlier in this chapter:

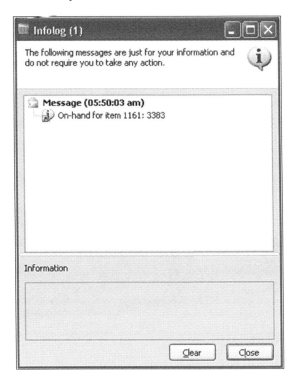

Summary

In this chapter, you learned how to let other applications access AX functionality by creating web services that expose the AX logic. You should also be able to create a new website in IIS and to publish web services to a website in IIS.

You also saw how we can add a service reference in AX in order for AX to consume web services.

The next chapter will guide you through the process of creating AX User Controls that expose AX data to the Enterprise Portal. You will also learn how to create a wizard that enables users to enter new records into an AX table.

12
Enterprise Portal

In this chapter, you will learn how to create the `.aspx` pages in **Microsoft SharePoint** based on the templates that come with the **Enterprise Portal**. You will also learn how to create Dynamics AX user controls that will expose data from AX to the Enterprise Portal.

Dynamics 2012 has taken a huge step with regards to the development of web content. In previous versions of AX, you could publish web content using Web Parts defined in AX. These Web Parts are now being phased out and replaced with a .NET-based Enterprise Portal framework in AX.

You will learn the basics so that you can explore the wonderful world of web development for Dynamics AX on your own. This chapter might not make you an expert in Enterprise Portal development, but it will give you a sense of how to work with it and how the different elements are tied together.

To learn more about Enterprise Portal development, please refer to the Dynamics AX 2012 SDK documentation here: `http://msdn.microsoft.com/en-us/library/aa493463%28v=ax.10%29.aspx`

In this chapter, we will go through the following topics:

- Creating a dataset containing the `RentalTable` table
- Creating a webpage that will display a grid consisting of the records from the `RentalTable` table
- Creating a wizard/tunnel that is used to create a new record in the `RentalTable` table
- Creating a toolbar that contains a menu item that is used to start the wizard
- Converting existing `WebForms` defined in AOT to .NET user controls

Enterprise Portal

Creating a dataset

First of all, let's see how we can create datasets in AX that will be used by .NET controls later on.

The datasets defined in AOT are used by the `AxDatasource` control in ASP.NET to fetch data from AX and send it back again when data is updated in a data-binding-enabled ASP.NET control.

A dataset can be considered as a replacement of the data source node in the web forms and web reports. Since web forms and web reports will eventually be removed from AX, we now need another way of connecting the fields in our .NET forms to fields in AX tables:

1. To create a dataset, open **AOT** and browse to **Data Sets**, right-click on it and select **New Data Set**.
2. Right-click on the new dataset and select **Properties** to see the **Properties** window. Then, change the name to `RentalDataSet`.
3. Go to the **Data Sources** node under **RentalDataset** and add a new data source by right-clicking on the **Data Sources** node and selecting **New Data Source**. Open the **Properties** window for the new data source and change the table and name property to **RentalTable**.

The dataset should now look like this:

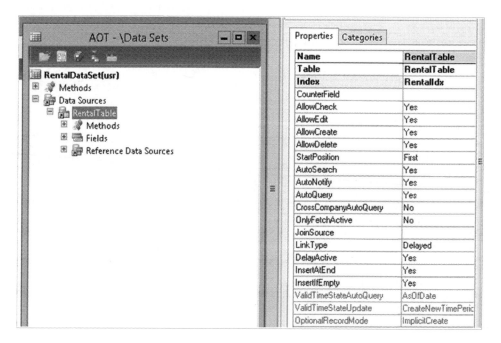

Creating a new Visual Studio project

Before you start creating a Visual Studio project, make sure that the Enterprise Portal development tools are installed on the same computer as the one installed with Visual Studio. Here are the steps to create a new Visual Studio project:

1. To create a new project in Visual Studio, open Visual Studio and go to **File | New | Web site**.
2. In the form that opens, select **Dynamics Data Web Site**, change the name, and click on the **OK** button.

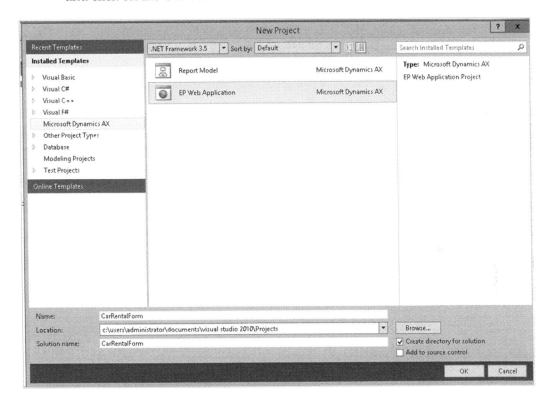

You are now good to go with a new project in Visual Studio. You will use this project for the rest of the examples in this chapter.

Enterprise Portal

Creating a grid

Follow these steps to create a grid control in ASP.NET that retrieves data:

1. Right-click on the website in the **Solution Explorer** in Visual Studio and select **Add New Item**, as shown in the following screenshot:

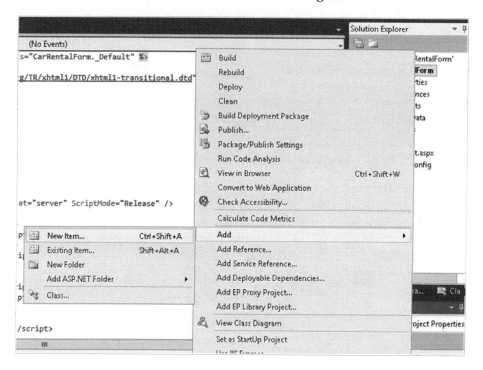

2. Select **EP User Control** and give it an appropriate name, as shown in the following screenshot:

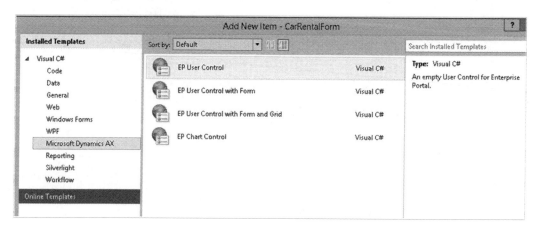

Chapter 12

3. Now that the control has been created, right-click on it in **Solution Explorer** and select **Add CarRentalForm to AOT**.

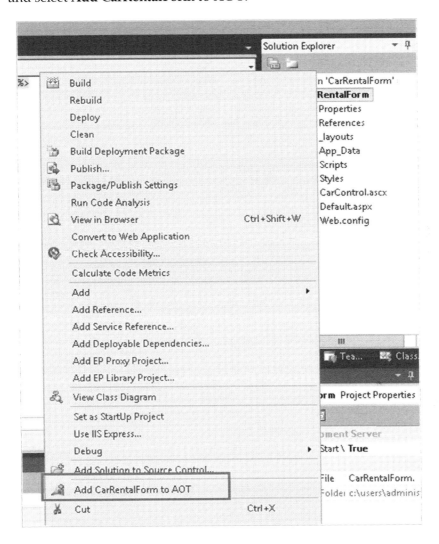

Enterprise Portal

4. When the previous step is done, the control is saved in AOT at **Visual Studio Projects | Web Application Projects**.

5. Click on **Dynamics AX** control and add an **AxDataSource** control to the user control by dragging it into the **Design** view, as shown in the following screenshot:

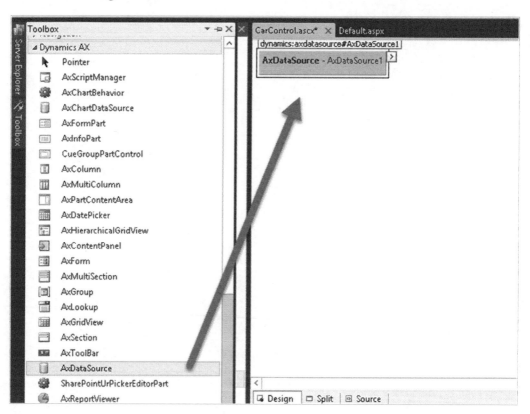

Chapter 12

The `AxDataSource` control extends `DataSourceControl` in ASP.NET to provide a declarative and data-store-independent way to read and write data in AX. Datasets that are created in AOT are exposed to ASP.NET through the `AxDataSource` control. The steps are as follows:

1. Click on the arrow to the right of the **AxDataSource** control in the **Design** view and change the **DataSet Name** property to be equal to the dataset you just created in AX, as shown in the following screenshot:

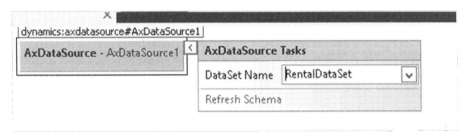

2. You can also do this by right-clicking on **Control** and selecting **Properties** to open the **Properties** window. Here, you can also change the rest of the parameters.

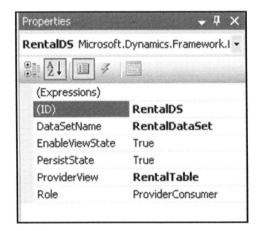

3. Now, go to **Toolbox** and drag the **AxGrid** control onto the design view.
4. Then, click on the arrow to the right of the control and select **Properties**.
5. Then, set the data source to be the data source that you have just created.

[315]

6. Also, if you would like the users to be able to edit and/or delete records from the grid, you have to check the **Enable Editing** or **Enable Deleting** checkboxes, respectively.

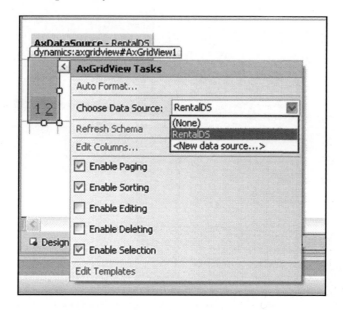

 You cannot insert records from a grid by using the `AxGrid` control. Instead, you can add an action in a toolbox that opens a tunnel/wizard that allows the user to create a new record.

7. Then, click on the **Edit Columns** link to select the columns from the data source that you want to use in the grid.

Chapter 12

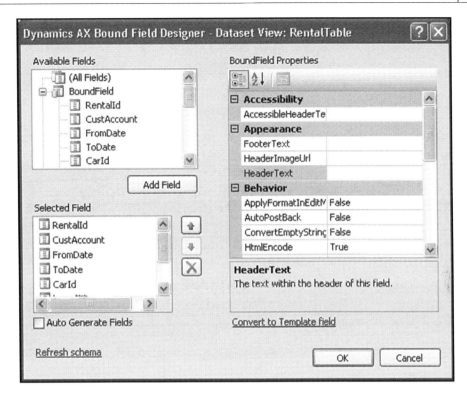

8. Available display and edit methods are also shown in the list of fields. Select all the fields in the list, except `dataAreaId`, `TableId`, and `RecId`. Then, click on the **OK** button.

The grid is now ready to be used by a Web Part page.

Creating a new Web Part page

To create a Web Part page, make sure you have installed and set up Enterprise Portal:

1. Start by opening the Enterprise Portal in a web browser, click on the **Site Actions** button in the upper-left corner, and then click on **More Options** button.

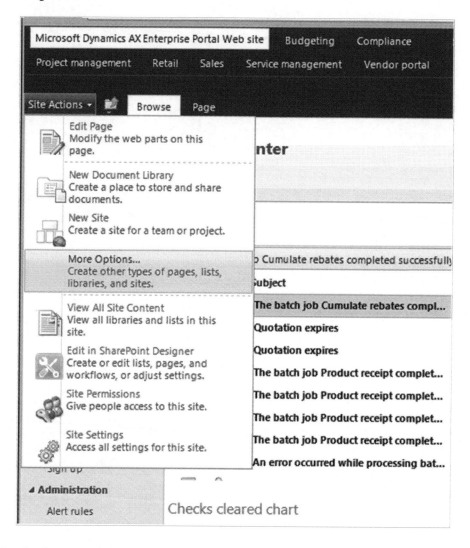

2. In the page that opens, click on the **Page** section on the left-hand side, and then click on the client **Web Part Page**, as shown in the following screenshot:

Chapter 12

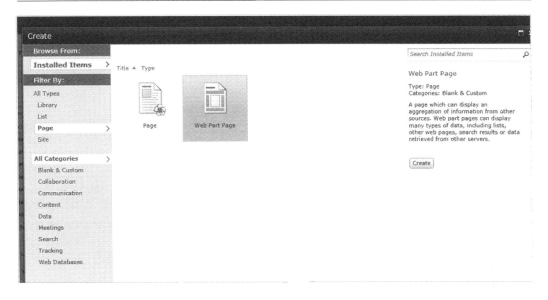

3. Then, you will be prompted to supply the name of the page, which template you would like to use, and in which document library you would like the page to be stored in.
4. Name the page `CarRental` and select the template called **Header, Left Column, Body** and store the page in the Enterprise Portal document library.

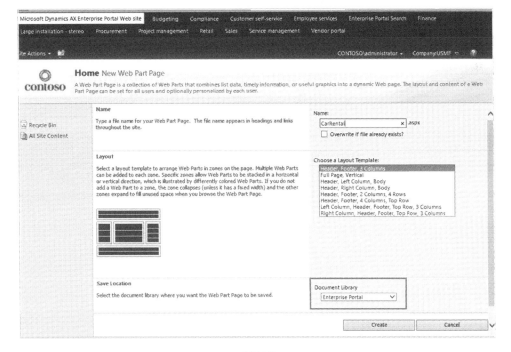

Enterprise Portal

5. The template page will now open in edit mode where you can add Web Parts. Add a new Web Part by clicking on the **Add a Web Part** button under the body section.

6. From the window that opens, find and select **Dynamics User Control Web Part** and click on the **Add** button.

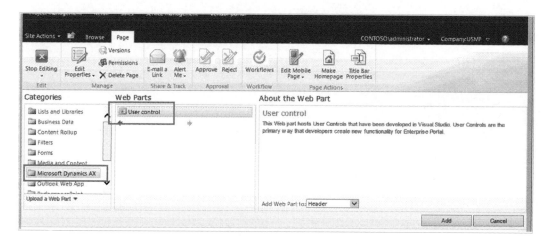

7. When you are back in edit mode, click on the **Edit** button in the new Web Part and select **Modify Shared Web Part**.

8. In the property window, you will find the user control you created in the list of managed content items, as shown in the following screenshot:

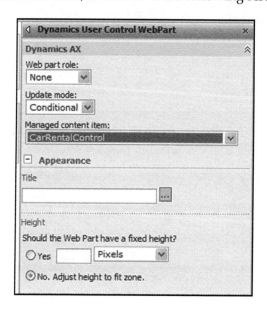

9. After selecting the created user control scroll down to the bottom and click on the **OK** button. In the edit mode, you can click on the link **Exit Edit mode** in the top-right corner to see what the page looks like.

The Web Part page should now look like this:

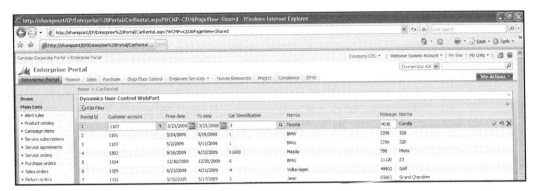

You have created a SharePoint page with a grid that lists records from the `RentalTable` tablewhere users can edit and delete records.

Now, we need to enable the users to enter new records as well. From a user's point of view, I would say that I should have been able to do this directly from the grid, but since that won't work, we can create a tunnel (also known as a wizard) to achieve this.

Creating a tunnel/wizard

Follow these steps to create a tunnel that enable the users to create a new record in `RentalTable` table:

1. Open the Visual Studio project that you worked with in the previous user control example and create a new Dynamics AX user control like you did with the grid. Name this user control `CarRentalCreateTunnel` and click on **OK** in the **Add New Item** form.

2. Now, remember to add the new control to AOT by right-clicking on it and selecting **Add to AOT**.

3. Open the user control in **Design** view and add an **AxDataSource** in the same way we did with the previous user control example. This data source should also point to `RentalDataSet`.

4. Now, drag an **AxForm** element from **Toolbox** and drop it onto the **Design** view.

[321]

5. Make sure that the properties for the form looks like this:

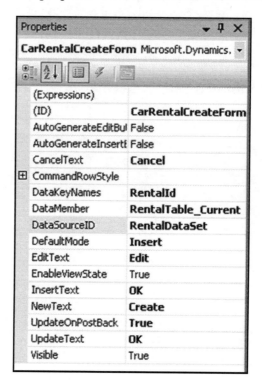

6. The next thing you need to do is to drag a wizard control from the toolbox and drop it onto **AxForm** in the **Design** view. The wizard is not a Dynamics AX component, but can be found under **Standard ASP controls** in the **Toolbox**.

7. Then, you have to set some of the properties of the wizard. Start by defining the steps that the wizard should consist of. In our example, we create three steps:
    - Select the customer.
    - Select the car to be rented.
    - Select the *from* date and *to* date and click on the **Finish** button.
    - To define these steps, click the arrow to the right of the control and bring up the **Wizard Tasks** window as seen in the following screenshot:

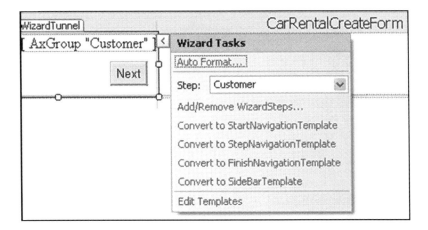

8. Now click on the **Add/Remove WizardSteps** link to bring up the following **WizardStep Collection Editor** window:

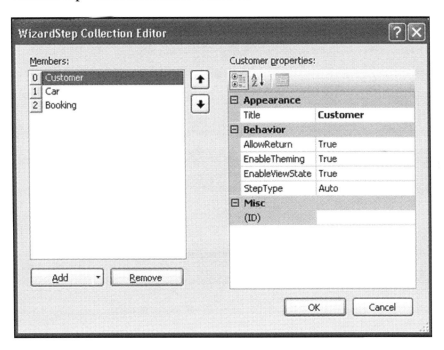

9. Just click on **Add** to add the steps and give each step a title. Click on **OK** when you are done to be taken back to the **Design** view.

Enterprise Portal

10. Now, click on the **Source** button at the bottom of the edit window (next to **Design** and **Split**) to see the source code of the control. The source code is an XML file that you now have to modify as shown here:

```xml
<asp:Wizard ID="WizardTunnel" runat="server" ActiveStepIndex =
"0"onfinishbuttonclick =
"WizardTunnel_FinishButtonClick">
<WizardSteps>
<asp:WizardStep runat="server" title="Customer">
<dynamics:AxGroup ID="Customer" runat="server"
FormID="CarRentalCreateForm">
<Fields>
<dynamics:AxBoundField DataField="CustAccount"
DataSet="RentalDataSet" DataSetView="RentalTable"
AutoPostBack="true" />
</Fields>
</dynamics:AxGroup>
</asp:WizardStep>
<asp:WizardStep runat="server" title="Car">
<dynamics:AxGroup ID="Car" runat="server"
FormID="CarRentalCreateForm">
<Fields>
<dynamics:AxBoundField DataField="CarId"
DataSet="RentalDataSet" DataSetView="RentalTable"
AutoPostBack="true" />
</Fields>
</dynamics:AxGroup>
</asp:WizardStep>
<asp:WizardStep runat="server" Title="Booking">
<dynamics:AxGroup ID="Booking" runat="server"
FormID="CarRentalCreateForm">
<Fields>
<dynamics:AxBoundField DataField="FromDate"
DataSet="RentalDataSet" DataSetView="RentalTable"
AutoPostBack="true" />
<dynamics:AxBoundField DataField="ToDate"
DataSet="RentalDataSet" DataSetView="RentalTable"
AutoPostBack="true" />
</Fields>
</dynamics:AxGroup>
</asp:WizardStep>
</WizardSteps>
</asp:Wizard>
```

In this XML file, we add groups of fields from the data source into each step of the wizard. As you can see from the first step here, the file will have a `dynamics:AxGroup` that consists of a fields node that contains the actual bound fields. In this case, it's the **CustAccount** field from the `RentalTable DataSetView` in the `RentalDataSet`. Here is the XML tag:

```
<dynamics:AxBoundField DataField="CustAccount"
DataSet="RentalDataSet" DataSetView="RentalTable"
AutoPostBack="true" />
```

Also, notice that I have added a reference to an event called `onFinishButtonClick`. I want to execute the `WizardTunnel_FinishButtonClick` method when this event occurs. To see the code of this event, open the code behind file by double-clicking on the wizard element in the **Design** view. As we have created the project as a C# project, the code behind is a `.cs` file.

When the user clicks on the **Finish** button, we want the record to be saved and the user to be redirected to the grid form again.

This is achieved by first getting a handle to the data source view and saving the content of that view by executing the `EndEdit` trigger.

The redirect is performed by creating a new object of the `AxUrlMenuItem` element that points to the URL menu item in AX that opens the desired SharePoint page; in our case, the `CarRentalList` URL menu item. Then, we simply use the `Response` class to redirect to the URL of that menu item. These steps are shown in the following code:

```
using System;
using System.Collections;
using System.Web;
using System.Web.Security;
using System.Web.UI;
using System.Web.UI.WebControls;
using System.Web.UI.WebControls.WebParts;
using System.Web.UI.HtmlControls;
using Microsoft.Dynamics.Framework.Portal.UI.WebControls;
using Microsoft.Dynamics.Framework.Portal.UI.WebControls.WebParts;

public partial class CarRentalCreateTunnell : System.Web.
UI.UserControl
{
    protected void Page_Load(object sender, EventArgs e)
    {
    ...
    }
```

Enterprise Portal

```
   protected void WizardTunnel_FinishButtonClick(object sender,
   WizardNavigationEventArgs e)
   {
      AxDataSourceView rentalTableView =
this.RentalDataSet.GetDataSourceView("RentalTable");

      if (rentalTableView != null)
      rentalTableView.EndEdit();

      AxUrlMenuItem carRentalsMenuItem = new
      AxUrlMenuItem("CarRentalList");
      Response.Redirect(carRentalsMenuItem.Url.ToString());
   }
}
```

Now, you can create a new SharePoint page like you did in the previous section of this chapter. Name the new page `CarRentalCreateTunnel` and use the same template as last time, and store this page in the Enterprise Portal document library.

Then, add the `CarRentalCreateTunnel` user control to this page and exit the edit mode to see what the page looks like. The first wizard page should look something like this:

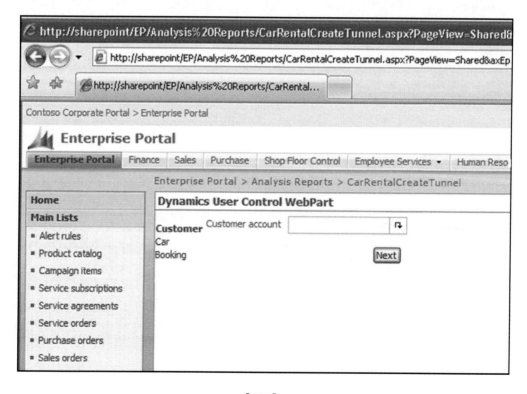

Note that the fields are already connected to the correct lookup forms so that you can easily find what you are looking for.

After filling in the **Customer account** field, click on the **Next** button and fill in all the information in all of the steps. Finally, click on the **Finish** button. A new record will be created in the `RentalTable` table and you will be directed to the `CarRental.aspx` page again, as specified by the `Response.Redirect` in the `FinishButtonClick` event.

Summary

In this chapter, you learned how to create Dynamics user controls from Visual Studio, make them use the datasets created in AOT to retrieve data and, put that data into a grid that is displayed to the users. You also learned how to create a wizard that enables the users to create new records and how to create a toolbar that consists of elements defined in a web menu in AX.

You should now be able to *webify* simple forms in AX and, hopefully, you have gained enough knowledge to start experimenting with the other AX elements that are available in Visual Studio for you to tinker with.

You have also learned how to convert `WebForms` to .NET user controls, a feature that can be very nice to use if you are converting an AX solution from an old version of AX to AX 2012.

A
Links

Throughout this book, there are references to websites and help files in AX. This section will structure these links so that it easier for you to find them again later. Other useful links are also added in this appendix.

All of the links can be imported into your browser by downloading a file from the book page at http://www.packtpub.com/support.

Websites

The tables given in the following sections contain links to some websites that you will become very familiar with after a while and others that are perhaps more like references if you want to delve deeper into the elements explained. The table is divided into the following parts:

- Official Microsoft websites
- Blogs
- Other relevant websites

Official Microsoft websites

The following links point to official Microsoft websites:

Description	URL
Microsoft Dynamics AX community	https://community.dynamics.com/ax/home.aspx
Microsoft Dynamics AX Developer Center	http://msdn.microsoft.com/en-us/dynamics/ax/default.aspx
Dynamics AX 2012 SDK	http://msdn.microsoft.com/en-us/library/hh881815.aspx
Information Source	https://informationsource.dynamics.com/

Blogs

Here is a list of technical AX blogs that you might find interesting:

Description	URL
Microsoft AX support blog	`http://blogs.msdn.com/b/axsupport/`
Michael Fruergaard Pontoppidan's blog	`http://blogs.msdn.com/mfp/default.aspx`
Issues concerning X++	`http://blogs.msdn.com/x/`
Enterprise Portal Blog	`http://blogs.msdn.com/epblog/`
Dynamics AX UK	`http://blogs.msdn.com/b/ukax/`

Other relevant websites

The following table lists miscellaneous links where you can find specific information about AX, .NET, and other technologies:

Description	URL
Axaptapedia repository	`http://www.axaptapedia.com/Main_Page`
Dynamics AX 2012 system requirements	`http://www.microsoft.com/en-us/download/details.aspx?id=11094`
Web Services Architecture	`http://www.w3.org/TR/ws-arch/`
Web services tutorial	`http://www.w3schools.com/webservices/default.asp`
SysEPWebFormConverter - Class that converts old AX WebForms into .NET User Controls	`http://msdn.microsoft.com/en-us/library/cc615339.aspx`
Codepages supported by Windows	`http://msdn.microsoft.com/en-us/goglobal/bb964653.aspx`
Common Language Runtime	`http://msdn.microsoft.com/en-us/library/ddk909ch(VS.71).aspx`
.NET Framework 3.5 SDK	`http://msdn.microsoft.com/en-us/library/w0x726c2.aspx`
Microsoft Dynamics Snap for Microsoft Dynamics AX	`http://www.codeplex.com/axsnap`

B
Debugger

In the first chapter of this book, it was briefly mentioned that the debugger was one of the most important tools when programming in AX. This appendix will give you a quick guide to how to use the debugger.

The debugger is installed as a separate application and can be opened directly from your Windows OS, or you can open it from AX. There are two ways to open the debugger in AX. You can open it before you start executing whatever you want to debug by clicking on the Start button (*Alt+M*) and navigating to **All Programs | Microsoft Dynamics AX | Debugger**.

The debugger is also started automatically when the code execution hits a breakpoint. If you are trying to debug code that is executed through the .NET Business Connector, there are certain steps you have to follow. Visit http://msdn.microsoft.com/en-us/library/gg860898.aspx to learn more about these steps.

If the code that you want to debug runs on the server, you will need to enable server-side debugging in the AX 2012 Server Configuration Tool.

To actually debug a piece of code, simply hit *F9* to add a breakpoint in the code. Try to do this somewhere in the `Collection_Set` job that we created in *Chapter 2, The X++ Language*. You can also modify the code and write the statement `breakpoint;` to set a breakpoint; this is especially helpful when debugging form controls.

> Make sure that the debugger is installed on your client's computer and debugging is enabled for your user by going to the Options form (click on the **Microsoft Dynamics AX button** (*Alt+M*) and go to **Tools | Options**). Go to the Development tab and make sure that the Debug Mode field is set to **When Breakpoint**.

Debugger

When you execute the job, it will stop at your breakpoint and will look like the following screenshot (without the red numbers that are put there for explanation):

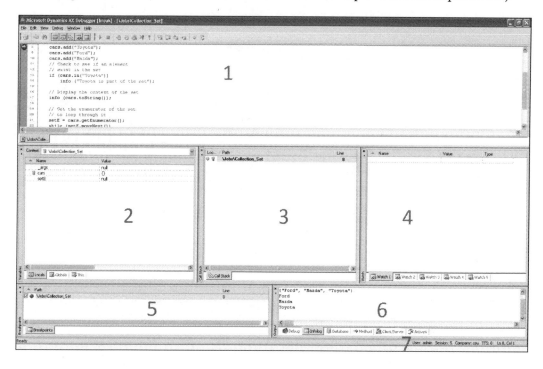

Let's discuss the various subwindows / snap-in windows shown in the preceding screenshot:

1. **Code window (1):** This window displays the code that is being executed. The red bullet to the left of the line numbering indicates a breakpoint. The yellow arrow on top of the breakpoint indicates the line about to be executed.

2. **Variable window (2):** The variables that are in the selected context are shown in this window. It is divided into three tab pages:
    - **Locals**: This tab shows the variables in the current execution scope
    - **Globals**: This tab shows the variables from the objects that are always created when AX runs (InfoLog, VersionControl, Classfactory, and Appl)
    - **This**: This tab shows the class member variables

3. **Call stack window (3):** This window displays the methods that have been executed in order to get to the current code. So, when the method A calls method B, which again calls method C; they will be listed in this window, with method C on the top and method A at the bottom. You can also double-click on a path in the call stack to see that method's code in the code window.

4. **Watch window (4):** In this window, you can look for certain variables regardless of their context. If they are in the current context, a value will be shown if they have any. You can mark a variable in the code window and drag it to the watch window to add it to the watch list.

5. **Breakpoints window (5):** This window shows all the breakpoint you have set in AX. You can also set new breakpoints and remove breakpoints directly in the debugger.

6. **Output window (6):** This window will display different kinds of output.
    - **Debug:** You can write statements like `Debug::printDebug("Test something");` in the code and have them traced in this windows
    - **Infolog:** All messages sent to infolog are shown in this tab
    - **Database, Method, Client/Server, ActiveX:** Any traces generated by these if their flag has been switched on under the Options form (by clicking on the **Microsoft Dynamics AX button** (*Alt+M*) and going to **Tools | Options**)

7. **Info bar (7):** This part of the debugger shows the following information related to the current session.
    - **User:** This is the user executing the current session
    - **Session:** This is the identifier of the current server session
    - **Company:** This is the three-letter ID of the current company account
    - **TTS:** This is the transaction level for the current session
    - **Ln Col:** This is the line number and the column number of the cursor in the code window

These are the main operations of the debugger (see a full list of shortcuts in the list of all standard shortcut keys at the AX link):

- **Step over** (*F10*): Using this operation, you can execute the current line without debugging methods called by the statement if any.
- **Step into** (*F11*): Using this operation, you can step into the method called by the current line. If more than one method is called, the innermost method will have priority, then the first one to the left of the line, and then the one towards the right.
- **Step out** (*Shift+F11*): Using this operation, you can step out of the current method and go back to the caller method (the previous method in the stack).
- **Go back**: You can drag the yellow arrow to a previous line of code in the current method to go back to it. Remember that the variables will not be automatically reset to the state they had when that line was executed the first time.
- **Run** (*F5*): Using this operation, you can continue the execution and jump to the next breakpoint, if any.
- **Run to cursor** (*Ctrl+F10*): Using this operation, you can continue to execute and break at the line where the cursor is in the code window.
- **Stop debugging** (*Shift+F5*): Using this operation, you can stop executing the code; none of the lines after the current execution position will be executed.

Index

Symbols

.NET Business Connector
　about 278
　static method, creating in AX 278
　used, in .NET classes 278
.NET class
　.NET Business Connector, using 278
　reference, adding to 273
　used, in X++ 274-277
.NET Framework 3.5 SDK
　URL 330

A

access options
　Correct 269
　Create access 269
　Delete 269
　Edit access 268
　No access 268
　View access 268
Account Receivable (AR) module
　about 241
　entity schema, base data 242, 243
　entity schema, orders 242
　transactions entity schema 244
Accounts Payable (AP) module
　about 241
　entity schema, base data 242, 243
　entity schema, orders 242, 243
　transactions entity schema 244
active method 109
aggregate select statements
　avg aggregate option 169
　count aggregate option 169
　group by parameter 171, 172
　maxof aggregate option 170
　minof aggregate option 170
　sum aggregate option 168
　writing 168
AifQueryTypeAttribute attribute 67
anytype datatype 43, 44
aosValidate methods 179
AOT
　about 8, 217, 241
　classes 10
　datasets 10
　forms 10
　jobs 11
　macros 10
　menu items 11
　menus 11
　project, adding to 279
　queries 11
　report libraries 11
　reports 10
　resources 12
　services 11
　SSRS reports 10
　system documentation 12
　Web node 11
　workflow framework 12
Application Developer Documentation 12
Application Explorer 280-282
Application Integration Framework (AIF)
　about 11, 198, 271
　URL 198
application object layers
　about 29, 30
　CUS 30
　FPK 30

GLS 30
ISV 30
SLN 30
SYS 30
USR 30
VAR 30
Application Object Server (AOS) 30
Application Object Tree. *See* AOT
area page 135
args.caller() method 62
Args class
  about 60-62
  parm 60
  parmEnum 60
  parmObject 60
  record 60
arithmetic operators 56
array 49, 70
assignment operators 55
AutoReport field 90
AvailableInclOrdered method 296
AvailableNow method 296
avg aggregate option 169
AX
  references 329
  static method, creating 278
Axaptapedia repository
  URL 330
AX architecture
  application object layers 29, 30
  dissecting 29
  network tiers 30
AX-Azure connector 291
AxGrid control 316
AX logic
  accessing, in external web service 304
  exposing 292-297
  exposing, web services used 292
AX logic, in external web service
  class, creating 306, 307
  service reference, creating 304-306
AX report
  creating, Visual Studio used 128-132
AX table
  data, inserting 282-284
  data, reading from 284-286

B

binary files 203
Boolean datatype 40
Breakpoints window 333
break statement 51

C

CalledWhen property
  Post 76
  Pre 76
callRentalInfo method 62
Call stack window 333
class
  about 46
  creating, for web service 306, 307
classDeclaration method 214, 217, 221, 222
classes, AOT 10
closeCancel method 107
close method 107
closeOk method 107
code
  inventory journal, entering from 235
  inventory journal, posting from 235
code permission, security hierarchy 267
code window 15, 332
collection classes
  about 70
  array 70
  list 71
  map 71
  set 72
  struct 73
common intermediate language (CIL) 69
Common Language Runtime (CLR)
  .NET class, using in X++ 274-277
  about 66, 271, 272
  reference, adding to .NET class 273
  URL 330
compiler
  about 16-18
  best practices 18
  Errors and warnings 18
  Status 18
  Tasks 18

components, forms
  about 106
  Data Sources 106
  Designs 106
  Methods 106
  Parts 106
  Permissions 106
composite datatypes
  about 44
  array 49
  class 46
  container 44
  table 47
configuration keys 264, 265
construct method 64, 220
container
  about 44
  container functions 45
functions 45
content page 135
content pane 136
continue statement 50
correct data retrieval method
  using 173
count aggregate option 169
create method 109
CreateNavigationPropertyMethods
    property 191
cross-references 21-23
current on-hand information
  finding 233, 234
CustTable 156

D

data
  inserting, in AX table 282-284
  querying, on inherited tables 99
  reading, from AX table 284-286
  reading, from database 209
  reading, from external database 209
  writing, to text file 199-201
  writing, to XML files 204-207
data retrieval
  data retrieval method, using 173
  field selects 173, 174
  improving 174

indexing 174
optimizing 173
views, used for optimizing 174
dataset
  creating 310
data sources
  adding 112
  joining, in query 146
data sources, forms 107
data sources, methods
  active 109
  create 109
  delete 109
  executeQuery 108
  init 108
  refresh 109
  reread 109
  research 109
  validateDelete 109
  validateWrite 109
  write 109
data sources, properties
  AllowCreate 108
  AllowDelete 108
  AllowEdit 108
  DelayActive 108
  Index 108
  JoinSource 108
  LinkType 108
  Name 108
  Table 108
datatypes
  about 34
  composite datatypes 44
  primitive datatypes 35
Date datatype 40
date-effective table
  creating 100, 101
debugger 28, 331
default parameter 60
default statement 53
delete action
  Cascade 94
  Cascade+Restricted 94
  creating 93, 94
  None 94
  Restricted 94

delete_from operator 177, 189
delete() method 177, 183
delete operation 183
design
  separating, form splitter used 115-119
Designs, forms 109
Designs, properties
  Caption 109
  Left/top 109
  TitleDatasource 109
  Width/Height 109
  WindowType 109
development tools
  cross-references 21-23
  debugger 28
  MorphX version control 23
  utilizing 20
dialog method 214
direct handling 193, 194
display methods
  about 120-122
  caching 123
  considerations 123
do-while loop 51
duties, security hierarchy 267
Dynamic property
  No 144
  Unselected 144
  Yes 144
dynamic query
  creating, X++ used 148, 149
Dynamics AX 2012 SDK
  URL 329
Dynamics AX 2012 SDK documentation
  URL 309
Dynamics AX 2012 system requirements
  URL 330
Dynamics AX development model
  about 7
  AOT 8
  Application Developer Documentation 12
  compiler 16-18
  features 7
  labels 19
  MorphX 8
  programming language 8
  Properties window 13

X++ code editor 14-16
Dynamics AX UK
  URL 330

E

edit methods
  about 122, 123
  considerations 123
else-if statement 52
else statement 52
Enterprise Portal (EP) 11
entity schema, tables
  CustGroup 243
  CustTable 243
  PurchLine 243
  PurchTable 243
  SalesLine 243
  SalesTable 243
  VendGroup 243
  VendTable 243
enum2int function 42
enum2str function 41
Enum datatype
  about 40, 41
  enum2int function 42
  enum2str function 41
event handler 75
exception classes
  about 286
  AlreadyLoggedOnException 287
  AXBufferNotValidException 287
  AXContainerNotValidException 287
  AXObjectNotValidException 287
  AXRecordNotValidException 287
  BusinessConnectorException 287
  ConnectionLostException 287
  DebuggerStopException 287
  ExecutionErrorException 287
  FatalErrorLoggedOffException 287
  InitializationFailedException 287
  InvalidReturnValueException 287
  LogonAsGuesNotSupportedException 287
  LogonFailedException 287
  LogonSystemChangedException 287
  LogonUserLockedOutException 288

MethodUnknownException 288
NoIISRightsException 288
NoSecurityKeyException 288
NotLoggedOnException 288
PermissionDeniedException 288
ServerCommunicationErrorException 288
ServerOutOfReachException 288
ServerOutOfResourcesException 288
ServerUnavailableException 288
SessionTerminatedException 288
UnknownClassHandleException 288
UnknownRecordException 288
UnknownTextException 289
UnknownXPPClassException 289
XppException 289
exception handling 54
executeQuery method 108
existing reference
  adding, in Global Assembly Cache 273
exist method 48
exists join 166
extended datatype (EDT)
  about 77, 78
  creating 78-81
extended datatype, properties
  DisplayLength 82
  Extends 82
  FormHelp 82
  HelpText 82
  ID 82
  Label 82
  Name 82
extended datatype, types
  Container 79
  Date 79
  Enum 79
  GUID 79
  Int64 79
  Integer 79
  String 79
  Time 79
  UtcDateTime 79
Extends property 96
external web service
  AX logic, accessing in 304

F

field group
  fields, adding to 89, 90
fields
  adding, to field group 89, 90
  adding, to table 87, 88
field selects 173, 174
filter pane 136
find method 47
first AX program
  creating 19, 20
five tracking dimension 232
for loop 50
form design
  creating 112-114
forms
  about 105
  adding, in AOT 124, 125
  components 106
  creating 111
  creating, with one data source 110
  creating, with two data sources 114
  design separating,
      form splitter used 115-119
  display method 120, 121
  edit method 120, 121
  lookup form, creating 124
forms, AOT 10
form splitter
  used, for separating design 115-119
form templates
  about 110, 111
  DetailsFormMaster 111
  DetailsFormTransaction 111
  Dialogue 111
  DropDialog 111
  ListPage 111
  SimpleList 111
  SimpleListDetails 111
  TableOfContents 111
form, with one data source
  data source, adding 112
  form, creating 111
  form design, creating 112-114
  form templates 110, 111
four item dimension 232
FPK 30

G

getFromDialog method 215
Global Assembly Cache
  existing reference, adding 273
GLS 30
Go back operation 334
grid
  creating 312-317
group by parameter 171, 172

H

hardcode values 10

I

if-else if-else loop 52
if statement 52
IIS
  web service, publishing to 298-303
ImpExp_Cars class
  about 220
  classDeclaration method 221
  readFile method 221
  writeFile method 222
ImpExpFile class
  about 217
  classDeclaration method 217
  construct method 220
  new method 218
  openFile method 218
  readFile method 219
  run method 219
  writeFile method 220
ImpExpFileDialog class
  about 213
  classDeclaration method 214
  dialog method 214
  getFromDialog method 215
  main method 217
  pack method 215
  run method 216
  unpack method 216
ImpExp_Rentals class
  about 222
  classDeclaration method 222
  readFile method 223
  writeFile method 224
import/export activity
  about 212
  ImpExp_Cars class 220
  ImpExpFile class 217
  ImpExpFileDialog class 213
  ImpExp_Rentals class 222
Independent Software Vendor (ISV) 30
index
  creating 90, 91
Info bar
  about 333
  Company 333
  Ln Col 333
  Session 333
  TTS 333
  User 333
info function 51
info method 42
inheritance 62, 63
initFrom method 48
init method 107, 108
InitValue method 180
inner join 164
insert() method 177, 179
insert operation 179
insert_recordset operator 177, 184, 185
integer datatype 37, 38
InventAdj classes 231
InventMovement classes 229
InventOnHand class 232
inventory dimensions
  current on-hand information,
      finding 233, 234
  finding 232
  five tracking dimension 232
  four item dimension 232
  inventory journal, entering from code 235
  inventory journal, posting from code 235
  on-hand information, finding by
      specific date 234
  six storage dimension 232
  working with 232
inventory journal
  entering, from code 235
  posting, from code 235

inventory module
  about 225
  InventTable entity schema 226-228
  InventTrans entity schema 228, 229
InventSum classes 232
InventTable entity schema
  about 226-228
  EcoResDistinctProduct 227
  EcoResProduct 227
  EcoResProductMaster 227
  InventDim 227
  InventDimGroup 227
  InventItemGroup 227
  InventItemInventSetup 227
  InventItemLocation 227
  InventItemPurchSetup 227
  InventItemSalesSetup 227
  InventModelGroup 227
  InventTable 227
  InventTableModule 227
InventTrans entity schema
  about 228
  CustTable 229
  InventDim 229
  InventSum 229
  InventTable 229
  InventTrans 229
  InventTransOrigin 229
  InventTransOrigin tables 229
  VendTable 229
InventUpdate classes 231
ISV 30
item
  price, finding for 245

J

job
  executing 332
JoinMode
  ExistsJoin 147
  InnerJoin 146
  NoExistsJoin 147
  OuterJoin 146
joins
  exists join 166
  inner join 164

notexists join 167
outer join 165
used, in select statement 163

L

labels 19
language-integrated query (LINQ) 8
Ledger entity schema, tables
  GeneralJournalAccountEntry 237
  GeneralJournalEntry 237
  Ledger 237
  LedgerEntry 237
  SubledgerVoucherGeneralJournalEntry 237
LedgerJournal class
  entering 238-240
  posting 238-240
Ledger module
  about 236
  LedgerJournal class, entering 238-240
  LedgerJournal class, posting 238-240
  ledger transactions, posting 238
  LedgerVoucher class, entering 240
  LedgerVoucher class, posting 240
ledger transactions
  Ledger Journal 238
  Ledger Voucher 238
  posting 238
LedgerVoucher class
  entering 240
  posting 240
license codes 263, 264
list 71
list page
  about 135
  action pane 136
  content pane 136
  creating 137-139
  filter pane 136
  preview pane 136
  working 136
local macro 74
LoginProperty class 209
lookup form
  creating 124
  creating, by adding new form
    in AOT 124, 125

creating, in lookup method 125, 126
parts 126, 127
lookup method
  about 125
  lookup form, creating 125, 126
loops
  about 50
  do-while loop 51
  for loop 50
  if-else if-else loop 52
  while loop 51

M

macro libraries 74
macros
  about 74, 75
  local macros 74
  macro libraries 74
  standalone macros 74
main class hierarchies
  about 229
  InventAdj classes 231
  InventMovement classes 229
  InventSum classes 232
  InventUpdate classes 231
main method 64, 217
map 71
maxof aggregate option 170
maxof option 168
menu bar 15
menu items
  about 133
  Action 133
  creating 133
  Display 133
  Output 133
  used, as button in form 134
menu items, AOT 11
menus 139, 140
menus, AOT 11
method access
  about 58
  private 58
  protected 58
  public 58
method list 14

methods 57
methods, forms
  about 106, 107
  close 107
  closeCancel 107
  closeOk 107
  init 107
  run 107
Microsoft AX support blog
  URL 330
Microsoft Azure 291
Microsoft Dynamics AX community
  URL 329
Microsoft Dynamics AX Developer Center
  URL 329
Microsoft Dynamics Snap
  URL 330
Microsoft SharePoint 309
minof aggregate option 170
minof option 168
Model View Controller (MVC) 66
MorphX 8
MorphX version control
  about 23
  setting up 24-26
  using 26-28

N

navigation pages
  about 135
  area page 135
  content page 135
  list page 135
NavigationPropertyMethodNameOverride property 191
network tiers 30
new method 218
next() method 150
notexists join 167
num2str function 39, 40
number sequence
  setting up 260
  using 262
number sequence reference
  setting up 254-257

[342]

O

ODBC
  about 209
  data, reading from database 209
  used, for reading from database 209
  used, for writing to database 211
official Microsoft websites 329
one data source
  form, creating with 110
on-hand information
  finding, by specific date 234
Open Database Connectivity. *See* ODBC
openFile method 218
operations, debugger
  Go back 334
  Run (F5) 334
  Run to cursor (Ctrl+F10) 334
  Step into 334
  Step out 334
  Step over 334
  Stop debugging (Shift+F5) 334
operators
  about 54
  arithmetic operators 56
  assignment operators 55
  relational operators 55, 56
options, menu bar
  Breakpoint 15
  Compile 15
  Display Changes 16
  Display Line numbers 16
  Enable/Disable breakpoint 15
  Help 16
  Lookup label/text 16
  Lookup properties/methods 16
  New 15
  Remove all breakpoints 15
  Run 15
  Save 15
  Scripts 16
  Source Code Controls 16
options, operations
  Append 199
  Binary 199
  Read 199
  Translate 199
  Write 199
order by parameter 162
outer join 165
Output window
  about 333
  ActiveX 333
  Client/Server 333
  Database 333
  Debug 333
  Infolog 333
  Method 333

P

pack method 215
parameter table
  about 257-260
  number sequence, setting up 260
  number sequence, using 262
parts 126, 127
parts, types
  Cue 127
  Form 127
  Info 127
pause statement 20
permissions, security hierarchy 267
policies, security hierarchy 267
preview pane 136
price
  finding, for item 245
primitive datatypes
  about 35
  anytype datatype 43, 44
  Boolean datatype 40
  Date datatype 40
  Enum datatype 40
  integer datatype 37, 38
  real datatype 38, 39
  string datatype 35, 36
  timeofday datatype 42
  utcdatetime datatype 43
print statement 37
private, method access 58
privileges, security hierarchy 267
process cycles, security hierarchy 268
programming language 8

project
  adding, in Visual Studio 279
  adding, to AOT 279
project, in Visual Studio
  Application Explorer 280-282
  data, inserting in AX table 282-284
  data, reading from AX table 284-286
  exception classes 286
Properties window 13
protected, method access 58
public, method access 58

Q

queries
  about 143
  data sources, joining in 146, 147
  dynamic query creating, X++ used 148, 149
  range, adding to 145, 146
  sort order, adding to 145
  static query creating, AOT used 143, 144
  using 150, 151
Query class 103
Query object model
  Query 148
  QueryBuildDataSource 148
  QueryBuildFieldList 149
  QueryBuildLink 149
  QueryBuildRange 149
  QueryRun 148

R

range
  adding, to query 145, 146
range operator
  , 145
  ! 145
  ? 145
  * 145
  < 145
  = 145
  > 145
  about 145
readFile method 219, 221, 223
real datatype
  about 38, 39
  num2str function 39, 40

str2num function 39
record-based manipulation 179
record-based manipulation, operations
  delete 183
  insert 179
  update 180-182
reference
  adding, to .NET class 273
  existing reference, adding in Global Assembly Cache 273
refresh method 109
RelatedTableRole property 191
relation
  creating 92, 93
relational operators
  ! operator 56
  != operator 55
  && operator 55
  < operator 56
  <= operator 56
  == operator 55
  > operator 56
  >= operator 56
  || operator 55
  about 55, 56
Report Definition Language (RDL) 128
Reporting Services
  about 128
  AX report creating, Visual Studio used 128-132
report libraries, AOT 11
reports
  about 127
  Reporting Services 128
reports, AOT 10
Request For Quotes (RFQ) 247
reread method 109
research method 109
resources, AOT 12
Response class 325
roles, security hierarchy 268
RunBase framework
  about 65
  Batch execution 65
  Dialog 65
  features 65
  Pack/unpack with versioning 66

Progress bar 66
Query 65
Run 65
run method 107, 216, 219
RunOn property 58, 59

S

sales/purchase updates
  posting 246-248
  printing 246-248
security framework
  about 263
  configuration keys 264, 265
  license codes 263, 264
  security hierarchy 266, 267
security hierarchy
  about 266, 267
  code permission 267
  duties 267
  permissions 267
  policies 267
  privileges 267
  process cycles 268
  roles 268
select statement
  about 154, 155
  aggregate select statements, writing 168
  CarTable 156
  CustTable 156
  joins, using 163
  parameters 155
  RentalTable 156
  sorting, using 162, 163
  writing 157-162
service reference
  creating 304-306
services, AOT 11
set 72
set-based data manipulation
  about 184
  delete_from operator 189
  insert_recordset operator 184, 185
  update_recordset operator 186, 187
six storage dimension 232
SLN 30

sorting
  used, in select statement 162, 163
sort order
  adding, to query 145
SQL Server Reporting Services (SSRS) 127
SSRS reports, AOT 10
standalone macros 75
statements
  about 50
  break statement 51
  continue statement 50
  exception handling 53
  switch statement 53
static method
  about 59
  creating, in AX 278
static query
  creating, AOT used 143, 144
static query, using AOT
  data sources, joining in query 146, 147
  range, adding to query 145, 146
  sort order, adding to query 145
Step into operation 334
Step out operation 334
Step over operation 334
str2num function 39
str2time function 42
strfmt method 36, 37
string datatype
  about 35, 36
  strfmt method 36, 37
  substr method 37
struct 73
substr method 37
subwindows / snap-in windows, debugger
  Breakpoints window 333
  Call stack window 333
  Code window 332
  Info bar 333
  Output window 333
  Variable window 332
  Watch window 333
sum aggregate option 168
SupportInheritance property 96
switch statement 53
SysEPWebFormConverter
  URL 330

SysOperation framework 66-69
SysOperationHelpTextAttribute
    attribute 67
SysOperationLabelAttribute attribute 67
system documentation, AOT 12

T

table
  about 47
  creating 82-86
  delete action, creating 93, 94
  exist method 48
  fields, adding to 87, 88
  fields, adding to field group 89-90
  find method 47
  index, creating 90, 91
  initFrom method 48
  relation, creating 92, 93
  table browser 94, 95
  table inheritance 96-98
  valid time state tables 100-103
table browser 94, 95
table browser, fields
  CreatedDateTime 95
  CreatedTransactionId 95
  dataAreaId 95
  ModifiedDateTime 95
  ModifiedTransactionId 95
  Partition 95
  RecId 95
  recVersion 95
table inheritance
  about 96-98
  data, querying on 99
table, properties
  Abstract 86
  ClusteredIndex 86
  ConfigurationKey 85
  CreatedDateTime 86
  CreatedTransactionId 86
  Extends 86
  FormRef 85
  ID 85
  Label 85
  ModifiedDateTime 86
  ModifiedTransactionId 86
  Name 85
  PrimaryIndex 86
  ReportRef 85
  SecurityKey 85
  SupportInheritance 86
  TableGroup 86
  TableType 85
  TitleField 85
TableType property
  In Memory 85
  Regular 85
  TempDB 85
text files
  about 198, 199
  data, writing to 199-201
  reading from 202, 203
TextIo class
  versus CommaTextIo class 199
timeofday datatype
  about 42
  str2time function 42
trade agreements 245
transactions entity schema 244
transactions entity schema, tables
  CustSettlement 244
  CustTrans 244
  VendSettlement 244
  VendTrans 244
ttsabort keyword 181
ttsbegin keyword 181
ttscommit keyword 123, 181
tunnel
  creating 321-327
two data sources
  form, creating with 114

U

unit of work 190-193
unpack method 216
update() method 177, 180
update operation 180-182
update_recordset operator 177, 186, 187
UseDefaultRoleNames property 191
utcdatetime datatype 43

V

validateDelete() method 109, 178, 183
validateField method 178
validateWrite method 109, 178
validation methods
  about 178
  validateDelete 178
  validateField 178
  validateWrite 178
valid time state tables 100-103
Value Added Resellers (VAR) 30
Variable window 332
Variable window, tabs
  Globals 332
  Locals 332
  This 332
Version Control System (VCS) 24
views
  about 152
  creating 152, 154
  used, for optimizing data retrieval 174
Visual Studio
  project, creating 279
  used, for creating AX report 128-132
voucher settlement 248, 249

W

Watch window 333
Web node, AOT 11
Web Part page
  creating 318-321
web service
  about 291
  class, creating 306, 307
  creating, for exposing AX logic 292-297
  publishing, to IIS 298-303
  URL 291
  used, for exposing AX logic 292

Web Services Architecture
  URL 330
websites
  about 329
  blogs 330
  official Microsoft websites 329
  other relevant websites 330
while loop 51, 202
while select statement 171
Windows Communication
    Foundation (WCF) 66
Windows Event Log 274
wizard
  creating 321-327
workflow framework, AOT 12
writeFile method 220-224
write method 109

X

X++
  .NET class, using 274-277
  about 33, 34
  syntax 33
  used, for creating dynamic query 148
X++ code editor
  about 14-16
  code window 15
  menu bar 15
  method list 14
XML files
  about 204
  creating 204-207
  data, writing to 204-207
  reading from 207
XppPrePostArgs object 76

Thank you for buying
Learning MS Dynamics AX 2012 Programming

About Packt Publishing

Packt, pronounced 'packed', published its first book, *Mastering phpMyAdmin for Effective MySQL Management*, in April 2004, and subsequently continued to specialize in publishing highly focused books on specific technologies and solutions.

Our books and publications share the experiences of your fellow IT professionals in adapting and customizing today's systems, applications, and frameworks. Our solution-based books give you the knowledge and power to customize the software and technologies you're using to get the job done. Packt books are more specific and less general than the IT books you have seen in the past. Our unique business model allows us to bring you more focused information, giving you more of what you need to know, and less of what you don't.

Packt is a modern yet unique publishing company that focuses on producing quality, cutting-edge books for communities of developers, administrators, and newbies alike. For more information, please visit our website at `www.packtpub.com`.

About Packt Enterprise

In 2010, Packt launched two new brands, Packt Enterprise and Packt Open Source, in order to continue its focus on specialization. This book is part of the Packt Enterprise brand, home to books published on enterprise software – software created by major vendors, including (but not limited to) IBM, Microsoft, and Oracle, often for use in other corporations. Its titles will offer information relevant to a range of users of this software, including administrators, developers, architects, and end users.

Writing for Packt

We welcome all inquiries from people who are interested in authoring. Book proposals should be sent to `author@packtpub.com`. If your book idea is still at an early stage and you would like to discuss it first before writing a formal book proposal, then please contact us; one of our commissioning editors will get in touch with you.

We're not just looking for published authors; if you have strong technical skills but no writing experience, our experienced editors can help you develop a writing career, or simply get some additional reward for your expertise.

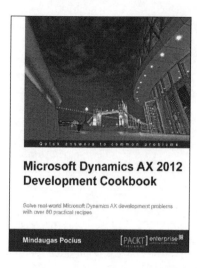

Microsoft Dynamics AX 2012 Development Cookbook

ISBN: 978-1-84968-464-4   Paperback: 372 pages

Solve real-world Microsoft Dynamics AX development problems with over 80 practical recipes

1. Develop powerful and successful Dynamics AX projects with efficient X++ code.
2. Proven recipes that can be reused in numerous successful Dynamics AX projects.
3. Covers general ledger, accounts payable, accounts receivable, project modules, and general functionality of Dynamics AX.
4. Step-by-step instructions and useful screenshots for easy learning.

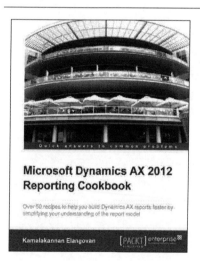

Microsoft Dynamics AX 2012 Reporting Cookbook

ISBN: 978-1-84968-772-0   Paperback: 314 pages

Over 50 recipes to help you build Dynamics AX reports faster by simplifying your understanding of the report model

1. Practical recipes for creating and managing reports.
2. Illustrated step-by-step examples that can be adopted in real time.
3. Complete explanations of the report model and program model for reports.

Please check www.PacktPub.com for information on our titles

Microsoft Dynamics AX 2012 Financial Management

ISBN: 978-1-78217-720-3   Paperback: 168 pages

Get to grips with how to successfully use Microsoft Dynamics AX 2012 for financial management with this concise and practical reference guide

1. Understand the financial management aspects in Microsoft Dynamics AX.
2. Successfully configure and set up your software.
3. Learn about real-life business requirements and their solutions.
4. Get to know the tips and tricks you can utilize during analysis, design, deployment, and operation phases in a project life cycle.

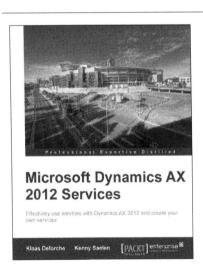

Microsoft Dynamics AX 2012 Services

ISBN: 978-1-84968-754-6   Paperback: 196 pages

Effectively use services with Dynamics AX 2012 and create your own services

1. Learn about the Dynamics AX 2012 service architecture.
2. Create your own services using wizards or X++ code.
3. Consume existing web services and services you've created yourself.

Please check **www.PacktPub.com** for information on our titles

Made in the USA
Columbia, SC
15 February 2018